CHORAL CONDUCTING AND THE CONSTRUCTION OF MEANING

Choral Conducting and the Construction of Meaning
Gesture, Voice, Identity

LIZ GARNETT

LONDON AND NEW YORK

First published 2009 by Ashgate Publishing

Published 2016 by Routledge
2 Park Square, Milton Park, Abingdon, Oxon OX14 4RN
711 Third Avenue, New York, NY 10017, USA

Routledge is an imprint of the Taylor & Francis Group, an informa business

Copyright © Liz Garnett 2009

All rights reserved. No part of this book may be reprinted or reproduced or utilised in any form or by any electronic, mechanical, or other means, now known or hereafter invented, including photocopying and recording, or in any information storage or retrieval system, without permission in writing from the publishers.

Notice:
Product or corporate names may be trademarks or registered trademarks, and are used only for identification and explanation without intent to infringe.

Liz Garnett has asserted her moral right under the Copyright, Designs and Patents Act, 1988, to be identified as the author of this work.

British Library Cataloguing in Publication Data
Garnett, Liz, 1970–
  Choral conducting and the construction of meaning: gesture, voice, identity
  1. Choral conducting 2. Nonverbal communication 3. Body language
  I. Title
  782.5'145

Library of Congress Cataloging-in-Publication Data
Garnett, Liz, 1970–
  Choral conducting and the construction of meaning : gesture, voice, identity / Liz Garnett.
      p. cm.
  Includes bibliographical references and index.
  ISBN 978-0-7546-6379-9 (hardback : alk. paper)
  1. Choral conducting. I. Title.

  MT85.G173 2008
  782.5'145–dc22
                                                                    2008041391

ISBN 9780754663799 (hbk)

Contents

List of Figures		*vii*
List of Tables		*ix*
DVD Track Listing		*xi*
Acknowledgements		*xiii*
1	Introduction: Choral Conducting in Context	1

PART I How To Study Conducting: Model, Method, Metalanguage

2	How do People Think about Conducting?	19
3	From Ethnography to Peer Research	31
4	How to Write about Conducting	43

PART II Choral Singing and Enculturation

5	Defining Choral Culture: What Counts as Choral?	63
6	Creating Choral Culture: The Dos and Don'ts	77
7	Maintaining Choral Culture: Policing the Boundaries	91

PART III Conducting Gesture and Musical Thought

8	Different Styles, Different Gestures	107
9	Different Styles, Common Ground	123
10	Metaphoric Gesture and Embodied Musical Meaning	137
11	Spontaneous Gesture and the Ensemble	153

PART IV The Conductor–Choir Bond

12   Monkey See, Monkey Do   169

13   Making Use of the Conductor–Choir Bond   183

14   Conclusion   195

Bibliography   *207*
Index   *221*

List of Figures

2.1	Transmission model of conducting	21
2.2	Interactive model of conducting	24
4.1	Efron's classification of gestures	52
8.1	Worcester Cathedral Choir	108
8.2	The White Rosettes	112
8.3	Birmingham Community Gospel Choir	116
8.4	City of Birmingham Symphony Chorus	119
10.1	Basic elements of the two-pattern and three styles of execution	147
10.2	Transformation of duple into quadruple metre	149
10.3	Basic topography of the four-pattern and its execution	150
10.4	Multilevel analysis of accent after Cooper and Meyer	150

List of Tables

4.1	McNeill's gesture classification continua, after Kendon	53
10.1	How emotion modulates gesture in sign-language and dynamics modulate gesture in conducting	142
10.2	Gestures for dynamic shaping and their metaphorical associations	144

DVD Track Listing

Adrian Lucas and the Worcester Cathedral Choir

1.1 'The Coventry Carol', trad., arr: Adrian Lucas

1.2 Jim Clements, 'Awake, Glad heart!'

1.3 Jim Clements, 'Awake, Glad heart!'

1.4 Jim Clements, 'Awake, Glad heart!'; Alick Rowe, 'Adam Lay Y-Bounden', arr: Roy Massey; 'Past Three O'Clock', trad., arr: Andrew Carter

Sally McLean and the White Rosettes

2.1 'Do I Love You', words and music: Cole Porter, arr: Paul Davies

2.2 'Gospel Medley', trad., arr: Ed Waesche

2.3 'Gospel Medley', trad., arr: Ed Waesche

2.4 'I'm Beginning to See the Light', words and music: Don George, Johnny Hodges, Duke Ellington and Harry James, arr: Greg Volk

Maxine Brooks and the Birmingham Community Gospel Choir

3.1 'Jesus Christ is the way', words and music: Walter Hawkins

3.2 'Holy Holy', words and music: Richard Smallwood

3.3 'Holy Holy', words and music: Richard Smallwood

3.4 'God of a second chance', words and music: Hezekiah Walker

Simon Halsey and the City of Birmingham Symphony Chorus

4.1   Igor Stravinksy, *The Rake's Progress*, Act III, Scene 1, 'Duet (Anne and Baba with Chorus and Sellem)', fig. 118–119

4.2   Igor Stravinksy, *The Rake's Progress*, Act III, Scene 1, 'Duet (Anne and Baba with Chorus and Sellem)', fig. 118–119

4.3   Igor Stravinksy, *The Rake's Progress*, Act III, Scene 3, 'Mourning Chorus', fig. 273–280

4.4   Igor Stravinksy, *The Rake's Progress*, Act I, Scene 2, 'Chorus', fig 114–129

Acknowledgements

First, and most importantly, my heartfelt thanks go to all the choirs and conductors who have let me visit their rehearsals during the course of the research for this book. Without their generosity and willingness to help, this project would quite literally not have been possible. I have learned an immense amount from them all, and have dedicated the book to them in the hope that I can offer back something that conductors and choirs might find of value.

Particular thanks must go to those who consented not only to the extra disruption of video cameras at their rehearsals, but also to letting me use footage from these videos to accompany the book. I am grateful to Maxine Brooks, Simon Halsey, Adrian Lucas and Sally McLean for their permission to show them in action, and to Elen Elis and Mike Flowers for their help in setting up the filming sessions.

I am grateful to Birmingham Conservatoire, and our parent institution, Birmingham City University, for supporting this project in many different ways from the provision of equipment to the peer review of funding applications. A period of four months' study leave in 2007–2008 was invaluable for putting the whole thing together, and my thanks go to my institution for providing it, and to my colleague Peter Johnson for taking over my course management responsibilities during my absence.

Many other people have given generously of their time and thoughts during the development of this project. Richard Cornock, Jonathan Day, Simon Hall and Nicola Plant offered much-needed technical help with the filming and production of the DVD. David Baltuch, Peter Johnson, Peter Litman, Areti Lymperopoulou, David Saint and Gavin Stewart were thoughtful and insightful readers, and Toby Balsley was a sympathetic and patient sounding-board. Discussions with five cohorts of Masters students in class and at our annual research study days have helped me develop and refine my ideas over the length of the project. Though they are too numerous to thank individually, it is important to acknowledge their contribution to creating a research culture that makes this kind of work possible, and I am sure that they and my colleagues will recognize how much this book owes to the intellectual and musical environment they have helped create. It goes without saying that the flaws are all my own work.

Finally, my thanks go to Jonathan Smith for his unwavering moral support, and for the way he expresses it through practical help when it is most needed.

Chapter 1
Introduction: Choral Conducting in Context

> The single element that most affects the eventual sound quality of a chorus in performance ... is the actual conducting technique or physical movements of the conductor.[1]

With these words, Abraham Kaplan summarizes a truism in choral practice: that the director should look like he or she wants the choir to sound. The character of the conductor's physical demeanour is believed to have a direct effect on how the choir sings, at a level that appears to be largely unconscious and involuntary. This effect encompasses not only deliberate conducting choices, but also habitual elements such as stance and mannerism.

It is also a matter of simple observation that different choral traditions exhibit not only different styles of vocal production and delivery, but also different gestural vocabularies. These are shared not only between conductors within that tradition, but also, to varying degrees, with the singers, and indeed the audiences. It is as possible to distinguish a gospel choir from a barbershop chorus or a cathedral choir by visual cues alone as it is simply by listening. John Blacking's category of 'sound groups' would thus appear also to be one of movement, or stance groups.[2]

There has been, however, little attempt to explain the nature of these forms of physical communication. Do they belong to a pre-cultural realm of primate social bonding, or do they rely on the context and conventions of a particular choral culture? Is kinaesthetic experience and body language an inherent part of musical performance styles, or does it come afterwards, in response to music? At a practical level, does one understand the music differently if one has or has not mastered the idiom's characteristic ways of using the self?

This book presents the outcomes of a long-term project that has explored these questions. The questions are simultaneously theoretical (in what ways is musical style stored in our bodily experiences, and how does it then relate to our sense of self?) and practical (how does one conduct a choir, especially in stylistic contexts that may feel 'foreign'?). It has examined the praxis of a variety of choral traditions, and has investigated the relationship between conductor demeanour and choral sound in general, and the ways it is constructed within the stylistic constraints of specific idioms. Its findings will be of interest both to those engaged in the study

---

[1] Abraham Kaplan, *Choral Conducting* (New York, 1985), p. 18.

[2] John Blacking, 'Music, Culture, and Experience', *Music, Culture and Experience: Selected Papers of John Blacking* ed. by Reginald Byron (Chicago and London, 1995), p. 232.

of music as a cultural practice and to practitioners involved in a choral conducting context that increasingly demands fluency in a variety of styles.

My central thesis is that the gestural languages of choral conducting, and their choirs' associated body languages and styles of vocal production, are integral to the way that musicians understand both the music they perform and – as a consequence – their own identities as performing musicians. My aim has therefore been to examine the ways in which choral practitioners inhabit the repertoires they perform (and vice versa) in order to analyse the processes by which people constitute themselves as choral conductors and singers. The pages that follow both theorize the relationship between musical style, social meanings and the performative construction of identity in choral performance, and draw practical conclusions regarding the transferability of good practice in choral conducting between different musical idioms.

Hence, this book lies at the intersection of two well-developed, but hitherto largely distinct disciplinary worlds in the study of music: critical musicology and choral practice. Members of each constituency might reasonably ask what is to be gained from their combination.

Critical musicology is accustomed to imagining the voice as a site where social processes and individual identity meet most intimately. The voice is singular and unique, to the extent that it acts as a standard image for originality and agency of thought throughout the arts and humanities: we talk of the poet's voice, or the composer's. At the same time it is generic, formed by forces beyond the control of the individual, whether those of nature (lungs, larynx, resonant cavities) or of nurture (language acquisition, gender roles, conventions of expression). The ideological, aesthetic, and – increasingly – technological contexts in which vocality is constructed have consequently been investigated in a plethora of idioms from bel canto to extended vocal techniques, from crooning to cock-rock.[3] The majority of this work, however, has focused on the singer as soloist; ensemble singing has received far less attention.

There are several reasons why it is valuable to critical musicology to redress this soloistic bias. First, the study of choral music presents interesting theoretical questions about the relationship between individual and corporate identities, between the personal and the supra-personal. The practical experience that choral practitioners have in melding disparate voices into a unified ensemble can usefully inform critical musicology's investigations into the role of musical participation in the 'project of the self'.[4] Related to this, it moves the focus away from the exceptional voice towards the 'typical'. While it is undoubtedly important to understand the passion that a diva, a torch singer or a rock star arouses in their

---

[3] See for example Leslie Dunn and Nancy Jones (eds), *Embodied Voices: Representing Female Vocality in Western Culture* (Cambridge, 1994) and Mary Ann Smart (ed.), *Siren Songs: Representations of Gender and Sexuality in Opera* (Princeton, 2001).

[4] Anthony Giddens, *Modernity and Self-Identity: Self and Society in the Late Modern Age* (Cambridge, 1991).

devotees, it is also important to understand how the 'ordinary' singer might experience their own voice. Choral singing (however broadly or narrowly one defines this) involves many more people in the act of musical performance than solo genres, and as such arguably represents a more fertile ground for the production of socio-musical meanings.

The widespread nature of the activity also gives it significance in its own right: many people experience choral singing as an integral part of their week-to-week lived experience. In particular, many choral organizations are deeply concerned with questions of social inclusivity, whether from an educational perspective, through the agenda of funding bodies, or simply from the pragmatics of recruiting and retaining choir members in an era of falling participation in organized leisure.[5] Contemporary choral music thus fulfils several of the theoretical interests that helped define critical musicology as a self-aware discipline: the concern with democratic, not just elite, musics; an interest in the cultural politics of classical music; and the desire to operate as an 'epic' theory, that is, a theory that addresses crises in the world, not just in theory.[6]

This in turn suggests where critical musicology can be of service to choral culture. In recent years choral singing has embraced an increasingly varied range of musical idioms and their associated cultural practices. The growth of international organizations and festivals has promoted an awareness of different national traditions, while national organizations have increased the contact between choral groups from a variety of different performing traditions within individual localities. These developments have produced much that is both artistically exciting and educationally enriching, opening up possibilities for the expansion of musical horizons and development of community ties in what is primarily an amateur art form.

Differences in approach, however, have also sometimes emerged as conflicts of taste and mutual misunderstanding that serve as barriers within the wider choral community. Indeed, there sometimes seems to be a greater continuity of approach and understanding between choral groups of different nationalities that share a common repertoire than between geographically close choirs performing in different styles. When these misunderstandings occur between a choir accustomed

---

[5] The concern for social inclusivity manifests in the range of projects and organizational initiatives aimed at enhancing the participation of specific social groups; see for example the range of Repertoire and Standards Committees supported by the American Choral Directors Association (details available online at http://acdaonline.org/R&S/ [accessed 1 December 2006]). Robert Putnam documents changing patterns in participative leisure in *Bowling Alone: The Collapse and Revival of American Community* (New York, 2001).

[6] The idea of an epic theory comes from Catharine MacKinnon, *Toward a Feminist Theory of the State* (Cambridge, MA, 1989); see also Liz Garnett, 'Musical Meaning Revisited: Thoughts on an "Epic" Critical Musicology', *Critical Musicology Journal* (1998), available online at http://www.leeds.ac.uk/music/Info/CMJ/Index/author.html#garnett_l.html [accessed 12 March 2008].

to performing in one idiom and a director that does not directly share this musical background, or a student director whose experience is in one idiom and a teacher with experience in another, the results can be unhappy for all concerned. The dilemma a performer faces when instructed to do something as a matter of 'good practice' that disconnects them from their experiential relationship with musical content needs handling with sensitivity. Critical musicology offers theoretical tools to analyse the nature and significance of both overlap and difference in performance practices and their associated meanings, and hence help individuals and ensembles involved in choral performance find their way through this stylistic pluralism. Negotiating between nature and nurture is a theoretical mainstay of the critical musicology project, as well as a constant practical challenge for the choral practitioner. Bringing the two together promises useful insights in both directions.

Contexts 1: Bodies of Knowledge

Within these broad disciplinary boundaries there are four specific bodies of knowledge that this study draws upon and to which it aspires to contribute. These are: theories of music and identity, with particular reference to voice; performance studies in music; the choral conducting literature itself; and theories of nonverbal communication.

Music and Identity; Voice and Identity

Music and its relationship with identity has been a central theme in the critical musicology project, not least because it was an interest shared by several of the subject areas whose interaction fed the growth of the 'new' musicology of the 1990s. Popular music studies, ethnomusicology, music and gender studies, and music psychology all shared a belief that traditional musicology's almost exclusive focus on the Western art music composer and 'his' (it was usually assumed) works took an unduly limited view of music's interest and importance in people's daily lives. What does music mean to us? Why and how do different people choose to align themselves with different types of music? In what ways is music integral to who we think we are? These were questions that all these disparate subject areas were asking in one form or another.

This heterogeneous origin has produced a literature that is vibrant and stimulating, but which also contains a potentially bewildering range of theoretical models and approaches to research method. Popular music studies started off in sociology departments in the days before they found favour in musicology, while ethnomusicology drew on the methods of anthropology. Music and gender studies drew on a range of feminist and literary/critical theories, while music psychology's disciplinary antecedents were visible in its more empirical approach. Music and identity as a subject area cuts across traditional lines not only between university departments but even faculties: it can sit not only in the arts or the humanities, but also the social sciences. It is something of a pleasant surprise, therefore, that it presents as coherent and stable a literature as it does.

Raymond MacDonald, David Hargreaves and Dorothy Miell, while writing from a music psychology perspective, make some useful points that generalize well across other approaches. First, they point out that theories of identity have moved away from the idea of the self as the stable core or essence of an individual towards a conception of identity as much more fluid and emergent. They describe the self as 'something which is constantly being reconstructed and renegotiated according to the experiences, situations and other people with whom we interact in everyday life'.[7] They attribute this shift to the rapid changes in peoples' lifestyles that accompany globalization and technological change, and indeed it may be that the dislocations of modern life bring to our attention how much psychological effort the individual needs to invest in order to maintain a sense of personal continuity. However, it is also worth pointing out this change has its theoretical origins in the work of critical and literary theorists from the 1960s onwards. The idea of a 'decentred' subject – that is, one that assembles him or herself from available cultural discourses rather than consisting of a central nucleus that pre-exists its encounter with culture – appears in various forms in the writings of Barthes, Lacan, Derrida, Kristeva and Foucault. It has subsequently infiltrated concepts of identity across many disciplines, including, of course, music.[8]

MacDonald et al. also make the distinction between identities in music, by which they mean aspects of identities defined, or at least shaped, by musical activities, and music in identities, by which they mean the ways that music acts as one of the resources people use to create their definitions of self. The first category relates more closely to the ethnomusicological tradition, with its interest in a culture's practising musicians and their cultural roles, while the second recalls the sociological interest popular music studies has taken in fandom and affiliation. The current study suggests that, useful as the distinction is, the two aspects cannot fully be separated: in Part II I shall discuss how the identity of 'choral singer' is crafted in terms that reference both 'purely' musical processes and wider social categories. That is, the identity in music is forged, at least in part, by reference to music in identity.

The foundational text in the study of voice and identity is Roland Barthes' 1972 essay 'The Grain of the Voice', in which he theorizes the indescribable but uniquely identifiable 'grain' of a voice as a result of the intersection between the

---

[7] Raymond MacDonald, David Hargreaves and Dorothy Miell (eds), *Musical Identities* (Oxford, 2002), p. 2.

[8] See for example Kevin Kopelson, *Beethoven's Kiss: Pianism, Perversion and the Mastery of Desire* (Stanford, 1996) and Judith Peraino, *Listening to the Sirens: Musical Technologies of Queer Identity from Homer to Hedwig* (Berkeley, 2005).

individual singing body and the culture-bound language it sings.[9] Barthes develops his argument by comparing two singers, Fischer-Dieskau and Panzéra, and much of the literature that has followed in his footsteps likewise evinces a fascination with individual, distinctive voices. Martha Mockus, for instance, takes the 'power, range, and depth' of k.d. lang's voice as her starting point, while Edward Baron Turk explores the reception of Jeanette MacDonald's voice in a series of film operettas from the late 1930s.[10] Other writers explore the encounter between culture and individual by focusing on the deeply personal response listeners can experience to certain voice types. For example, Elizabeth Wood identifies a voice type she calls 'Sapphonic' in the singers with whom Ethel Smyth worked as an opera composer, and discusses the specific meanings this mode of singing accrued within a lesbian aesthetic in early-twentieth-century Britain. Michel Poizat, meanwhile, explores the transcendent experiences reported by opera fans in response in particular to the soprano voice.[11]

John Potter's *Vocal Authority* takes a much broader purview than these case-study approaches, and undertakes an explicitly ideological analysis of voice production over the history of Western art music.[12] His starting-point is to question the very different uses of the voice mandated by classical and popular singing styles that he had found himself negotiating as a professional singer. From this he develops a narrative of the history of vocal music driven by a dialectic between a populist urge to communicate text intelligibly and an elitist tendency to privilege the voice as sound-object. His analyses of ideological processes that shape vocal production are incisive and original, but there is a tendency to posit a kind of Marxian vocal 'false consciousness', whereby the voice's 'natural' state is distorted by the workings of cultural politics. Popular vocal styles are just as culturally constructed as classical ones, after all, if generally less expensive to acquire. Notwithstanding these reservations, the current study (particularly Part II) shares much of Potter's critical perspective. Indeed, if the ambitious scope of Potter's work both establishes its status as a key text and represents its most significant weakness, then more focused studies such as this will inevitably read as both amplification and critique.

---

[9] Roland Barthes, (1977), 'The Grain of the Voice', in *Image Music Text*, trans. by Stephen Heath (London, 1977).

[10] Martha Mockus, (1993), 'Queer Thoughts on Country Music and k.d. lang', in Philip Brett, Elizabeth Wood and Gary C. Thomas (eds), *Queering the Pitch: The New Lesbian and Gay Musicology* (New York, 1994); Edward Baron Turk, 'Deriding the Voice of Jeanette MacDonald: Notes on Psychoanalysis and the American Film Musical,' in Dunn and Jones.

[11] Michel Poizat, *The Angel's Cry: Beyond the Pleasure Principle in Opera*, trans. by Arthur Denner (Ithaca, 1992).

[12] John Potter, *Vocal Authority: Singing Style and Ideology* (Cambridge, 1998).

Performance Studies

The area of performance studies can be seen as part of the critical musicology project in that it developed in part as a critique of academic music's prior focus on the composer and the work. Indeed, it is rather surprising how recently performance studies has emerged; for instance, it had its first dedicated session at the American Musicological Society Conference only in 1995.

Of course, musical performance has been studied in the academy since music training first moved from an apprenticeship to an institutional model, but this study traditionally operated within clear boundaries of activity and authority. Musical performance was studied almost exclusively as a practical activity, in which the aim was accurately to reproduce the work according to the composer's intentions. Any scholarship surrounding performance was focused on questions of technique, pedagogy or interpretation in service of this aim. The appropriate object for the academic study of music, meanwhile, remained the composer.

The single most significant development for the growth of performance studies was simply a decision to take seriously what practitioners do. Rather than assuming that the full meaning and artistic significance of the musical work was imparted by the composer, with the performer's role merely to transmit these meanings to the listener, scholars started to examine what performers themselves did as artistically autonomous beings. Instead of asking what a particular analysis of a work could tell a performer about how to play it, people started asking what particular performances can tell us about how to analyse a work.[13]

This shift of perspective was facilitated in several ways by technological change. First, by the 1990s, there was the best part of a century's worth of recordings available for study. While the exact status of recordings as documents and their relationship with live performance is subject to debate, this historical breadth permitted the comparison of stylistic traits across time in a way that had previously only been possible with textual sources. Robert Philip's *Early Performance and Musical Style* of 1992 was the groundbreaking text that demonstrated how the use of a host of orchestral performance devices – rubato, vibrato, portamento – that would nowadays be considered vulgar or self-indulgent were at one time mainstays of expressive performance.[14]

Philip's study was the formal outcome of work in the National Sound Archives that had started in the 1960s, and had produced many radio broadcasts en route. It was digital recording technology, however, that facilitated the dissemination and emulation of its insights. The reprocessing and reissue of old recordings on compact disc made the performance styles about which Philip wrote much more

---

[13] See for instance Nicholas Cook, 'Analysing Performance and Performing Analysis', in Nicholas Cook and Mark Everist (eds), *Rethinking Music* (Oxford, 1999); and John Rink (ed.), *The Practice of Performance: Studies in Musical Interpretation* (Cambridge 1995).

[14] Robert Philip, *Early Recordings and Musical Style: Changing Tastes in Musical Performance, 1900–1950* (Cambridge, 1992).

accessible to other scholars and their students, and thus permitted the growth of performance studies outside of specialist archives, and its infiltration into university and conservatoire curricula.

The other significant way in which technology assisted the development of performance studies was in the empirical study of performance. Whereas performance pedagogy had traditionally specified what performers *should* do, the increase in computer memory and processing power by the 1990s meant that it was now possible to measure what in fact they *did* do. Tempo variation, loudness, tuning and tone colour could all be measured, both from recordings and in the laboratory. The elements of music that lie 'between the notes' had previously been relegated to the margins of academic study as overly 'subjective' compared to the solidly verifiable elements of notation; when technology made these details available for study, the qualitative became quantifiable.[15]

I will discuss this study's relationship with empirical methods in more detail in Part I; for now, it suffices to note that the ethos of performance studies lies at the heart of this book. My central thesis sees performing individuals as integral to the construction and transmission of musical meanings, and my focus will be on these individuals almost to the exclusion of the composer's text. I will also be exploring the gap between what theorists recommend and what practitioners actually do, and will be doing so without making a priori assumptions about which is most likely to be 'right'. For while there are few conductors who would lay claim to flawless technique, there is also much that conductors do very effectively that nonetheless appears to contradict theory, or is simply not documented. By making these practices visible, then, this study recognizes the work of those who keep choral traditions alive, as well as giving them a sense of perspective on each other's praxis.

The Choral Conducting Literature

The distinction between pedagogical and empirical approaches noted in performance studies is also very clear within the choral conducting literature itself. This study has a somewhat different relationship with this body of knowledge from those discussed above, in that the choral conducting literature represents both a principal disciplinary context to which this book aims to contribute and a significant primary source. That is, the distinction that scholarly writing traditionally makes between 'literature review' and 'data analysis' becomes very blurred when the people for whom and about whom one is writing are substantially the same. I will discuss the ethical and epistemological issues this raises in more detail in my discussion of peer research in Part I; here I will simply outline what the choral conducting literature comprises and how I will use it in this book.

---

[15] See for example Peter Johnson, '"Expressive Intonation" in String Performance: Problems of Analysis and Interpretation' in Jane Davidson (ed.), *The Music Practitioner: Research for the Music Performer, Teacher and Listener* (Aldershot, 2004).

The pedagogical literature I draw on consists of texts for the instruction of choral conductors published in Britain and the United States between 1914 and 2004. Some (primarily American) are intended for use in structured courses in choral conducting and/or by those intending to pursue choral conducting as a career; others (both British and American) are aimed at the aspiring amateur. Virtually all, though, are written by practitioners and strongly reflect their authors' personal experience as choral conductors; consequently, I refer to this body of work as the practitioner literature.

These texts both draw upon and constitute a complex and constantly renegotiated discourse that shapes cultural practice. They are the discursive flotsam left behind by a century of music-making in two countries, and they give us vivid pictures of their authors' practical experiences, and the frameworks of value in which these occurred. At the same time, the texts are claiming the power to shape their readers' activities and their beliefs about their activities in ways that will directly impact upon the lived experience of the singers those readers direct. It is notable that the intertextual relationships within this literature are strongly mediated by praxis; authors are in general far more likely to refer to another conductor's or choir's good practice to support their recommendations than they are to another writer's book. Practitioners are the primary storage device for this discourse, and the literature is commensurately personal and practical.[16]

The empirical literature is much more recent, and much more firmly based in the academy. It is strongly linked to American university departments that run DMA programmes in choral conducting, and is often published in education journals, although the development of specialist journals since the turn of the millennium attests to the growth of this area as a discipline in its own right. The empirical literature both critiques and draws upon the practitioner literature. Its primary rationale is that the practitioner literature is unscholarly in its reliance on anecdote and uncorroborated experience; consequently common themes found within the practitioner literature provide many of its hypotheses for testing. I shall discuss in Part I the merits of this critique, and the implications of the methods chosen to produce the desired intellectual rigour.

The empirical literature thus represents a change in attitude as to what constitutes reliable knowledge: the scientifically demonstrable becomes valued above the

---

[16] Hence, in 1975 Darrow notes that a 1959 article classifies articulation styles into legato, marcato and staccato; this classification also appears in 1970 and 1996 in books by Garretson and Jordan respectively, and is developed in 2002 by Neuen. This classification probably first appeared in print in 1950 in Max Rudolf's book on orchestral conducting, but in all of these cases except Darrow, there is no reference to any literary provenance. See Gerald Darrow, *Four Decades of Choral Training* (Metuchen, 1975), p. 152; Robert Garretson, *Conducting Choral Music*, 3rd edn (Boston, 1970), p. 24; James Jordan, *Evoking Sound: Fundamentals of Choral Conducting and Rehearsing* (Chicago, 1996), p. 119; Donald Neuen, *Choral Concepts: A Text for Conductors* (Belmont, 2002), p. 224; and Max Rudolf, *The Grammar of Conducting*, 3rd edn (New York, 1995).

merely expert. It does not, however, represent a shift in what this knowledge aims to achieve. Like traditional instruction manuals, most empirical studies in choral conducting seek to identify what is effective in order that practitioners might change what they do for the better. That is, despite the adoption of very different methods and modes of discourse, these studies remain primarily pedagogical in intent. This contrasts with the empirical work in performance studies discussed above, which explicitly refused to assume that the theorist is entitled to instruct the practitioner.

For this study, the practitioner literature provides a significant source of evidence for how choral conductors understand what they do, and I use this evidence in several ways. First, like the empirical studies in choral conducting, I use practitioner texts to document the rationale for my central questions. While any one writer may be deemed anecdotal in approach, together they demonstrate a broad community of understanding. Second, I use this shared understanding to test methods and theories applied to the study of choral conducting, both by myself and others. Hence my critique of empirical approaches to conducting in Part I is based on the way they rely on marginalizing elements that practitioners value most highly. The criterion by which I select theories of nonverbal communication to discuss in Part IV is likewise whether they explain practitioners' experiences. Third, I analyse the practitioners' discourse for evidence of the musical and cultural values that inform and shape their practice; the practitioner texts accordingly provide much of the primary source material for my discussion of enculturation in Part II.

Nonverbal Communication Studies

Conducting, as many writers on the subject contend, is a form of nonverbal communication. It is perhaps surprising, then, that the extensive literature in nonverbal communication studies is not referenced more widely in studies of conducting. This is the final major body of knowledge to inform this book, and it is both the most obvious and – in its manifestations to date – the least musical.

Nonverbal communication studies is an interdisciplinary field which brings together aspects of anthropology, neuropsychology and semiotics, although its primary disciplinary home is in social psychology. It embraces a range of areas of enquiry, including the study of body language (gesture, stance, mannerism); of facial expression, particularly in relation to emotional state; of how people interact physically in social situations; and the non-linguistic elements of speech (tone, inflection, speed).[17] It thus shares a number of questions of both theory and method with the study of conducting.

---

[17] For general overviews of the field, see Michael Argyle, *Bodily Communication*, 2nd edn (London, 1988), and Mark Knapp and Judith Hall, *Nonverbal Communication in Human Interaction*, 5th edn (London, 2002).

Key theoretical questions surround the nature and function of gesture and body language. To what extent are gestures part of a shared cultural vocabulary, and to what extent are they idiosyncratic to the individual? Is body language expressive or communicative? That is, to what extent do gestures and facial expressions reflect a person's interior state, and to what extent are they a means to convey information? What relationship does gesture have to thought? Is it a descriptive gloss to aid communication, or does it participate in the formulation of ideas?[18] Gesture studies has a well-developed theoretical framework within which to address these questions, including a collection of systems by which to classify gestures according to the degree to which they are conventionalized and their relative dependence on or independence from verbal content.[19]

This work, though, has been developed almost exclusively in the context of spoken language. Musical systems of gesture, such as conducting and solfège, rarely feature among the case studies in this literature, which include such otherwise varied examples as American Sign Language, theatre studies and primatology. And some of the most significant theoretical developments in gesture studies, such as David McNeill's concept of the 'growth point' – the moment at which a thought is formulated – see language and gesture as so intimately related that one could hardly exist without the other.[20] In this context, simply applying the pre-existent theories from nonverbal communication studies to conducting is easier said than done. Still, there is a growing interest in gesture theory among musicologists (if relatively little in conducting studies itself), and the explanatory possibilities are rich enough that it is worth teasing out how gesture studies' answers to the common questions outlined above might illuminate what goes on in the choral rehearsal. Indeed, a subsidiary aim of this project is to offer back to theorists of nonverbal communication some insight as to how effectively their models work with regard to musical discourses.

Nonverbal communication studies also grapples with similar questions of method to those that face the researcher in conducting. These include, first, questions of how to capture details of the behaviours to be studied: whether to set up situations in which the behaviours will unfold, or whether to go out and observe the behaviours occurring in daily life. Second, there are the questions of documentation: how best to record or describe the behaviours, particularly

---

[18] These issues are explored in Adam Kendon, 'An Agenda for Gesture Studies', *Semiotic Review of Books* 7/3 (1997): 8–12; and Paul Ekman, 'Should We Call it Expression or Communication?', *Innovations in Social Science Research* 10/4 (1997): 333–44.

[19] Classification systems are presented in Bernard Rimé and Loris Schiaratura, 'Gesture and Speech' in Robert Feldman and Bernard Rimé (eds), *Fundamentals of Nonverbal Behaviour* (Cambridge, 1991); David McNeill (ed.) *Language and Gesture* (Cambridge, 2000); and David McNeill, *Gesture and Thought* (Chicago, 2005).

[20] David McNeill, *Gesture and Thought* (Chicago, 2005) and 'Gesture, Gaze, and Ground', available online at http://mcneilllab.uchicago.edu/pdfs/McNeill_VACE.pdf [accessed 12 March 2008].

with regard to qualitative (as opposed to formal) elements. Related to this is the question of interpretation, especially as it relates to the researcher's own cultural background: to what extent, and in what circumstances, can one reliably ascribe expressive qualities to a gesture? These issues are equally fundamental whether one is studying human interaction in conversational groups or in vocal ensembles, and the solutions developed in nonverbal communication studies have usefully informed my discussions of method and approach in Part I.

Contexts 2: Communities of Practice

So who are the choral practitioners whose music-making this study attempts to understand? In addition to the British and American practitioners whose voices come through the literature, this study draws on visits to over 40 choirs in rehearsal. The majority of these were based within an hour's travel from Birmingham, UK; this was a choice of pragmatism rather than principle, however, and I took opportunities as they arose to observe choirs from further afield, either when they visited the West Midlands or when I travelled elsewhere. Hence I also have notes on groups from North America, Ireland, Korea, the Netherlands and New Zealand, as well as from around the UK, although some of these were in staged open rehearsals and so do not offer direct comparison with ensembles observed 'in the wild'. They nonetheless offer some wider perspective. The choirs were selected to represent a variety of choral traditions, and included large choral societies, small community choirs, cathedral choirs (men and boys, and mixed), gospel choirs (both church and performance), Jewish choirs (again, both synagogue and performance), barbershop choruses (male and female) and male voice choirs. The majority of singers, though not all, were amateur, and the directors included the full gamut from seasoned professional, though semi-professional to relatively inexperienced amateur. Contact came variously by telephoning around choirs listed in local directories and by personal introductions, and the selection process therefore aimed to balance opportunism as I developed my relationship with the region's choral networks with the need for breadth in the overall picture.

This broad picture, then, gives rise to several further questions. What is the relationship between insights gained from the practitioners represented in the literature and the practitioners observed in person? Should we see this as a cross-cultural, inter-cultural or intra-cultural study? How, in fact, does one define the identity of a choral group?

To start with the question of primary sources: for the purposes of this study, the medium in which material is accessed is largely irrelevant to its usefulness. That is, it does not matter if one learns of a conductor's view that, in articulating a text, 'you can never have too much consonant' through reading it in an instruction manual or hearing it spoken in rehearsal. Either way, it acts as evidence of a particular set of beliefs about choral performance. Given that the practitioner literature both arises from and seeks to shape actual practice in rehearsal and performance, there is a broad continuity of discourse and cultural meanings between published texts and observed practice.

Within this general premise, however, a couple of caveats are in order, and these start to impinge on our questions about group identity. The first caveat is to consider how the two classes of material are situated in time and place. That is, they both present bodies of evidence of beliefs and practices within choral music-making, but the profiles of the samples are quite different. One covers two continents and the time-frame of a century, and presents the world from the perspective of the conductor, while the other is focused on the early years of the twenty-first century in central England, and presents the world from the position of an informed observer. It is clear, therefore, that generalizing across the bodies of evidence needs to be undertaken with some care; it is unlikely, for instance, that Henry Coward's views on social class and singing ability would be as acceptable in Sheffield today as they were in 1914.[21] On the other hand, the two bodies of evidence are not as distinct as this might suggest. There are genealogies of practice that run through both: choral practitioners will routinely quote other conductors' points of principle or *bons mots* to both their choirs and their readers to lend authority to their statements. And, while it varies considerably how much today's practitioners engage with the literature aimed at them, all the texts cited are available to them and thus have at least the potential to inform their discursive world.

The second caveat relates to how we delineate the group 'choral practitioners'. The impression one gains from a cursory read of the practitioner literature is that choral music is a relatively self-evident and obvious category with a clear set of shared norms. Likewise, festivals and networking organizations suggest that, while different choral groups present different performing traditions and repertoires, we all know what choral singing involves and will be able to recognize it when we hear it. And of course at one level this is the case; the common-sense understanding clearly works well as a useful part of our musical world. But it also hides within it assumptions about what choral music is, and what choral practitioners do, that do not necessarily generalize to all parts of choral culture. I will analyse this issue in detail in Part II, but it is relevant here because it affects the points about both evidence and cultural identity outlined above.

The definition of 'choral practitioners' affects the relationship between text-based and ethnographic evidence because writers on choral music are more likely to come from certain traditions than others. This should not be surprising, of course. A person's relationship with educational institutions, and thereby with formalized knowledge, is a significant component of identity, and it is thus only to be expected that those whose background includes the expectation that music is something to be written about would provide the published literature. Still, it should remind us that when a writer makes a point about choral music in general, they are nonetheless writing from a specific position in relation to choral music as a whole. That is, their statements do not necessarily carry more authority than those

---

[21] See p. 92 in Chapter 7 for a discussion of this.

of practitioners whose rehearsals I have observed. The fact of publication can give some indication about an individual practitioner's esteem and influence among his or her peers, but this is only relevant within those parts of choral practice that have an established relationship with the infrastructure of publication. In effect, this is to restate my earlier point about evidence base – that the medium is largely irrelevant to the effectiveness of material to demonstrate beliefs and practices – but with a particular precautionary note.

The question of a 'choral' identity and how to define it also affects how this project is framed in general, whether it should be seen as a cross-cultural or within-culture study. This looks as if it should be an easy question, but actually depends significantly on how one formulates concepts such as 'culture' and 'identity'. If we use standard sociological markers of social groups – race, class, age, nationality – we will come to rather different answers than if we define the groupings by the cultural practices that identify people as choral practitioners – lay clerk, soprano, barbershopper. From the first perspective, this looks like a within-community study that investigates British choirs, with the few groups from abroad offering a little breadth of perspective but not significantly distracting from this focus. Indeed, all the choirs were English-speaking, in that rehearsals were conducted in English (although the Korean choir was clearly doing this for a British audience, and the Dutch group was working in English for the benefit of an English-speaking educator).

Beyond this basic common denominator, however, the cultural homogeneity starts to break down. The demographic profiles of different choral groups in the same area can be strikingly different: one can find an all-white, explicitly secular group rehearsing in the same venue as an all-black, faith-based ensemble. And even language is not as stable a factor as one might suppose. Several of the UK-based choirs have repertoire in languages other than English (Hebrew, Welsh, Latin) that act as significant markers of religious and/or ethnic identity, or educational background. The extent to which these sociological markers would be regarded as essential to the group's identity varies: one is more likely to be excluded from a choir because one is the wrong religion than because one did not learn Latin at school. It is clear, though, that there is a significant degree of cross-cultural comparison involved in studying different choral traditions within the same geographical area.

This suggests that it can make more sense to delineate choral singers' identities in terms of musical repertoires and their associated performance traditions. These remain somewhat tangled up with sociological categories of identity, as we have seen, but are more likely to be experienced as central to a singer's identity within the context of that group. Some choral traditions are relatively easy to identify as distinct musical communities: barbershop and gospel, for instance, have boundaries that are relatively visible and audible, sustained not only by repertoires and performance practices but also by institutions and belief systems.[22]

---

[22] See for example Liz Garnett, *The British Barbershopper: A Study in Socio-Musical Values* (Aldershot, 2005a) for a discussion of the ways in which barbershop creates and maintains its sense of identity.

Male voice choirs present a less clear-cut example. Some maintain a strong sense of heritage and continuity of tradition, articulated by, for example, Welsh-language repertoire, while others position themselves more simply as singing organizations that offer single-sex leisure. The English collegiate and cathedral tradition is easily identified in its typical locations, but the strength of this tradition as a training-ground for British musicians means that one frequently finds directors from this background leading many choral societies and chamber choirs. Other choral societies, meanwhile, have directors with a background of conducting instrumental ensembles. Here, then, the boundaries between traditions and repertoires are fuzzier; the meme-pool is larger and more freely shared.

Hence, this study has elements both of cross-cultural and intra-cultural work, depending on how one chooses to define cultural groupings. It cannot claim to speak for all choral practitioners everywhere – even at its widest reach it remains focused on the UK and the US. But it does embrace a sufficient range of performing traditions to give a sense of perspective, and thus to draw conclusions that have the potential to offer insight beyond the case studies from which they are drawn.

Before embarking on the cultural, gestural and interpersonal questions that lead to these conclusions, however, it will be useful to consider how to go about research in conducting. Hence Part I will examine questions of research method and its implications for the kind of knowledge that different approaches will produce. Readers whose primary interest is in the practice of conducting may wish to skip ahead to later sections, although they will need to come back to Part I if they find themselves wondering why I have gone about the research in the ways that I have.

The following three sections travel a path along the nature–nurture axis from an analysis of the social construction of the choral singer to a discussion of how ensemble singing relies on instinctual behaviours we share with other primates. Part II considers questions of choral culture and identity, examining the ways that choirs establish and uphold their customs and conventions. It shows that practices that most readers will find so familiar as to be almost invisible are in fact sustained by a collection of deeply embedded belief systems and expectations for behaviour that are enforced by conductors and singers alike. Part III focuses on the conductor and explores how it is that they can come to 'look like the music'. This section includes detailed discussion of gestural vocabulary, illustrated by footage on the accompanying DVD, and uses this to theorize how these gestures become meaningful. This section is the heart of the book: it is where practical detail meets theoretical analysis most directly, and thus allows us to see how genre-specific traditions arise from processes shared across styles. Part IV moves away from questions of cultural values towards the mechanisms of interpersonal interaction. We may know how gestures become meaningful, but how is it that they can have such an audibly direct effect on the way choral singers use their voices? As Part II provides the cultural context for the construction of meaning, Part IV explores the inborn infrastructure that permits choral traditions to develop and disseminate their distinctive practices.

The Conclusion draws these threads together to show how these processes interact, how the conductor's generation and communication of musical meaning relies on both cultural-discursive processes and instinctive, inherited behaviours. It goes on to ask what the implications of these findings are for conducting studies in general and for the reflective practitioner in particular. My central research questions arose from experience in real-life situations, and I have therefore evaluated the theories that I have used to answer them by their capacity to explain phenomena observed in regular choral practice. The overall aim, therefore, is to offer ideas that will enable directors to develop a new level of self-knowledge at the level of both technique and interpersonal interactions, make wiser and more sensitive choices when moving between stylistic worlds, and make sense of their musical experiences in new ways that will enhance their conducting and their teaching. The essence of a good theory, after all, is that it helps us not only to understand the world around us, but also to act more effectively within it.

PART I
How to Study Conducting: Model, Method, Metalanguage

Research into conducting has become something of a growth industry since the start of the twenty-first century, particularly in the USA, with articles spilling over from their traditional home in music education journals into new specialist publications. Indeed, two such journals appeared during the five years I have spent working on this project: the *International Journal of Research into Choral Singing* in 2003 and *The Choral Scholar* in 2007. The discipline is developing a level of scholarly confidence, and shows a desire to move beyond anecdote and individual experience towards a more systematic approach to knowledge.

It has not yet reflected extensively on the nature of this knowledge, however. There is a broad consensus that findings need to be based in something more solid than hearsay, and a set of standard methods are emerging to this end. But there has been little discussion of the implications these methods might have for the use-value of their results. The relationship between what we know, how we know it and how we go about discovering it – the relationship between epistemology and method, that is – is less obvious than it may first appear.

Part I explores what counts as knowledge in the study of conducting in order to explain how I have approached the research for this book. It is necessarily more abstract than the sections that follow, and less intimately engaged with the detail of either conducting technique or choral rehearsal. Nonetheless, it remains an important part of the overall argument, since it lays the foundations for my decisions about research method, and therefore what kind of knowledge this research can produce. Moreover, given the pedagogical impulse of most conducting research – the desire to produce conclusions that will change what people do – it seems to be a valuable enterprise in its own right to take a step back to consider the basis upon which these changes are proposed.

Part I thus addresses three interrelated questions: how to think about conducting (model); how to go about researching conducting (method); and how to write about conducting (metalanguage).

Chapter 2 explores the question of model: How do people conceptualize the process of conducting? It outlines the two competing models in evidence in the conducting literature, a signalling model and an interactive model. Both are present in the practitioner literature, but the empirical literature relies much more heavily on the signalling model, probably in response to the requirements of experimental design. The chapter continues with a discussion of the consequences of this model and its associated methods for the production of knowledge, and suggests that the imperative to isolate variables makes it difficult to generalize from the experimental situation to real life.

Chapter 3 turns to the interactive model of conducting and considers its implications for method. It argues for the study of choral practice in naturalistic settings, and explores the distinctive set of insights that ethnographic approaches can offer. The ethos of performance studies is important too: by taking what practitioners do, and what they say about what they do, seriously, one can discover aspects of practice that might otherwise be ignored. Hence, this chapter explores a model of peer research that attempts to avoid the separation of subject and object, or insider and outsider, as a basis for the researcher's authority to draw conclusions. This includes questions of ethics, representation and accountability, and suggests that Thomas Lindlof's notion of qualitative research as 'catch and release fishing' is significantly inflected when one considers the 'fish' themselves as a primary audience for the research's outputs.[1] The chapter includes a description of the rehearsal observations on which much of the rest of the book draws.

Chapter 4 moves on to consider how to write about conducting. The problem of metalanguage is an issue in any study of semiotics or communication, and has been discussed at length in both musicology and gesture studies. This chapter outlines the various possible approaches for describing conducting gesture, from the musically interpretative to the anatomical, and weighs up their various merits and limitations. There is a trade-off between analytical rigour and detail on the one hand and readability on the other; descriptions that 'chunk' together movements into meaningful phrases risk inscribing the researcher's assumptions into their results, whereas descriptions that break them down into the smallest units risk overwhelming the reader with detail.

Part I has another, more global and arguably more important, aim: to mediate between the two contrasting bodies of knowledge associated with choral conducting. On the one hand there are the instruction manuals written by and for choral practitioners, and on the other the empirical studies emerging from university departments in the form of dissertations and scholarly articles. This mediation is necessary not only to provide a coherent context for the sections that follow, but also to bring together the disparate musical constituencies associated with these literatures. For when the academic dismisses the practitioner as 'subjective' and the practitioner dismisses scholarship as 'irrelevant', they both have a point. Part I seeks to understand this divide and to find a way of thinking about choral practice that is meaningful to both.

---

[1] Thomas Lindlof, Qualitative Communication Research Methods (London, 1995), pp. 282–3.

Chapter 2
How do People Think about Conducting?

> Fundamental beliefs require fundamental questions. There are many things that music educators hold to be true or obvious, but ... music education would be better served by pursuing the underpinnings of beliefs to gain better insights into their foundations. In this way, we would see whether they stand up to systematic examination. In spite of appearance [sic] to the contrary, the Earth is not flat; if you examine the data, you will find that it is round – sort of.[1]

In these words, from his editorial introduction to Julie Skadsem's 1997 study of conductor behaviour and choir response, Harry Price places the endeavour of empirical studies in choral conducting firmly within the Enlightenment project. Old certainties, the myths of a discipline that are handed down from sage to student as eternally true, are to be held up to the light of day. Nothing is too sacred to be questioned.

And indeed, there is much in the practitioner literature that is arbitrary, unsupported or, as Kevin Ford puts it, 'largely anecdotal'.[2] The reader is expected to trust assertions as truth on the strength of the writer's track record as a practitioner, and the only means to decide between competing or conflicting instructions is therefore by recourse to the reader's own practical experiences. There is good reason to 'venture beyond ... the "this works for me" approach' and attempt to test these unsubstantiated assertions.[3]

However, if an individual's personal experience is an insufficient claim to authority, we should be equally chary of accepting an appeal to scientific method as conferring an automatic alternative source of legitimacy. Various branches of the arts and humanities have sought to share the cultural power that accrued to the sciences during the second half of the twentieth century, and not all have fared

---

[1] Harry E. Price, Editorial introduction to Julie A. Skadsem, 'Effect of conductor verbalization, dynamic markings, conductor gesture, and choir dynamic level on singers' dynamic responses', *Journal of Research in Music Education*, 45/4 (1997): 508.

[2] Kevin Ford, 'Preferences for Strong or Weak Singer's Formant Resonance in Choral Tone Quality', *International Journal of Research in Choral Singing*, 1/1 (2003): 29–47, p. 30.

[3] James F. Daugherty, 'On Pursuing Unusually Stubborn and Persisting Efforts to Think by the Intelligent Gathering and Use of Data,' *International Journal of Research in Choral Singing*, 2/1 (2004): 1–2, p. 1.

equally well.[4] Indeed, the debate in the social sciences about the relative merits of qualitative and quantitative research is in large part a debate about the limits of positivism: when and in what ways can methods developed for the study of the natural world transfer usefully to the study of human activities?[5]

This chapter examines how empirical studies in choral conducting have gone about the task of controlled, systematic research, and in particular what the conceptual bases are for their approaches. It starts with the question of model: when people think about conducting, what is the mental structure that they use to represent it to themselves? It then goes on to show why one of the two common models is overwhelmingly chosen in empirical conducting studies, and the consequences of that choice for the results produced. It will argue that the shibboleths of objectivism are just as dangerous as the myths of artistic expertise, that how one conceives the process of conducting is integrally related with the choices one makes in research design, and that these decisions in turn affect what kind of knowledge the research can produce.

Two Competing Models

There are two basic models for the conducting process: a signalling model and an interactive, or ensemble model. The first is represented by Figure 2.1, and sees conducting as a process of the transmission of information. The conductor is understood to encode information, which is signalled to the performers via the channel of visible gesture, and the performers decode this information in order to act upon it. It is a very common model of communication, characterized by George Lakoff and Mark Johnson as the 'conduit' metaphor: it draws attention to the way that information is passed from one person to another, and conceives the means by which that information travels from one person to the next as a link

---

[4] An example that may be familiar to music scholars lies in music theory, where the imperative to be 'scientific' and 'objective' found in 1970s semiotics had been quietly dropped by the 1990s. Compare, for example, Jean-Jacques Nattiez's two books, *Fondements d'une Sémiologie de la Musique* (Paris, 1975) and *Music and Discourse*, trans. by Carolyn Abbate (Princeton, 1990). The ideals of rigour and transparency remain in the later book, but the attempt to base analytical insight on purely positivistic methods has largely disappeared. A similar process in the study of literature was parodied brilliantly by David Lodge in his campus novels *Changing Places* (London, 1975) and *Small World* (London, 1984).

[5] A good introduction to these issues can be found in John Creswell, *Research Design: Qualitative, Quantitative, and Mixed Methods Approaches*, 2nd edn (London, 2002), and a more nuanced discussion of the philosophical and ethical aspects of the debate is presented in Paul Smeyers, 'Qualitative versus Quantitative Research Design: A Plea for Paradigmatic Tolerance in Educational Research', in Mike J. MacNamee and David Bridges (eds), *The Ethics of Educational Research* (Oxford, 2002).

or path between them.[6] It is a paradigm based on the model of the telegraph, and, just as telecommunications have become a technologically pervasive aspect of our lives, the concept of communication they spawn has become culturally pervasive, in music and beyond.

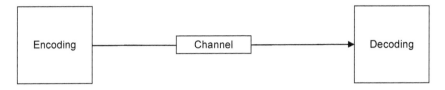

Figure 2.1   Transmission model of conducting

Figure 2.1 itself, for example, is based on the way that Michael Argyle presents the basic model of information transmission between people in his introduction to nonverbal communication studies.[7] In this case, the 'channel' refers to the sense involved – sight, sound, or touch – although visual signals are often broken down into separate channels: facial expression, posture, gesture or gaze behaviour.[8] Umberto Eco uses a similar model in his *Theory of Semiotics*, and Edward Venn uses this as the basis for his semiotic analysis of the conducting process, with the conductor's motions construed as the channel.[9]

This model has also been used more abstractly. Leonard Meyer evoked the metaphor of the telephone directly in his discussion of musical meaning based on information theory.[10] Likewise, the 'neutral level' in the tri-partitional model that Jean-Jacques Nattiez adopts from Jean Molino conceives the score as a conduit between the composer of a message and its receiver.[11] The performance process is also often implicitly – and sometimes explicitly – modelled

---

[6]   George Lakoff and Mark Johnson, *Metaphors We Live By* (Chicago, 1980), pp. 10–11.

[7]   Michael Argyle, *Bodily Communication*, 2nd edn (London, 1988), p. 2.

[8]   Arvid Kappas, Ursula Hess and Klaus R. Scherer present a similar diagram to represent vocal communication in 'Voice and Emotion', in Robert S. Feldman and Bernard Rimé (eds), *Fundamentals of Nonverbal Behavior* (Cambridge, 1991), p. 201.

[9]   Umberto Eco, *A Theory of Semiotics* (Indianapolis, 1976); Edward Venn, 'Towards a Semiotics of Conducting', paper presented at the *Music and Gesture* conference, University of East Anglia, June 2003. My thanks to the author for supplying a copy of this paper.

[10]   Leonard B. Meyer, 'Meaning in Music and Information Theory', in *Music, The Arts, and Ideas: Patterns and Predictions in Twentieth-Century Culture* (Chicago, 1967).

[11]   Jean-Jacques Nattiez, *Music and Discourse*. Nattiez actually states (p. x) that his theory of musical semiotics is not about communication per se, on the grounds that there is no guarantee that the meaning intended at the poietic level will match that which is decoded at the esthesic level. Nonetheless the model is very clearly structured using the conduit metaphor.

this way. Both Hindemith's notorious attack on performers and Stravinsky's polemics against interpretation cast the performer as a passive channel between composer and listener. Hindemith calls the performer an 'intermediate transformer station between the generator of a composition and its consumer' and Stravinsky states that the 'proper function' of a performer is 'to transmit music to the listener'.[12] The best one can hope from a telephone wire, after all, is that it does not distort the message too much.

The evidence for this model in writings by conductors themselves, however, is less clear-cut than one would expect given its general popularity in wider culture. It is evoked in some of the vocabulary used to describe the conducting process: Robert Garretson, John Hylton, Donald Bostock and Mike Brewer all use the verb 'to convey', while Leslie Woodgate, and Harold Decker and Colleen Kirk use the visual metaphors of 'to indicate' and 'to picture' respectively.[13] Other writers refer to it directly, but suggest that it is only a partial explanation for what a conductor does. For instance, Max Rudolph regards the elementary gestures of beat patterns and tempo changes as 'hardly more than traffic signals'.[14] David Hill, Hilary Parfitt and Elizabeth Ash, meanwhile, state that the clarity of the 'code' that the conductor uses 'to give messages to [their] choir members' is only half of the process; the conductor also needs the 'capacity to respond' to them in turn.[15]

Hence, practitioners find the transmission model as somewhat meaningful to describe what they do, but inadequate or incomplete as a full account. Rather, they conceive conducting as an inherently interactive process that creates an intimate and vital connection between conductor and ensemble. Indeed, there is some stringent critique for those who consider conducting to be a one-way process. Bostock complains that, 'Too many people regard the choir as a sound-producing machine, which may be manipulated by means of a score, two arms and a stick.'[16] Brock McElheran, meanwhile, recommends that the conductor 'throw himself into the task of drawing music from the performers rather than merely going through

---

[12] Paul Hindemith, *A Composer's World: Horizons and Limitations* (New York, 1952), p. 153; Igor Stravinsky, *Poetics of Music*, trans. by Arthur Knodel and Ingolf Dahl (Cambridge, MA, 1947), p. 122.

[13] Robert L. Garretson, *Conducting Choral Music*, 3rd edn (Boston, MA, 1970), p. 5; John Hylton, *Comprehensive Choral Music Education* (Englewood Cliffs, 1995), p. 96; Donald Bostock, *Choirmastery: A Practical Handbook* (London, 1966), p. 25; Mike Brewer, *Kick Start Your Choir* (London, 1997), p. 10; Leslie Woodgate, *The Chorus Master* (London, 1944), p. 27; Harold A. Decker and Colleen J. Kirk, *Choral Conducting: Focus on Communication* (Englewood Cliffs, 1988), p. 6.

[14] Max Rudolph, *The Grammar of Conducting: A Comprehensive Guide to Baton Technique and Interpretation*, 3rd edn (New York, 1995), p. xv.

[15] David Hill, Hilary Parfitt and Elizabeth Ash, *Giving Voice: A Handbook for Choir Directors and Trainers* (Rattlesden, 1995), p. 40.

[16] Bostock, p. 6.

studied mechanical actions.'[17] This sense of drawing sound out of the ensemble, rather than pushing information over to them, is a common metaphor. Paul Roe describes what kind of gestures allow a director to 'pull' sound from the choir, Colin Durrant writes of 'releasing' sound from the singers, while James Jordan entitles his book on choral conducting *Evoking Sound*.[18]

The organ that drives this process, according to many writers, is the conductor's ear. 'How well do you hear?' Howard Swan asks directors, 'How well do you listen? How much do you hear at rehearsal?'[19] Jordan locates the origin of the conductor's movements in this capacity: '[G]esture is a byproduct of listening', he says. 'Conducting gesture, like spontaneous dance, should be a reaction to something heard.'[20] Other writers articulate the vital communication between conductor and choir through metaphors of physicality. Hill, Parfitt and Ash identify '*being in touch*' as the primary characteristic of conducting, while John Bertalot instructs the director to 'conduct every rehearsal so that you hold your singers in the palms of your hands'.[21] William Ehmann develops this image into a very concrete metaphor: 'The choir director must feel somewhat like an extremely skilled glassblower, who with his highly trained hands and fingers forms with greatest dexterity, the stream of hot liquid glass while it is being poured into a work of art.'[22] Archibald Davison and Samuel Adler, meanwhile, offer a more dynamic metaphor when they both liken conducting singers to throwing a rubber ball at a stone wall: 'There is as much rebound as there is force in the throw.'[23] This sense of real-time connection, of ensemble, is developed by some writers into a notion almost of telepathy; indeed, Coward actually uses this term to evoke the way the depth of the conductor's preparation speeds up the choir's process of learning.[24] Bertalot defines 'creative and interactive eye contact' as meaning 'when your eyes meet, each of you knows what the other is thinking'.[25]

---

[17] Brock McElheran, *Conducting Techniques for Beginners and Professionals* (Oxford, 1966), p. 84.

[18] Paul Roe, *Choral Music Education*, 2nd edn (Englewood Cliffs, 1983), p. 217; Colin Durrant, *Choral Conducting: Philosophy and Practice* (London, 2003), p. 141; James Jordan, *Evoking Sound: Fundamentals of Choral Conducting and Rehearsing* (Chicago, 1996).

[19] Howard Swan, *Conscience of a Profession* (Chapel Hill, 1987), p. 42.

[20] Jordan, p. 139.

[21] Hill, Parfitt and Ash, p. 41 (emphasis in the original); John Bertalot, *How to be a Successful Choir Director* (Stowmarket, 2002), p. 107.

[22] William Ehmann, *Choral Directing*, trans. G. Wiebe (Minneapolis, 1968), p 116.

[23] Archibald Davison, *Choral Conducting* (Cambridge, MA, 1954), p. 9; cited by Samuel Adler, *Choral Conducting: An Anthology* (Fort Worth, 1971), p. 12.

[24] Henry Coward, *Choral Technique and Interpretation* (London, 1914), p. 265.

[25] Bertalot, p. 119.

Lewis Gordon presents a diagram to illustrate the complexity of the relationships not just between conductor and singers, but between the singers themselves (reproduced as Figure 2.2).[26]

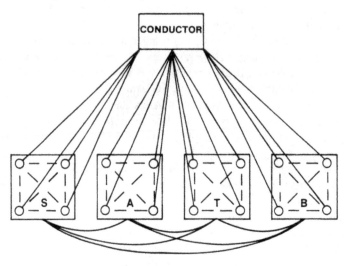

Figure 2.2   Interactive model of conducting

At first glance, this may appear to be simply a concatenation of multiple versions of Figure 2.1: there are a good many more parties involved, but each is basically encoding information to be passed over to all other parties, who will decode it. However, two features suggest that we should consider this to be a fundamentally different way of conceiving the communication process between director and ensemble. The first is the way that Gordon characterizes the connecting lines in his commentary: 'The choral director should develop the constant image that he or she is connected by several strings to each member of the ensemble. Whenever hands, arms or chest are moved, there should be a *physical* feeling of directly controlling the singer's response.'[27] This not only resonates with the physical metaphors cited above, but articulates very clearly their contrast of instantaneous interaction with the time-bound idea of a conduit. However quickly a channel may carry a message, the encoding-transmission-decoding process is essentially sequential. By contrast, to pull on the end of a taut string is to exert force on the entire object at once; to affect one end is to affect both. Second, the very complexity changes the nature of the interactions. If all parties are simultaneously both sending and receiving messages to and from multiple interactants, this is no longer a collection of one-to-one relationships but a many-to-many relationship. Each connection impinges

---

[26] Lewis Gordon, *Choral Director's Rehearsal and Performance Guide* (West Nyack, 1989), p. 96.
[27] Ibid., p. 96, emphasis in original.

on all its neighbouring connections, and it becomes impossible to take one out without affecting all the others. These contrasts become important as we turn our attention to empirical studies in choral conducting, and the relationship between conceptual model and research design.

Conducting Experiments

Empirical studies in conducting aspire to systematic, controlled enquiries that can verify or debunk the subjective assertions of the traditional practitioner literature. The way that many of them exert this control is by designing their experimental procedures around the transmission model of communication. The reasons for this decision lie not only in its currency within wider culture, but also in specific attributes that suit it to the scientific method. However, as we shall see, choosing a model that prefers the worldview of a research culture over those of the practice it investigates presents some problems when applying these results back into the field.

The basic procedure for this kind of study is to identify a specific aspect of conducting and/or rehearsal technique to test, and then see what difference it makes to an ensemble's performance when that aspect is varied. That is, it makes carefully defined changes to the input at the encoding stage, and measures the differences in the output. For example, Rhonda Fuelberth tests the effects of various left-hand gestures on singers' perceptions of inappropriate vocal tension, and Gregory Fuller tests whether a specific variant on a standard pattern produces a more effective performance in particular musical contexts than standard patterns, sub-divided patterns or no conducting at all.[28]

Designing studies around this model provides the opportunity to fulfil two significant requirements of the scientific method. The first is the imperative to isolate variables, that is, the need for the research design to guarantee that observed differences in result can be attributed to the specific aspects of technique under inspection, and not to some other, incidental factor. The second is the imperative that that experiments be replicable, that another researcher could reproduce the same experimental procedure to verify the results. Clearly, neither of these is possible in a complex many-to-many model of conducting as proposed by practitioners.

---

[28] Rhonda F. Vieth Fuelberth, 'The Effect of Conducting Gesture on Singers' Perceptions of Inappropriate Vocal Tension: A Pilot Study', *International Journal of Research in Choral Singing*, 1/1 (2003): 13–21 and 'The Effect of Various Left-hand Gestures on Perceptions of Anticipated Vocal Tension in Singers,' *International Journal of Research in Choral Singing*, 2/1 (2004): 27–38; Gregory Fuller, 'Effects of Metric Conducting Patterns, Subdivided Patterns, Managed Preparatory Gestures, and No Conducting on Choral Singers' Precision and Expressiveness at Phrase Punctuation Points Less than the Unit Pulse', (Ph.D. Thesis, University of Missouri, Columbia, 2000).

However, reducing the conductor–ensemble relationship back to a one-to-one model produces problems of its own. First there is the pragmatic question about how possible it actually is to isolate a single variable from the conducting context. Many studies succeed in reducing the number of variables, but still leave room for alternative explanations for their findings. For example, Fuelberth's study used a video recording of the conductor to guarantee that all participants experienced identical stimuli, and the six different left-hand gestures were performed to the same musical content to ensure that participants' different responses were to the conductor and not to the music. The publication of these video clips along with the report on this research, though, reveals that the conductor's attempts to follow the instruction to 'maintain a neutral facial expression throughout each of the six examples'[29] were only partially successful. The gestures used encompass more than the left-hand movements by which they are described: not just facial expression, but head and upper body movement, gaze behaviour and levels of bodily tension all change when the conductor switches from the baseline conducting behaviour to the introduction of left-hand gesture. The 'fisted' and 'stabbing' gestures, for instance, are accompanied by a dipping forward of the head, muscular tension in the arm, back and neck, and the adoption of a more determined facial expression. These ancillary behaviours are all congruent with the sorts of expressive functions these gestures would carry in practice, so it could be argued that the word 'gesture' should be understood as the total complex of bodily actions that carry a particular performance instruction, not simply the action of the left hand. While this may make musical sense, however, it does not help identify which aspect of bodily action induced the inappropriate vocal tension identified by participants.

The attempt to isolate gestural variables by neutral conducting is an aim that is itself open to question. Such techniques as maintaining a neutral facial expression, or keeping all beats the same size 'with no dynamic implications', are intended to close off communication channels in order that they do not interfere with the channels to be measured.[30] However, if the conductor is still visible, the 'removal' of information itself carries information: a pattern that shows '*only the direction of the beats by absolutely expressionless straight-line motion in the baton*' is a technique that Elizabeth Green terms the 'dead gesture', and has the purpose of showing a beat without inviting the musicians to play.[31] Rather than cutting off all channels except one, these studies keep the channels open and use them to send bland information.

It could be argued that the failure to fully isolate variables is a weakness of individual studies, and that it remains a worthy ideal to strive for. After all, some studies do find ways around these practical issues of experiment design.

---

[29] Fuelberth, 'Effect of Conducting Gesture', p. 16.

[30] Fuller, p. 80.

[31] Elizabeth Green, *The Modern Conductor: A College Text on Conducting based on the Technical Principles of Conductor Nicolai Malko as set forth in his 'The Conductor and his Baton'*, 6th edn (Englewood Cliffs, 1997), p. 58, emphasis in original.

For example, Geoff Luck avoids the interference of other elements of nonverbal communication by abstracting the conducting pattern entirely from its musical or performance context.[32] This study used point-light representations of beat patterns produced by two conductors, and measured their relative predictability when the parameters of tempo and curvature were varied by asking participants to tap on a computer's space bar in time with the patterns presented.

Luck's study, in its very success in isolating variables, demonstrates the deeper problem with the aim itself: to the extent that experimental design succeeds in isolating variables, it also divorces the experimental conditions from the real-life conditions in which their results would be applied. His findings about the relationship between rhythmic accuracy and the tightness of a beat's loop are fascinating in themselves. However, it is hard to predict how they would transfer into a context where there was musical content as well as a visual stimulus involved in regulating the rhythmic flow, or where the shape of the ictus is involved in expressive functions such as articulation as well as in regulating tempo. It is telling that this study found no difference in eliciting accuracy between a novice and an experienced conductor: it is even possible that the variable measured here is not especially significant in overall conductor effectiveness.

Of course, researchers are only too aware of the limitations that the exigencies of research design place on their results. Discussion sections routinely caution against assuming their findings are relevant to other circumstances, and outline future lines of research that would test their transferability.[33] This suggests that the consequence of a reductive research design is to limit the study's potential to inform theory. That is, if the purpose of empirical research into choral conducting is to improve praxis, the usefulness of its data depends on their capacity to be generalized into other circumstances. Results whose claims to truth are predicated on the specifics of an explicit and replicable experimental procedure may be verifiable, but their very particularity prevents their readily making the transition from the status of information to that of knowledge.[34] The essence of a theory

---

[32] Geoff Luck, 'An investigation of Conductors' Temporal Gestures', paper presented at the *Music and Gesture* Conference, University of East Anglia, June 2003. My thanks to the author for supplying me with a copy of this paper. This work was published in a more developed form just before the completion of this manuscript; see Geoff Luck and Sol Nte, 'An Investigation of Conductors' Temporal Gestures and Conductor-Musician Synchronization, and a First Experiment', *Psychology of Music*, 36/1 (2008): 81–99.

[33] See Ford, 'Preferences for Strong or Weak Singer's Formant Resonance', p. 45; James F. Daugherty, 'Choir Spacing and Formation: Choral Sound Preferences in Random, Synergistic, and Gender-Specific Chamber Choir Placements', *International Journal of Research in Choral Singing*, 1/1 (2003): 48–59, pp. 57–8; and Richard Earl House, 'Effects of Expressive and Nonexpressive Conducting on the Performance and Attitudes of Advanced Instrumentalists' (DMA dissertation, University of Arizona, 1998), pp. 86–7.

[34] As Peter Johnson points out, these caveats are also often lost when a study's findings are summarized by a subsequent researcher, giving a possibly misleading impression of the breadth of their applicability. Peter Johnson, Review of Richard Parncutt and

is, after all, that it is abstracted from the particular in order that it should be transferable to new situations. The anecdotal assertions from the practitioner literature thus arguably present a greater theoretical robustness than the empirical studies that critique them, in that they represent conclusions drawn from a range of experiences, even if that process of abstraction is unsystematic and/or under-documented.

The problems that researchers face in generalizing back to practice are particularly acute where their results appear to contradict accepted good practice. In one sense, this is precisely the sort of information that empirical studies should be producing, since the whole point of testing received opinion is to separate mythology from fact. However, researchers sometimes seem reluctant to assert the validity of their findings over conventional wisdom.

For example, Skadsem appears troubled by her finding that verbal instruction was a more effective channel in its impact on singers' performance than written instructions in the score, conductor gesture or the vocal behaviour of other singers.[35] Her discomfort is unsurprising, given the unanimity of the practitioner literature in exhorting the choral conductor to minimize verbal instruction in rehearsal – her results appear to be directly contradicting widely held beliefs about good practice.[36] Her discussion identifies the problem of 'mixed messages' affecting her results – that is, of giving written or verbal instructions that are not reinforced by conductor gesture or aural feedback – and proposes further studies to combine communication channels as a means to overcome this. I should like to suggest, however, that the problem of mixed messages is both more fundamental and trickier to surmount than her discussion implies, because it stems from the conflict between the two models of conducting discussed earlier. A method predicated on measuring a one-to-one relationship simply stalls when it is required to account for a many-to-many relationship. Hence, elements of experimental design driven by the imperatives of her empirical approach (such as the videotaped conductor and his/her deliberately neutral demeanour) both directly interfere with the interdependent ideal espoused by practitioners and limit the applicability of her

---

Gary E. McPherson (eds), *The Science and Psychology of Music Performance: Creative Strategies for Teaching and Learning*, (Oxford, 2002), *Musicae Scientiae* 9/1 (2005): 196–202.

[35] Julie A. Skadsem, 'Effect of Conductor Verbalization, Dynamic Markings, Conductor Gesture, and Choir Dynamic Level on Singers' Dynamic Responses,' *Journal of Research in Music Education*, 45/4 (1997): 509–20.

[36] See Adler, p. 12; Davison, p. 40; Jordan, p. 269; Roe, p. 272; Leonard Davis, *Practical Guidelines for Orchestral and Choral Conducting: For Those Wishing to Build on their Existing Experience rather than for Complete Beginners* (London, n.d.), p. 10; Steven Hart, 'Evolution of Thought and Recurrent Ideas in Choral Conducting Books and Secondary Music Education Texts Published from 1939 to 1995', (Ph.D. Thesis, University of Colorado, Boulder, 1996), p. 36; and Imogen Holst, *Conducting a Choir: A Guide for Amateurs* (Oxford, 1973), p. 46.

findings to situations that achieve this ideal. Indeed, one could interpret Skadsem's results as suggesting that verbal instructions become necessary when one has failed to establish the desired interactive rapport with one's singers.

Conclusion

The old saw that 'if all you have is a hammer, everything looks like a nail' is a common recognition that we imagine the world via the technologies with which we act instrumentally on it. Telecommunications, with their capacity to disembed time from place, are the archetypal technologies of modernity. Hence it is not surprising that they have become not only a standard model with which to theorize the communication process, but also the model of choice for a discipline that seeks to align itself with the forces of rationality and modernity against the superstitions of the past. Technological metaphors make intuitive sense as a way to conceptualize quantitative research.[37]

We should also note, however, that developments in telecommunications technologies over the last century have been driven overwhelmingly by an ideal of presence, by ever more ambitious attempts to recapture the qualities of live, real-time, face-to-face encounters. So, radio was succeeded by television, then by surround-sound home cinema; Web 2.0 vaunts itself as a collection of devices that allow people to be more genuinely interactive over the internet. The enhancements to entertainment of 'stereovision' and the 'feelies' imagined by mid-twentieth-century science fiction have yet to emerge, but broadband connections have brought its long-imagined desire for video telephony to fruition.[38] The digital, it seems, aspires to the condition of the analogue; that technologies have had to sacrifice this immediacy in solving the problem of communication at a distance is seen as a necessary compromise to be overcome by any means possible.

It is therefore by no means obvious why it is appropriate to theorize complex, nuanced interpersonal behaviours using a paradigm that not only erases much of this complexity, but that regrets doing so. Analytical structures inevitably simplify and abstract from the phenomena they are invoked to explain, but to configure our understanding of choral conducting around a process that unsuccessfully strives for

---

[37] This explanatory strategy has also been observed in other domains. Kim Stanley Robinson, for instance, remarks on how theories of the human mind change along with the dominant technologies of the time: 'clockwork for Descartes, geological changes for the early Victorians, computers or holography for the twentieth century'. Freudian concepts, meanwhile, are glossed as modelled on the steam engine: 'application of heat, pressure build-up, pressure displacement, venting, all shifted into repression, sublimation and the return of the repressed' (Kim Stanley Robinson, *Blue Mars* (London, 1996), p. 55).

[38] Robert Heinlein writes about stereovision in *Stranger in a Strange Land* (London, 1961); Aldous Huxley posits the 'feelies' in *Brave New World* (London, 1932); telephones with television screens appear in Stella Gibbons, *Cold Comfort Farm* (London, 1932).

the richness of detail such interpersonal situations entail is to impose an equivalent impoverishment on the studies based on that understanding. I would argue, along with scholars such as Ramona Wis and Dwayne Dunn, for such activities to be studied if not in fully naturalistic settings, at least in ways that do not require the erasure or distortion of the practices under scrutiny as part of their method.[39] This may still be in the laboratory, or by using positivistic methods to gather data. Indeed, in the five years that have elapsed between embarking on this project and completing the manuscript, the technological possibilities for measuring movement have expanded remarkably, and I would anticipate that future studies of conducting will take full advantage of these developments.

So, this is not a rejection of either quantitative or empirical work in conducting. It is, however, a plea for researchers to consider the implications of the models they choose to structure their experiments. For, as we have seen, the way that people imagine a phenomenon is fundamentally linked with the way they choose to research it, and this in turn shapes the kinds of knowledge that result and the uses to which it can be put. With this in mind, Chapter 3 will turn to the second, interactive model of conducting, and discuss the ways in which the practitioners' vision of their activity has shaped the research processes for this book.

---

[39] Ramona Wis, 'Gesture and Body Movement as Physical Metaphor to Facilitate Learning and to Enhance Musical Experience in the Choral Rehearsal' (Ph.D dissertation, Northwestern University, Evanston, 1993), p. 184ff; Dwayne E. Dunn, 'Effect of Rehearsal Hierarchy and Reinforcement on Attention, Achievement, and Attitude of Selected Choirs', *Journal of Research in Music Education*, 45/4 (1997): 547–67, p. 563.

Chapter 3
From Ethnography to Peer Research

During the research for my last book, an interview subject started to question me about how people become musicologists. I told him about the typical requirements for entry into music degree programmes in the UK, and this prompted the follow-up question: 'So, in order to become a musicologist, do you first have to be a musician?'

This incident encapsulates nicely the two questions that underpin this chapter: what is the relationship between knowledge and practice and what is the relationship between the researcher and the researched? While these are both questions about how theory and practice can and should inform each other, they consider this relationship in two different places. The first question asks what goes on inside the individual. It is about epistemology, about how we develop knowledge, and whether knowledge can be separated from experience. The second question asks about social interactions and the politics of knowledge, about who is entitled to collect information from and draw conclusions about whom. By quizzing me about my professional life and genealogy as I had probed his musical pedigree, my interviewee asserted his right to determine the content of our discussion. This changed the dynamic of the conversation from that of a semi-structured interview in which I set the agenda, to a much more reciprocal relationship of two people who were interested in each other's activities.

This chapter continues the investigation into the relationship between model and method started in Chapter 2, by turning its attention to the interactive model of conducting. It starts by exploring the interactions at three levels: within the process of conducting itself, in the choral rehearsal as social environment, and in wider choral cultures. This leads to a discussion of the ethnographic approach and why it is well suited to study phenomena conceived using this interactive model. A description of my procedures in rehearsal observations follows, and this in turn provides the context for a return to my opening questions about theory and practice. The chapter ends by outlining a model of peer research that is informed both by these philosophical questions and by the practical experience of doing ethnographic research among musical communities of which I am already a member.

Rehearsal as Social Environment

The interactive model of conducting presented in the practitioner literature sees conductor gesture and choral sound working in a symbiotic relationship. The choir members adapt their vocal behaviours in response to the stimuli of conductor, the demands of the music and the actions of their fellow singers, and at the same time conductors adapt their directing in response to the music and to what they hear from the singers. It sees a choral ensemble as a microcosmic social world, or as an environment for patterns of behaviour to evolve and propagate themselves. Elements of technique that produce good results (where 'good' is a set of qualities recognized by that choir's peers) will tend to proliferate and survive, and those that achieve less effective results are not repeated. The wider choral networks provide the macro-environment for the development of distinct traditions, as conductors observe the techniques others use to achieve musical success, while the individual relationship between choir and director is the micro-environment in which both personal directing styles and characteristic choral sounds are cultivated.

Indeed, the evolutionary metaphor works well to describe not just specifically musical behaviours, but also the rituals and etiquette of the wider social context of the choir. The musical interactions take place within and are consequently shaped by the cultural context of the choir as an organization, with its particular profile of values, belief systems and expectations from its participants. This in turn will both draw on and inform the choir's broader institutional and cultural affiliations, whether these be religious, political or artistic.

And of course not all behaviours that persist necessarily improve the choir. Most choirs have at least some habits that are artistically either irrelevant or even harmful, but which nonetheless flourish in the micro-climate of that choir's culture. John Bertalot captures this kind of co-dependent relationship when he comments on directors who have to tell their choir the same thing two or three times: 'If you suffer from this problem, the reason is that your choir has trained you to repeat your instructions'.[1]

This environmental approach also sheds light on the way that different choral traditions develop and maintain distinctive stylistic profiles, via the concept of speciation. One of the foundational observations of Darwin's work was that populations of a single species that are separated become more unlike each other until eventually they can no longer interbreed – that is, they have become two separate species.[2] As I discussed in Chapter 1, the choral cultures this book examines maintain varying degrees of separation from one another. There is a broad continuity of repertoire, practice and personnel between Western classical and Anglo-Catholic liturgical traditions, whereas the gospel and barbershop traditions, and to a lesser extent male voice choirs, have much clearer boundaries. Understanding the mechanisms and extent of choral speciation is important at a practical level for any choral practitioners who move between genres, in order to

---

[1] John Bertalot, *How to be a Successful Choir Director* (Stowmarket, 2002), p. 38. The rationale for empirical studies is of course the possibility that standard practices accepted throughout the profession might be this kind of sub-optimal behaviour that nonetheless succeeds in reproducing itself.

[2] Charles Darwin, *The Origin of Species*, ed. by J.W. Burrow (London, 1968).

judge how much of their technique and knowledge is applicable to the new context, and how much should be left behind as irrelevant or even counter-productive.[3]

This complex, interactive concept of choral practice is one reason why my research method focuses on the rehearsal, as this is the primary setting in which meanings and values are negotiated and maintained. This is not to say that performance is not important. Indeed, the nature of the intended performance is one of the most significant factors in shaping how a choir operates: one develops very different regimes to prepare for a daily service, a termly concert or a yearly competition. But at the point of performance, conductor and choir have reached a stage of at least provisional agreement about what they are doing and how they are doing it. Performances can demonstrate a relationship between conductor gesture and choral sound, but they cannot show us how those gestures became meaningful.

A model that sees any action by a participant as both shaped by and contributing to the actions of all other participants is particularly well suited to an ethnographic approach. Anthropology, and its specialist manifestation as ethnomusicology, has a well-developed methodological framework for researching rich cultural products, and a well-developed theoretical framework for dealing with the philosophical and ethical questions this can raise.[4] Before outlining the detail of my procedures, it is worth highlighting a few aspects of this method that resonate particularly well with the model developed here.

First, and most important, is the study of a practice in a naturalistic setting. In order to study a phenomenon consisting of complex, many-to-many relationships, those relationships need to be left intact, and ethnography traditionally takes a holistic approach that values the richness and texture of the cultures it studies. It is certainly possible to bring a choir into a laboratory setting and retain the richness of the specifically musical interactions, as represented by Lewis Gordon's diagram cited in Chapter 2. But going out to meet choirs on their home ground also gives access to the cultural and social norms of the choir that form the wider social environment within which these musical interactions operate. The third level of interactions, those between choirs that make up the extended choral worlds with which individual choirs align themselves, can be seen two ways: first, by comparing the individual choirs to find the cultural continuities between them, and second, through the events (concerts, festivals, conferences, training days) and literature produced by umbrella organizations.

---

[3] The analysis of cultural products by analogy with evolutionary theory is generally undertaken under the disciplinary heading of memetics, using the central concept of the meme, coined by Richard Dawkins in *The Selfish Gene* (Oxford, 1976). I am proposing the comparison here as a concept which provides a useful model for thinking about conducting, rather than as a full-blown explanatory structure. I should think that a memetic approach to conducting gesture could well prove fruitful, however.

[4] A good overview is presented in Bruno Nettl, *The Study of Ethnomusicology: Thirty-One Issues and Concepts* (Urbana, 2006).

The second important feature of an ethnographic approach is the principle of ethnotheory, that is, of deciding on areas of focus and deriving analytical categories to account for them according to what is considered important to members of the culture. Hence, a second reason to focus on the rehearsal is that that is what matters to the conductors: while the instructional literature on orchestral conducting focuses on stick technique and to a lesser degree interpretation, the choral practitioner literature concerns itself primarily with training choirs. This resonates with performance studies' commitment to taking practitioners' views seriously, which was discussed in Chapter 1. If we are to understand what people are doing, it makes sense to pay attention to what they say they think they are doing. In this sense, the practitioner texts are part of the ethnographic evidence base, representing the voices of expert informants, and part of the means by which choral culture's mythologies are preserved and disseminated.

Ethnotheory is also important from an ethical perspective, since it is one of the ways that researchers can show respect for the cultures they investigate. It acknowledges the insider's expertise about their own social world, and it presents the researcher's findings in categories that will be transparent to members of that community. As a result, it puts researchers in a position where their work is meaningfully subject to critique by those about whom they write; it makes researchers accountable not only to the academic community, but also to the communities they research. The principle of ethnotheory thus underlies my promotion of the interactive rather than the transmission model of conducting, since this is the conception that is overwhelmingly in evidence in texts by practitioners.

Finally, the method itself, like the model of conducting I am using it to investigate, is interactive. Its standard techniques of cultural immersion, participant observation and interviews construe researcher and subject not as separated, but in a relationship in which each affects the other. I would not suggest that one's research methods should have to be structured in the same way as one's conceptual models in order to produce useful results, not least because arguments by analogy are usually more useful as ways to engage the imagination than as fully fledged explanatory structures. In this case, however, the comparison has proved useful for two reasons. First, it has provided a means to reflect on questions of method, particularly in relation to the two questions with which this chapter started. Second, like the principle of ethnotheory, it acts as a check on my accountability to the communities I am researching: it makes me ask not only 'what would an ethnomusicologist think of this?' but also 'what would be a choral conductor's opinion?' I will return to both of these points at the end of the chapter.

Method

The aim of the rehearsal observations was to develop what Clifford Geertz called 'thick' descriptions, that is, descriptions that not only state what happened, but also seek to understand the meaning of these actions.[5] As well as the interaction between conductors and their choirs, I wished to observe the full social context in which these interactions occurred. Each visit sought to develop as detailed a picture as possible of what constituted 'business as usual' at that choir.

Of course, my presence necessarily made the rehearsals I visited slightly other than 'business as usual', but my aim throughout was to minimize my impact – not only for the sake of my observations, but also so as not to disrupt the choirs' work. On arrival, I would introduce myself to the conductor and appropriate choir committee members, and answer their questions about the project. Sometimes the choir had been told about my visit in advance; at others I was introduced at an appropriate moment, or asked to address the choir to explain my visit. I was at pains to emphasize both when setting up the visits and on arrival that the choirs should do nothing special for my visit – it was the opportunity to observe their regular rehearsal that I sought.

I would find somewhere to sit where I could observe the conductor during the rehearsal, preferably where I could also see some of the choir, and where I was not in direct line of sight of either director or choir. It became clear very quickly if I had chosen a place where I distracted anybody, and I would move as soon as there was a moment in which I could do so discreetly. I would chat with choir members before the rehearsal and in the breaks and aim to get into position to observe as the singers got into position to sing, so that I was able to take notes from a minute or two before the formal start.

My note-taking routine started with the global choral situation, and focused in on the particular as the session progressed. I would start with the demographic profile of the choir: number of singers, age range, race, gender, norms of dress, accent. My conversations with choir members gave valuable information about the choir's wider social framework, as did announcements made by committee members and notices on choir noticeboards. As the choirs settled into singing, their rehearsal rituals would become apparent: what kind of warm-up regime they had, how latecomers were treated, how much the choir rehearsed seated or standing, whether the atmosphere was serious or jocular, when and for what reasons choir members were permitted to speak. The musical norms also became clear in this early part of the process: how much was rehearsed with accompaniment, how much they worked from notation and how much by ear, how much the rehearsal discourses focused on vocal or musical issues, and whether these were approached via technical or metaphorical language.

The second stage of note-taking focused in on body language, particularly the conductor's, but also the choir's. Taking notes on conducting technique in real time is a challenge, since note-worthy events occur far more quickly than one can log them. On the other hand, conductors are reasonably consistent in their gestures, so after 20 minutes or so of watching any one individual, one starts to

---

[5] Clifford Geertz, 'Thick Description: Toward an Interpretive Theory of Culture', in *The Interpretation of Cultures: Selected Essays* (New York, 1973).

understand not only what their characteristic ways of doing things are, but also how much variability there is in their gestures. If someone places their ictus at sternum level 95 per cent of the time, a downbeat placed at shoulder level will have a very different meaning from a high ictus delivered by a director who regularly varies the placement of their beats. Notes on the choir's body language were more general, covering posture, degree of uniformity in body language across the choir and any relationship with the conductor's posture and gestures.

The final stage of the note-taking was writing up the notes after the rehearsal. This was usually the morning following an evening rehearsal, though I was able to do this even sooner in the case of the few daytime rehearsals I watched. The purpose of this was to clarify my notes while the events they referred to were still clear in my memory, and fill in enough detail so that they would be able to reawaken the memories after months or years had elapsed. It also allowed me to reflect on what I had seen in a way that was not possible in the midst of the rehearsal, and make comparisons between rehearsals. This stage of processing the notes produced many of the insights developed in Parts III and IV. In some ways, then, the structure of the book echoes the shape of the rehearsal observation process: moving from the social context and conventions within which musical meanings were negotiated, through detailed examination of the conductor's craft, to theorizing the mechanisms by which conductor and choir interacted.

Rehearsal is a private space, in which musicians necessarily find themselves in a state of some musical undress. Consequently, all material from the rehearsal visits has been anonymized. It may be possible for conductors and choirs I visited to recognize themselves in the examples I present, although I would expect that they will have long forgotten the sorts of details I report by the time the book appears since they will have experienced so many more rehearsals since. There are no details given that could identify the choirs to people who did not know I had visited them. While I regret not thanking the choirs and conductors individually in print, it was more important that they could not be identified in what I write about them.

The filmed rehearsals came at a much later stage, and these were intended to provide material with which to illustrate the argument. That is, they were more about presentation of ideas to the reader than about primary data gathering. As such, there were some differences in approach. While the choirs I observed in rehearsal were selected to give a wide range of both genre and skill level, the conductors presented on the DVD were selected specifically as good representatives of their style. 'Good representative' here means two things: first, that the conductors are respected as competent, and second, that their peers will recognize their approach as in many ways typical. This is not to say that they do not have distinctive personal styles – indeed, it would be difficult to imagine a conductor who was highly regarded without also being individual in approach – but simply that other practitioners in each genre represented would recognize shared gestural, musical and cultural traditions. Brilliant gestural mavericks, interesting as they are, would not help readers understand common gestural conventions.

The other major difference is that of anonymity, which is of course compromised by the very process of filming. When discussing the project with choirs and conductors prior to filming, I undertook not discuss choir members individually. They can be heard en masse on the DVD, and I have presented still pictures to give the reader a sense of the choir's size and rehearsal layout; hence individuals can be recognized by people who already know them. But I have not presented footage to illustrate my discussions of choir body language: I decided that the singers' right to privacy was more important than the readers' need to be shown what I have described. The behaviours I discuss are sufficiently widespread that the reader will find opportunity to observe them in their real-life interactions with choirs. They are also considerably less complex than the conductors' gestures, so verbal descriptions will be enough to represent them adequately.

The conductors on the DVD, by definition, could not be anonymized. One of the interesting things about artistic activities is the way that individuals are recognizable from their products, so it is not possible to remove evidence of identity from a conductor on video without also removing the information that the DVD is intended to demonstrate. Obscuring a conductor's face would still leave his or her distinctive body language visible, and even removing all visual cues would still leave phrasing and approach to choral tone audible in the choir's voices. Besides, established directors are accustomed both to people looking at them in action, and to taking public credit for their artistic activities, so the DVD does not represent an intrusion in quite the same way. Still, the rehearsal is a private space, and they may not wish to submit everything that goes on there to public scrutiny, so I sent all the conductors copies of the edited material from their rehearsals and what I had written about it for them to approve before publication.

On the other hand, the basic premise – that the rehearsal is the crucible in which musical meanings are forged, and that this process is best observed in naturalistic settings – remained the same. Hence, the filming process aimed to be as unobtrusive as possible. One camera was set up pointing at the conductor from behind the choir, and was simply left running throughout the rehearsal. While this was visible to the conductor throughout, it presented relatively little distraction because it remained static. A second camera was placed off to the side to take footage of the choir to show the general rehearsal context, and to follow the conductor when they moved around the rehearsal space. This camera did move, but was placed carefully to remain outside the peripheral vision of both conductor and choir. In practice, though, this second camera produced little that was useable except general establishing shots: the ways that the conductors interacted with their choir members as they moved out of their default directing position usually served to create more intimate groupings that excluded those not directly involved in the conversation, including the camera operator.

This hands-off approach to filming necessarily produced results that are less interesting from a filmic perspective than a more active approach would have done. However, it was important that the conductors and choirs could get on with their regular work without disruption, both for their own sake, and for the purposes the DVD is designed to serve. I was confident from the experience of the rehearsal observations that the gestures and processes I wished to demonstrate would occur during the course of these rehearsals, and that the total nine hours or so of filming would produce more than enough material to illustrate my discussions. This indeed turned out to be the case, and the editing process was thus one of selecting combinations of passages that illustrated most efficiently the points I wished to discuss. Subsidiary criteria for editing were musical coherence and topic continuity. That is, I tried wherever possible not to cut people off mid-flow, either in musical or rehearsal terms, although this principle had to be sacrificed in places in service of either pragmatics or content. I introduce the conductors and their choirs in Chapter 8 as a prelude to discussing the content of the DVD.

The Researcher-Subject Relationship

In my last book, I was concerned with the classic ethnographic distinction between the emic and the etic – the perspectives of the insider and the outsider. My conclusion there was that it was the act of writing about a practice that places one outside it – or, more specifically, the act of writing as a scholar.[6] The very discourses that will present one's findings as credible or authoritative tend to cast the people one writes about as 'them' rather than 'us'. A similar effect can be seen in the empirical literature discussed in Chapter 2. Many of the scholars writing about conducting are conductors themselves, and their practical interest is what motivates their formal research. Their results, however, are often framed in terms of what practitioners can learn and/or do differently on the basis of this research, presenting an us–versus–them structure in which the theorist instructs the practitioner how they should go about their craft. This is not the researchers' intentions, I am sure – no doubt they themselves are the practitioners to whom their instructions are addressed – but is a function of the way that the empirical approach positions the researcher as fundamentally separate from their subject. The question of the researchers' relationship with their subject is something that the ethnographer experiences not only through discourse, but also at a practical, personal level.

During the rehearsal observations and filming sessions my role was mostly as an emic, but non-participant observer: I was an insider to the choral culture, but not participating in the activity itself on that occasion. However, the degree to which I was an insider varied. In classical choral societies and chamber choirs, and in barbershop contexts, I was on home ground both musically and culturally, and was nearly as inside in church/cathedral contexts. With gospel, male voice choirs and Jewish choirs I was quite explicitly an outsider culturally, though the common interest in choral singing served to place me in a category that was recognizably 'like us' to an extent. It was clear both that my presence was more of an intrusion

---

[6] Liz Garnett, *The British Barbershopper: A Study in Socio-Musical Values* (Aldershot, 2005a), Chapter 9.

in those rehearsals where I shared less cultural background with the choirs, and that the purpose of my visit was the main factor that mitigated this.[7]

In all cases, informal conversations with choir members served as a means to minimize the inside–outside relationship. As in the vignette with which I started this chapter, the opportunity for the research subjects to become the interrogators introduced a degree of reciprocity into the encounter, and diminished the power differential between observer and observed that researchers set up when they assume the power to gaze. While these conversations in one sense made me more visible, they made my presence less disruptive, since they served to integrate me into the group. Nonetheless, that I was watching them without also singing did make a number of the conductors self-conscious. They were all able to move beyond this and get on with the business in hand, but this was less to do with anything I could do to smooth over the issue than the simple fact that conducting a rehearsal requires a lot of attention. The conductors had so much to do once into the swing of rehearsal that they did not have the time or the mental space to find my presence more than momentarily distracting.

Throughout the time I was doing the research, I continued to be active as a choral practitioner myself – as a director, a singer, a teacher and a festival adjudicator. This substrate of activity, while not formally articulated as part of the research process, was important to it in several ways. First, and most obviously, it was the source of my primary research questions. Second, it established my credibility with the choirs and conductors I visited, and made it possible to meet them as a peer rather than an interloper. Third, it was an important means to process the ideas and insights I was gaining from the rehearsal observations and reading. Research and praxis moved into a dialogue in which my reading and observations gave me the means to theorize my practical experiences, while my week-to-week engagement with choral practice helped me make sense of what I was seeing and reading. This meant I was able to test hypotheses both analytically and experientially, which was important if I were to produce findings that would be realistic and relevant to both theorists and practitioners.

This reflective process takes us back to the question raised at the start of this chapter. It is a standard tenet of ethnomusicology that the researcher needs to learn how to perform the music they study if they are to fully understand it: experience is seen as central to knowledge. And, as my interview subject brought to my attention, the institutional structures of musicology tend to make the same demands, if less explicitly. This fundamental requirement of experiential knowledge, however, is often obscured by music's scholarly discourses. The performer is conceived as the

---

[7] Another factor that affected the relative ease with which choirs met my visits was my status as a representative of a Higher Education music college. For choirs most closely aligned with the Western classical tradition, this increased my attractiveness as a visitor; for choirs in traditions less commonly represented in formal music education, this affiliation was, if anything, a source of mistrust. In these cases, my previous work with the barbershop movement was a significant factor in allaying anxieties about musical snobbishness.

conduit or 'transformer station' between composer and listener as discussed in the last chapter, or as the 'handmaiden' that serves music.[8] These ideas have tended to position the performer as subservient both to the will of the composer whose ideas animate their praxis, and to the instruction of the theorist who analyses the music to instruct them what it means. If the discourses of Western art music acknowledged the need for an embodied, experiential knowledge to underpin and make sense of our declarative knowledge as candidly as ethnomusicology does, performers might not find it so difficult to have their work recognized as 'research-valid'.

Towards a Model of Peer Research

Thomas Lindlof has characterized qualitative research as a process of 'catch-and-release fishing'.[9] This is a telling metaphor: it evokes a research method that may collect less comprehensive data than if one killed the fish and dissected it, but it preserves the essential quality of how the organism works when it is alive, a quality that can never be recaptured after dissection. It also asserts an implicit ethical superiority over quantitative methods that remove the research subject from its natural environment: the fish returns to its previous life almost as if nothing had happened. At the same time, though, the metaphor maintains a categorical distinction between fish and angler: there is no chance that the roles may become blurred, and as a result the power differential is absolute. Other anglers may be impressed by the ethical claims, and may be convinced by the results of the research, but nobody asks the fish for an opinion.

In the research for this book, I have endeavoured to work towards a model of peer research based on a simultaneous identification with and stepping-out from a practice. As I intimated earlier, this is in some ways modelled on the process of conducting itself. Both choral and orchestral conductors are expected to have the skills to participate as members of the ensemble in some fashion as the basis for their authority with fellow musicians, and indeed they will have participated as performers within ensembles before stepping out to direct. Their competence to conduct is predicated on a prior competence to participate. Likewise, the musicologist is expected to have a competent practical knowledge of the practices they investigate, or, in the case of the ethnomusicologist, to acquire it as part of the research process.

But conductors also stand outside the ensemble; they see and hear a bigger picture than is perceptible from within. This broader perspective, and the judgements it enables them to make, is in turn the basis of the trust the audience places in them. Similarly, musicologists also step out of the practices they research. This can mean standing aside in a literal sense, as in my rehearsal observations,

---

[8] Harriet Cohen, *Music's Handmaid*, 2nd edn (London, 1950).
[9] Thomas Lindlof, *Qualitative Communication Research Methods* (London, 1995), pp. 282–3.

but more fundamentally, it refers to the critical distance from a subject that is created by a discipline's analytical discourses. And it is the perspective that these discourses give researchers that is the basis of their authority with their academic peers.

Archibald Davison articulates the interactive model of conducting by saying, 'To say that the conductor and choir must be in sympathy is not enough. They must be *one*'.[10] This ideal can only ever be fulfilled at a level of artistic purpose; however united director and singers are in their vision of the music they sing, their roles ultimately remain distinct. Likewise, the model of peer research I am proposing here can never truly dissipate the distinction between researcher and subject: the person who publishes the findings is the one who gets to draw the conclusions. But what it does offer is accountability. Peer review is the mainstay of academic accountability, and I would suggest that the ethical difficulties surrounding questions of representation and authority can be significantly ameliorated if we extend the category of 'peer' to include the musicians about whom we write.

---

[10] Archibald Davison, *Choral Conducting* (Cambridge, MA, 1954), p. 8, emphasis in original.

Chapter 4
How to Write about Conducting

> Almost everyone agrees that performing and listening to music are primary activities; writing about music is secondary, parasitical.[1]

The questions of how to think about conducting and how to study it spill over into the question of how to write about it. This is a practical question, but, as the Charles Rosen quote above suggests, it is an ethical question too. There is an underlying suspicion in Western musical culture – both classical and popular – that words betray music. Robert Schumann worried that there was 'something unseemly and charlatanlike'[2] in narrative programme notes, and the aphorism that 'talking about music is like dancing about architecture' is both widely quoted and widely attributed.[3] Choral conductors seem to share this mistrust of musical literature. One director I visited spoke warmly of how much he had learned watching Bernard Rose at Magdalen College, Oxford, and rather dismissively of how little he had learned from the one book on conducting he had read. It was useful enough for the basic patterns, he said, but he was more interested in directing phrases. If music can reveal 'a higher significance than feeble words … can communicate', it is possibly not surprising that musical practitioners can find the literature about their art not only inadequate, but at times dangerously so.[4]

Jean-Jacques Nattiez called this the 'problem of metalanguage'.[5] That is, how do we choose the terms with which to discuss other, non-linguistic forms of communication? How we solve the problem is not just about the communication

---

[1] Charles Rosen, 'Music à la Mode', *New York Review of Books*, 41/12 (23 June 1994): 55–62.

[2] Robert Schumann, 'Berlioz' *Symphonie Fantastique*', in Henry Pleasants (ed.), *The Musical World of Robert Schumann: A Selection from Schumann's Own Writings* (New York, 1965), p. 84.

[3] This statement has been attributed to Elvis Costello, Laurie Anderson and Thelonius Monk among others, although the identification of a definitive origin remains elusive. Its very currency, however, attests to its continuing resonance with contemporary popular culture. See Alan Scott, 'Talking about Music is like Dancing about Architecture', available online at http://www.pacifier.com/~ascott/they/tamildaa.htm [accessed 9 January 2008].

[4] E.T.A. Hoffmann, 'Beethoven's Instrumental Music', in David Charlton (ed.), *E.T.A. Hoffmann's Musical Writings: Kreisleriana, The Poet and the Composer, Music Criticism* (Cambridge, 1989), p. 102.

[5] Jean-Jacques Nattiez, *Fondements d'une Sémiologie de la Musique* (Paris, 1975), p. 45.

medium, but also depends on how we position ourselves relative to the knowledge we produce and to our various readerships. There is the purely presentational level of how to use the written word and/or other media to communicate meaningfully about what conductors and choirs do. But this both relies upon and informs what we think conductors are doing and also the means we use to record our observations. Metalanguage is not just the final stage of the research process, the means by which we present out findings, but is integrally related with our models and our methods, the means by which we find them.

This chapter explores some of the metalanguages that are available to write about conductor gesture and choral sound, and assesses their respective advantages and disadvantages. These metalanguages have been developed both within musicology and further afield, particularly in the study of nonverbal communication. The two primary criteria for assessment are (a) their user-friendliness in presentational terms, and (b) their completeness and accuracy; that is, their value to readers and scholars respectively. There is a degree of tension between these two criteria. Descriptions couched in terms chosen to resonate with a reader's cultural experience risk reinscribing the researcher's assumptions into the results (which was of course the basis of the empiricists' critique of practitioner literature discussed in Chapter 2). On the other hand, descriptions that aim to expunge all preconceptions in order to give insight into what was really going on, rather than what the researcher would expect to happen, risk becoming impenetrable to the reader, or simply overwhelming them with data.

Metalanguage is thus related to our questions of insider and outsider discussed in Chapter 3. An emphasis on readability privileges the practitioner over the academic, while a preference for rigour sets up an insider relationship between scholars, at the risk of excluding the practitioner. Given that so many scholarly writers on conducting are themselves also practitioners, negotiating between these obligations is not always straightforward. Moreover, the world of the 'practitioner' is less homogenous than this blanket term suggests, and performers in different musical worlds have very different levels of access to scholarly discourses. Hence, there is no single, ideal way to write about conducting, but there is a good range of partially useful possibilities.

Metalanguages 1: Writing about Gesture

Ethnotheory

Chapter 3's emphasis on ethnotheory for making a study transparent and accountable to its subjects makes this the obvious metalanguage with which to start. There is a good general consensus, both in manuals and among practitioners, for the basic vocabulary of conducting technique. The primary beat patterns and their constituent parts of preparatory beat, ictus, rebound and subdivision are shared widely and applied with little or no controversy. There may be differences of opinion about how best to execute these elements, but their definitions are widely agreed. There are also more specialist terms in use, such as those used in particular conducting methods: Leonard Atherton's 'vertical plane focal point', for example, or the various types of beat proposed by Hideo Saito.[6] Again, these are unproblematic because, although they do not enjoy the same level of currency, their association with specific approaches means they can be used unambiguously.

What is more problematic with the vocabulary of conducting technique is how much it omits. As the conductor cited earlier pointed out, conducting manuals are good on how to execute beat patterns, but the 'left-hand function', or the gestures performed by the non-dominant hand, is remarkably under-theorized. This is partly because it is generally classed as the 'expressive' rather than 'technical' hand, and as such is considered inherently subjective. Emil Kahn, for instance, advises that, 'the exact manner of gesturing depends on the conductor. The student should discover for himself which way feels most natural.'[7] This elides the emotional or intuitive with the natural or untutored to produce a concept of individual, authentic expression: it is in the spontaneous, idiosyncratic gestures that the unique genius of a conductor's imagination is thought to reside. However, that one can clearly identify gestural traditions in these undocumented gestures suggests that, while they may indeed represent the individual conductor's unique imagination in the way they are used, they are nonetheless learned elements of behaviour.

We should also not assume that textbook conducting technique actually matches what practitioners do. This is partly because some musical traditions have a closer relationship with the academy and its structures of formal training than others; as we shall see in Part III, the conductor of a symphony chorus shows a much more 'textbook' technique than the director of a gospel choir. But even within those idioms that recognize a formalized grammar of conducting technique, there are widely used gestures that are either absent from the instruction manuals, or are even directly prohibited by them.

A more generalist approach to ethnotheory would use interpretive musical vocabulary to describe gestures, for example, 'a sweeping, legato gesture'. This moves the focus from the technical (what the conductor does) to the artistic (what the conductor intends), from the quantitative to the qualitative. This vocabulary sometimes appears in conducting manuals – for instance, Max Rudolph categorizes types of ictus by styles of articulation: legato, staccato, marcato[8] – but it most closely matches the vocabulary of the rehearsal. As we shall see in Part III, there is a strong link between the words conductors use to verbalize their musical intentions (whether this is technical musical or more figurative vocabulary)

---

[6] Leonard Atherton, *Vertical Plane Focal Point Conducting* (Muncie, 1989); Joseph A. Valent, 'An Examination of the Conducting Method of Hideo Saito' (DMA Dissertation, Ball State University, 2000).

[7] Emil Kahn, *Elements of Conducting* (New York, 1975) p. 85.

[8] Max Rudolph, *The Grammar of Conducting: A Comprehensive Guide to Baton Technique and Interpretation*, 3rd edn (New York, 1995).

and the gestures they use to make them visible. Consequently, such musically interpretive vocabulary has the strength of an inherently meaningful relationship with the activities it describes.

The disadvantage of this vocabulary is that, because it is interpretive, it may reflect the assumptions of the researcher more than the intentions of the conductor.[9] The danger of this decreases in proportion to the researcher's familiarity with the conductor's musical world, of course. The researcher can never know exactly what the conductor is thinking, but if they are a reasonably competent member of that musical culture, they will have as much chance of inferring it as the singers who are expected to respond to the gestures. Similarly – and more importantly in a study that moves between different traditions – the meaningfulness of the description depends upon the reader's familiarity with the musical-gestural world described. We may think we know what musical terms mean, but one of the main goals of the historical performance practice movement and, more recently, the study of early twentieth-century recordings, has been to make us aware how much styles of execution can change between different times and different places.[10] Musical descriptors, then, risk inscribing the assumptions of both researcher and reader into the account of what happened.

Conductor-Scholars

A variant on ethnotheory is the work of conductor-scholars, that is, researchers who position their studies within an academic context, but who are themselves also practitioners. In one sense, to separate this work out from the vocabularies of instruction manuals and conductors in rehearsal is somewhat arbitrary, since conductor-scholars are typically both familiar and fluent in these vocabularies through both their research and their praxis; in particular, it is quite unclear whether to consider highly systematized conducting methods as ethnotheoretical or scholarly metalanguages. On the other hand, the desire to locate their ideas in the academy leads conductor-scholars to develop metalanguages that are more systematic and/or more clearly grounded theoretically than the vocabularies developed within purely practical contexts.

Systematic approaches include a variety of analytical frameworks that break down conducting gesture into a number of elements by which any single conducting gesture can be classified. Frederik Prausnitz, for example, identifies four qualities

---

[9] Arvid Kappas, Ursula Hess and Klaus V. Scherer discuss similar difficulties in developing a vocabulary to describe vocal qualities in speech: 'The terms used in everyday language to describe voice and speech characteristics are frequently confounded with descriptors of speaker state or are too general to apply to a specific vocal feature.' See 'Voice and Emotion', in Robert S. Feldman and Bernard Rimé (eds), *Fundamentals of Nonverbal Behavior* (Cambridge, 1991), p. 200–201.

[10] See Robert Philip, *Early Recordings and Musical Style: Changing Tastes in Instrumental Performance, 1900-1950* (Cambridge, 1992).

of any beat: timing, direction, size and impetus.[11] Many scholars and teachers use Rudolf Laban's concept of 'effort shapes' as a means to analyse conductor gesture along the axes of space, weight and time.[12] These kinds of approach are excellent for analysing the qualitative aspects of the execution of pattern, since they give clear conceptual categories into which to organize observed gestures, but allow considerable scope to deal with the complexity and variability of what conductors do by means of their multidimensional structure. This clear structure makes these systems particularly suitable for teaching conducting, since they provide a means for student directors to control individual parameters of a gesture.

There seems to have been little attempt in conducting studies, however, to develop any kind of systematic and complete notation akin to Labanotation for dance. This is in some ways surprising – however complex the conductor's movements, they are considerably simpler than those that concern choreographers – but in other ways less so – the purpose of notating dance is so that it can be reproduced exactly, whereas conductors are rarely interested in repeating their own gestures exactly, let alone other people's. And, while these analytical strategies have the potential to provide an exhaustive analysis of a conductor's actions, the result would be both time-consuming to produce and difficult to read.

The other main type of metalanguage used by conductor-scholars is to discuss gestures metaphorically as if the conductor were manipulating physical objects. This has some connection with Laban's theory, which gives the eight different combinations of weight, space and time tactile labels such as dab, wring or glide. But the language of object-manipulation is much more varied than this, and much less systematic. This is particularly interesting in that it engages with elements of technique on which the conducting manuals often remain silent. Hence, Rhonda Fuelberth names two of the left-hand gestures she investigates 'fisted' and 'stabbing', and Peter Litman includes terms such as 'rubberband stretch' and 'left-hand support' in the list of gestures he observes in rehearsal.[13] This sense of

---

[11] Discussed by Edward Venn in 'Towards a semiotics of conducting', paper presented at the *Music and Gesture* conference, University of East Anglia, June 2003.

[12] For example, Gail B. Poch, 'Conducting: Movement Analogues Through Effort Shape', *The Choral Journal*, 23/3 (1982): 21–2; Michele Menard Holt, 'The Application to Conducting and Choral Rehearsal Pedagogy of Laban Effort/Shape and its Comparative Effect upon Style in Choral Performance' (DMA Dissertation, University of Hartford, 1992); and Therees Tkach Hibbard, 'The Use of Movement as an Instructional Technique in Choral Rehearsals' (DMA Dissertation, University of Oregon, 1994).

[13] Rhonda F. Vieth Fuelberth, 'The Effect of Conducting Gesture on Singers' Perceptions of Inappropriate Vocal Tension: A Pilot Study', *International Journal of Research in Choral Singing*, 1/1 (2003): 13–21 and 'The Effect of Various Left-Hand Gestures on Perceptions of Anticipated Vocal Tension in Singers', *International Journal of Research in Choral Singing*, 2/1 (2004): 27–38; Peter Litman, 'The Relationship Between Gesture and Sound: A Pilot Study of Choral Conducting Behaviour in Two Related Settings', *Visions of Research in Music Education*, 8 (2006), available online at: http://www-usr.rider.edu/~vrme/v8n1/vision/Litman_Article.pdf [accessed 13 March 2008].

handling the sound also resonates with the physical metaphors for conductor–choir interaction discussed in Chapter 2: Ehmann's glass-blowing metaphor, for instance, or Adler and Davison's idea of bouncing a rubber ball.

Penny Boyes Bräm and Thüring Bräm present an analysis of orchestral conductors' expressive gestures that grounds this potentially rather ad hoc approach to taxonomy in George Lakoff and Mark Johnson's theories of metaphor.[14] While Bräm and Bräm are not conductors themselves, I am including this study here because it accounts so well for the terms that conductor-scholars often use. Moreover, Lakoff and Johnson's ideas have also been used to good effect by choral practitioners exploring the role of participant gesture (rather than conductor gesture) in rehearsal.[15]

Lakoff and Johnson first developed their theory of metaphor in 1980 in the book *Metaphors We Live By*, and each has developed and extended these key ideas in subsequent work.[16] Their central point is that metaphors – often regarded as a surface feature of figurative language – are actually fundamental to the way in which we think and act in the world. They define the metaphor as 'understanding and experiencing one thing in terms of another', or the mapping of concepts from one domain of experience onto another domain that has comparable attributes.[17] For example, to talk of 'undermining someone's authority' is to understand their social position as a building. This mapping is necessarily partial, and thus metaphors simultaneously highlight and hide different aspects of the concepts they articulate. Metaphors are both physical and cultural: all human beings share the orientational structure of front–back, for example, but some cultures use this to conceptualize time with the future stretching out in front, others the past. Hence, metaphors are not only not just about poetic language; they are also not just about spoken language. Verbal metaphors are a perceptible, surface effect of our fundamental ways of understanding the world through interacting with it.

Bräm and Bräm thus see conducting as mapping the domain of sound onto the domain of physical objects, and use this framework to analyse a variety of left-hand gestures displayed by two conductors in terms of acting on those objects. These include gestures to 'pull sound out' of the orchestra, with the shape of the hand (fingers tight together or cupped more widely) indicating whether a thin or

---

[14] Penny Boyes Bräm and Thüring Bräm, 'Expressive Gestures Used by Classical Orchestra Conductors', in Cornelia Müller and Roland Posner (eds), *The Semantics and Pragmatics of Everyday Gestures* (Berlin, 2004).

[15] See Ramona Wis, 'Gesture and Body Movement as Physical Metaphor to Facilitate Learning and to Enhance Musical Experience in the Choral Rehearsal' (Ph.D dissertation, Northwestern University, Evanston, 1993).

[16] George Lakoff and Mark Johnson, *Metaphors We Live By* (Chicago, 1980). See also Mark Johnson, *The Body in the Mind: The Bodily Basis of Meaning, Imagination, and Reason* (Chicago, 1987), and George Lakoff and Mark Johnson, *Philosophy in the Flesh: The Embodied Mind and its Challenge to Western Thought* (New York, 1999).

[17] Lakoff and Johnson, *Metaphors We Live By*, p. 5.

full sound is required, and indications to stop playing by metaphorically taking the sound 'out of view'. This is a powerful link to make, since it is a theory that has strongly informed gesture studies, and has also garnered some considerable interest in music theory.[18] It therefore has a well-established relevance to the two primary domains involved in conducting. It also posits a strong theoretical link between the verbal language used by conductors in rehearsal and the gestures they use, which adds further support to the value of ethnotheoretical categories as a metalanguage.

This kind of synthetic approach produces descriptions that are much more accessible to the reader than analytical descriptions that disaggregate conducting technique into their constituent parts. But they still only present atomized, momentary slices of meaning. Even when presented with pictures that show a gesture's direction, size and position relative to the gesturer's body, as in Bräm and Bräm's work, this is still removed from the musical context that motivated the gesture. It is a useful metalanguage, and one that I join other conductor-scholars in favouring, but it still has significant limitations.

'Objective' Accounts

The logical opposite to ethnotheory is an objective account that aims simply to describe what a conductor does without attempting, in the process of documentation, to ascribe meaning to it. Notwithstanding the rise of an objectivist ethos in empirical conducting studies, there has been little attempt to develop such notation systems for conducting in any systematic way. Still, the theoretical possibility has had an impact on the development of this study and as such is worth a brief discussion.

The idea of an 'objective' descriptive notation for conducting echoes in its aspiration for completeness and accuracy the notional Labanotation posited above, but would use anatomical descriptions rather than analytical/interpretive categories. Clearly, it would share the disadvantages of that notation of being time-consuming both to operate and to interpret, overwhelming both analyst and reader with indigestible quantities of data. Indeed, it would experience these problems to a much greater extent if it aspired to document gestures not by abstracted analytical categories but by accounting for the activity of each part of a conductor's skeleton and all the muscle groups that effect the action. This desire for extra-cultural anatomical description could consequently be seen as a *reductio ad absurdum* that proves the futility of the desire for objectivity.

On the other hand, there is a precedent for such a detailed, fastidious approach to human behaviour in the form of Paul Ekman and Wallace Friesen's Facial

---

[18] See for example Janna Saslaw, 'Forces, Containers, and Paths: The Role of Body-Derived Image Schemas in the Conceptualization of Music', *Journal of Music Theory*, 40/2 (1996): 217–43; Laurence Zbikowski, 'Conceptual Models and Cross-Domain Mapping: New Perspectives on Theories of Music and Hierarchy', *Journal of Music Theory*, 41/2 (1997): 193–225; and Michael Spitzer, *Metaphor and Musical Thought* (Chicago, 2004).

Action Coding System.[19] Originally published in 1976, and developed extensively over the years that followed, this is a taxonomy intended to codify every possible human facial expression by identifying the specific combination of muscular movements or action units involved.

This is indeed painstaking work, and it takes a lengthy training to be able to undertake it. It is only really effective for detailing actions that occur over short passages of time. But it can make distinctions between very similar behaviours that cultural/interpretive categories may elide, and has thus provided the basis for Ekman's extensive and influential theoretical work on facial expression and emotion.[20] An objectivist approach certainly has its obstacles, but it still has a useful contribution to make to the intellectual world of conducting studies.

Moreover, although the process of taking notes on rehearsals in real time precluded any attempt at the level of completeness to which such objectivist methods would aspire, anatomical description emerged as a significant element of the metalanguage I used to record rehearsal observations as a primary means for pinpointing accurate detail of behaviour. My notes record the level of a conductor's ictus as defined in relation to his or her body (waist, sternum, shoulder, eye level), which joint or joints were involved in a gesture (shoulder, elbow, wrist, knuckles) and at what angles, and the orientation of the hands (palm up, palm down, palm towards the choir). These were all essential details for producing notes that contained enough information to allow me to recall gestures vividly, and to make meaningful comparisons between directors observed over a period of several years. This is not necessarily a metalanguage that is helpful to the reader (except in small doses), but as a tool for reflection on, and therefore theorizing from, rehearsal observations it proved invaluable.

We should also note that the aspiration for completeness and accuracy of documentation without cultural interpretation is increasingly susceptible to realization using motion capture technology. A significant pioneer in this area was Teresa Marrin Nakra, whose 'Conductor's jacket' was designed to measure muscle activity, respiration, heart rate, temperature and galvanic skin response of the conductor wearing it.[21] Like many researchers into motion capture technology, Nakra was primarily interested in the use of movement as a creative tool, and was studying conducting to improve the technology's usefulness for composing and/ or improvising; moreover, developments in wireless technology, which were not

---

[19] Paul Ekman and Wallace V. Friesen, *Facial Action Coding System: A Technique for the Measurement of Facial Movement*, (Palo Alto, 1978).

[20] For a comparison of this system with other methods of codifying facial expressions, see Paul Ekman and Maureen O'Sullivan, 'Facial Expressions: Methods, Means and Moues', in Robert S. Feldman and Bernard Rimé (eds), *Fundamentals of Nonverbal Behavior* (Cambridge, 1991).

[21] Teresa Marrin Nakra, 'Inside the Conductor's Jacket: Analysis, Interpretation and Musical Synthesis of Musical Gesture' (Ph.D. Dissertation, Massachusets Institute of Technology, 2000).

yet available when she completed this project, offer considerable improvements on her methods at the level of hardware.[22] Nonetheless, her study contains many useful insights about conducting gesture.

It also demonstrates very neatly how the two functions of metalanguage – the researcher's record of what happened, and the presentation of this to the reader – separate out into the layers of evidence and analysis, and the more detailed the researcher's record, the more separate these layers become. Although the reader needs to see extracts from the evidence base if they are to understand and believe the conclusions, whether that evidence base is a graph of galvanic skin responses or a written account of a rehearsal strategy, without the extra layer of interpretation, the metalanguage presents merely data, or at best information – not knowledge. It is interesting to note that Nakra takes a largely ethnotheoretical approach to her analytical metalanguage, drawing her main areas for discussion from a selection of conducting manuals.

Gesture Studies

Finally, it is worth turning to the discipline of gesture studies to examine how researchers here have dealt with these questions. It is not surprising that scholars of gesture in human culture at large have grappled with the same questions of analytical categories and notation in their metalanguages as musicians have. It is perhaps more surprising that there has been so little interest in musical gesture among nonverbal communication specialists, and so little interest in nonverbal communication studies among researchers in conducting.

To start with the question of analytical categories: gesture studies has produced a profusion of classification systems for gestures, many of which provide useful categories for discussing conducting, but few if any are exact fits. Many taxonomies build on the work of David Efron, whose main categories are summarized in Figure 4.1.[23]

---

[22] See also Eric Lee, Marius Wolf and Jan Borchers, 'Improving Orchestral Conducting Systems in Public Spaces: Examining the Temporal Characteristics and Conceptual Models of Conducting Gestures', available online at http://media.informatik.rwth-aachen.de/materials/publications/lee2005a.pdf [accessed 7 December 2007].

[23] David Efron, *Gesture, Race and Culture* (The Hague, 1972). Figure 4.1 summarizes in graphic form the account of Efron's system given in Bernard Rimé and Loris Schiaratura, 'Gesture and Speech', in Robert S. Feldman and Bernard Rimé (eds), *Fundamentals of Nonverbal Behavior* (Cambridge: Cambridge University Press, 1991).

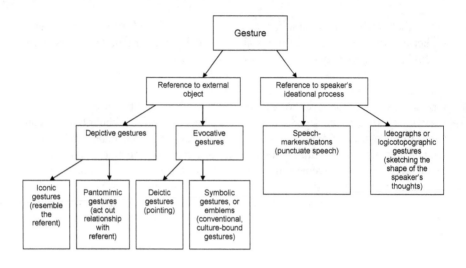

Figure 4.1   Efron's classification of gestures

This is a useful taxonomy and, while it contains implicit assumptions that thought is inherently verbal, and that gesture necessarily accompanies speech, its categories will transfer to music-associated gestures quite meaningfully. Possibly more of a problem is its fundamental division between internal and external referents that results from its hierarchical structure: this suggests that one could not use a culture-defined emblematic gesture as part of one's thought process.

David McNeill, building on the work of Adam Kendon, has produced analytical structures that classify gestures along continua rather than in discrete categories, and that usefully breaks down the internal/external division in Efron's list. This has the advantage of giving a more flexible system than a categorical taxonomy can offer, but presents problems for musicians by organizing gestural content primarily according to its relationship with speech. Table 4.1 collates the first three of McNeill's continua into a single chart.[24]

---

[24]   David McNeill, *Gesture and Thought* (Chicago, 2005), pp. 7–9.

Table 4.1   McNeill's gesture classification continua, after Kendon

	Gesticulation →	Emblems →	Pantomime →	Sign Language
Continuum 1: Relationship to speech	Obligatory presence of speech	Optional presence of speech	Obligatory absence of speech	
Continuum 2: Relationship to linguistic* properties	Linguistic properties absent		Some linguistic properties present	Linguistic properties present
Continuum 3 Relationship to conventions	Not conventionalized		Partly conventionalized	Fully conventionalized

*   In this context, 'linguistic' means having characteristics such as grammatical structures, vocabularies, and an inherently sequential way of putting together an utterance: words come one after another in a sentence.

It is harder to apply this system to music than Efron's, although it is not impossible. If we replace the word 'speech' with 'music', and gloss 'linguistic' as 'sequential or analytical', these continua do make sense, to an extent, of the classic distinction conductors make between 'time-beating' and 'expressive gesture'. There is a general sense that the formal 'grammar' of conducting patterns convey their conventional meanings without the need for sounding music, and that the creative, spontaneous gestures that remain untheorized in conducting manuals only arise and become meaningful within the musical flow. However, as we shall see in Part III, these distinctions, useful as they are, keep deconstructing themselves in musical contexts. The formal, conventional elements of technique such as pattern turn out to be meaningful by the same metaphorical processes as the spur-of-the-moment, expressive gestures, and these idiosyncratic, spontaneous gestures turn out to belong to well-established gestural traditions.

An earlier, simpler classification from McNeill, clearly influenced by Efron, presents fewer strong explanatory possibilities, but is one of the easiest formulations to apply to conducting I have found.[25] This includes iconics (gestures that have a close formal relationship with their object), metaphorics (like iconics, but representing an abstract idea), deictics (pointing) and beats (simple up-down or in-out gestures that mark particular words as important). Beats clearly make up the basic building blocks of pattern, and also of non-metrical conducting styles such as psalm chants, and deictics account for cueing gestures. Metaphorics include the manipulative gestures discussed above, while iconics will tend to become direct modelling in a conducting situation: an orchestral conductor asking for more vibrato is arguably not so much representing an idea as inciting the string

---

[25]   David McNeill, *Hand and Mind: What Gestures Reveal about Thought* (Chicago, 1992).

section to join in with the action. As a basic tool for classifying conductor gesture, this works well. We will also find that the category of ergotic, or work-associated gesture, becomes a useful additional category to this list.[26]

The descriptive, as opposed to the analytical, metalanguages of gesture studies have tended to rely on a combination of anatomical description and interpretive/metaphorical accounts that chunk separate movements into complete gestalts. The potential problems of cultural bias and researcher assumption are acknowledged by these writers, but three factors keep these under control. First, their metaphorical accounts avoid ascribing emotional states or expressive intentions to gesturers, but are limited to metaphorical associations at a physical level. Second, the overwhelming focus on gesture as it relates to speech provides a ready-made substrate of agreed meanings to ground the interpretation of gestures; ascribing a meaning to a gesture is much less problematic when the gesturer provides a simultaneous verbal statement as part of the same communicative act. Indeed, there are a number of notational conventions designed to show how gestures and speech are coordinated. Third, verbal descriptions are almost always supplemented by some kind of visual representation, whether line drawings, video stills or video footage.[27] This not only grounds the verbal descriptions, but allows them to remain much briefer and more readable than they would be were they required to evoke the full image alone. Dane Archer advocates the use of videography in cross-cultural work on the grounds that verbal description will never capture the full character of a gesture well enough for someone who is not already familiar with it to grasp it.[28] I have chosen to follow this advice here, since readers from one musical tradition may be less familiar with the gestural worlds of other genres, and also because it is important for the reader to understand the specific musical contexts in which gestures emerge.

Metalanguages 2: Writing about Choral Sound

It is not only gestures that require description. Given this study's central concern with the relationship between conductor gesture and choral sound, we also need a metalanguage to account for the vocal responses that conductors' gestures elicit. However, musicology has developed far more sophisticated and systematic means to analyse notated music than performed sound, largely due to

---

[26] See Axel Mulder, 'Hand Gestures for HCI', available online at http://xspasm.com/x/sfu/vmi/HCI-gestures.htm [accessed 22 January 2008].

[27] Examples that display all of these characteristics can be found in David McNeill (ed.) *Language and Gesture*, (Cambridge, 2000), and Jürgen Streeck, 'Gesture as Communication I: Its Coordination with Gaze and Speech', *Communication Monographs*, 60 (1993): 275–99.

[28] Dane Archer, 'Unspoken Diversity: Cultural Differences in Gestures', *Qualitative Sociology*, 20/1 (1997): 79–105.

the historical privileging of the composer's work over the performer's, but also because it holds still for analysis more readily than the fleeting experience of real-time performance. Nonetheless, scholarship and praxis have generated a similar set of possible metalanguages here as for gesture, with similar advantages and disadvantages. As the intellectual and practical issues are substantially the same, I do not propose to discuss these in the same level of detail. It is worth walking through the possibilities, however, since it is important to find ways of talking about both that can correlate with each other.

At the level of ethnotheory, the most obvious set of descriptors are those derived from instructions for musical performance: legato, staccato, cantabile, dolce. The meaningfulness to the activity is very direct here, if potentially verging on the circular; to say a staccato gesture results in a staccato sound tells us that the director is communicating effectively with his or her choir, but is rather unsatisfying as a description.

The practitioner literature also has a plethora of (often pejorative) terms that form a colourful and ad hoc vocabulary with a considerable consistency of currency. Henry Coward, for example, classifies untrained voices into the categories of 'weak and quavery, worn and tinny, harsh and shrill, strident, metallic, shouty, throaty, cavernous, hooty, scoopy, and nondescript'.[29] This is a more informal classification than standard musical vocabulary, and also therefore rather less stable, since it is the area to which individuals are most likely to contribute creatively in the course of working with choirs. It shares the advantage of being meaningful to practitioners, but presents the attendant problem that it may not transfer meaningfully to practitioners in neighbouring idioms.

Practitioner-scholars have produced a variety of schemata for discussing choral sound. Like the analytical frameworks for conductor gesture, these are primarily intended to give practitioners leverage to work more effectively in practical situations. A common formulation is to classify voice timbres into types named after orchestral groups in order to aid choir stacking: 'flutes' and 'reeds' are particularly common, while some add 'strings' to the taxonomy.[30]

'Objective' accounts likewise fall into those that account for production and those that analyse the physical results. The former describes vocal tone in terms of the anatomical processes of production (degree of vibrato, placement, type of contact between vocal folds). This has the value of relating directly to singers' use of the self. The problem of course is that the technical vocabulary of singing is itself contested: one practitioner's 'breath support' is another's 'anchoring'.

---

[29] Henry Coward, *Choral Technique and Interpretation* (London, 1914), p. 19.

[30] This is a technique that goes back at least to the 1950s, and is sufficiently widespread that later writers refer to voices' 'flutiness' or 'reediness' as commonly understood terms, without further reference to their use in a formal method. See John W. Molnar, 'The Selection and Placement of Choir Voices', *Music Educators Journal*, 36/6 (1950): pp. 48–9; Gerald F. Darrow, *Four Decades of Choral Training* (Metuchen, 1975), p. 190; and Brian R. Busch, *The Complete Choral Conductor: Gesture and Method* (New York, 1984), p. 240.

Arguably, terms derived from singing technique might better sit in the category of ethnotheory, even when based on a method that prides itself on its physiological credentials. The latter involves acoustic analysis of recorded sound, and is considerably more developed, at the levels both of technology and disciplinary conventions, than motion capture. Like the 'Conductor's jacket', these approaches make a clear separation between the graphic presentation of empirical results and the culturally bound metalanguages used to make sense of them. For instance, Nicholas Bannan, Gillyanne Kayes and Jeremy Fisher use spectrographic analysis of vocal sound in conjunction with a voice production vocabulary derived from the Estill method,[31] while Jon Sakata cross-references such analyses with traditional score analyses.[32]

Practicalities

It will be clear by now that the choice of metalanguage goes hand in hand with choice of method. Any attempt to document activities in real time will entail the use of metalanguages that group details of movement or sound into gestalts, and which provide the means to make judgements about salience: what, of all these myriad actions, matters? Any attempt to capture detail comprehensively without making a priori judgements of meaning or significance will require technological intervention, either as some kind of measuring device, or simply recording an activity to be examined in detail later. One has to make one's intellectual commitments in the context of their practical ramifications, and one's practical decisions about method in the context of the kind of knowledge one wishes to produce. In this sense, the choice of metalanguage occurs at the point of research design, as a decision that comes prior to embarking on research. Hence, the decisions about method outlined in Chapter 3 provided the primary constraints on how I charted my course between the competing demands of usability and precision during rehearsal observations.

At the same time, however, the development of descriptive vocabularies went hand in hand with the development of observational skills (both visual and aural) through many hours of rehearsal observations over a period of some years. It is a truism of learning music that theoretical and experiential learning feed off one another: learning new concepts allows us to perceive musical elements that were already there but we did not know to listen for, while new musical

---

[31] Nicholas Bannan, Gillyanne Kayes and Jeremy Fisher, 'Correlations between tone, blend and the experience of emotion in group singing', paper in preparation. This study also used a grid with a vertical dimension of light–heavy and a horizontal dimension of dark–bright as stimulus material for the choir when recording the examples.

[32] Jon Sakata, 'The First Recitative-Chorus from Haydn's *The Creation*: Rendering Forces of Darkness and Light Audible', *SAPAAN* 1 (2003), available online at http://www.sapaan.com/vol1/sakata.htm [accessed 9 January 2008].

experiences can help us make sense of concepts we had been taught but had not previously understood. Indeed, this is the rationale behind the practitioner-scholars' taxonomies: the distinction between 'flutey' and 'reedy' voices increases a director's aural acuity by providing a filter through which to organize otherwise undifferentiated sense data. So, the post-observation reflective process I outlined in Chapter 3, with the internal dialogue between theorist and practitioner, both fed off and nourished my perceptions as an observer. The development of a metalanguage is thus an iterative process.

It is also a creative process. None of the pre-existent metalanguages at my disposal – even the more colourful practitioner texts – were adequate to account for the variety, both formal and qualitative, of the gestures I observed in choral directors' routine praxis. This is in some ways not surprising; the pedagogical thrust of both the scholarly and the practical conducting literature will lead writers to present a reasonably 'purist' view. And, as we have seen, the personal, spontaneous aspects of conducting have largely been consigned to a box marked 'Magic: do not theorize'. Consequently, the observation process presented a continual challenge to find descriptors that would evoke the distinctive characters of gestures vividly enough and their formal shapes accurately enough to make the memory of watching them accessible to reflection. My notes are littered with ad hoc terms for the ictus such as the self-explanatory 'karate attack' and the less obvious 'Kermit accent' and 'micro-Zorro' down-beat. Few of these terms have survived in the metalanguages I use to present my findings – they are too idiosyncratic, and are only genuinely meaningful in the context of observing them – although I have retained the term 'Sistine wrist' for the characteristic angle found in Michelangelo's depiction of Adam and in the gestures of many directors from the British cathedral/collegiate tradition.

Moreover, what I was looking for developed over the course of the research. I started off expecting to produce accounts of what conductors were doing, but as research progressed, it became increasingly clear that it would be necessary to discuss not only the conductor's physical demeanour and the choir's sound, but the choir's physical demeanour too. There were often shared body languages to be seen among singers, which may or may not be shared with the director. Indeed, observation of these common currencies of demeanour within choirs led to two key hypotheses that I will discuss in Part IV, namely that (a) it is the choir's use of the self that effects the mediation between director gesture and vocal sound, and (b) that it may be more useful to see the director's arm movements as extensions of their more general use of the self than as the primary focus of study. For descriptive purposes, languages of social behaviour seemed appropriate here, combined with anatomical descriptions to clarify. I also became more willing to use descriptors that related to emotional state when discussing a whole choir than just the conductor. This was partly because one can just be more certain of one's inferences about sentiment from the demeanour of 30 people than of only one, but was also grounded in my explorations of theories of emotional contagion for Part IV.

Overall, then, the aim has been to draw on these various possible descriptive vocabularies with a certain degree of pragmatism. As a researcher, I can never escape the cultural filters that shape my perceptions nor the connotations of the vocabularies I use to describe them, but I can commit myself to the twin imperatives of usefulness and rigour, and be transparent about the way my research design has constrained each. The inclusion of video examples on DVD should allow the reader to triangulate between the various metalanguages and the practices they describe.

After all, when scholars talk of 'documenting' something, they intend not simply to provide a concrete record of it, but to create knowledge about it. The act of writing is part of how things become known. Written accounts, however lavishly illustrated, will always feel mono-dimensional and impoverished compared to real musical experience, and the more they try to capture this lost detail, the further they seem to stray from the aesthetic response that prompted the writing. The metalanguages contained in these accounts, however, provide the means we have to think about what we do; they offer what Nicholas Cook characterized 'a repertoire of means for imagining music'.[33] Charles Rosen may see talking about music as 'parasitical' on the primary activities of composing and performing, but this would appear to be a parasite that promotes the health of its host. Indeed, my observations suggest a strong correlation between the richness of a conductor's metaphorical vocabulary (both spoken and gestural) and the quality of the performance a choir produces; conversely, choirs that aspire only to follow literally the instructions in the score produce much more mechanical results.

The existence of many possible metalanguages signals that there are many possible types of knowledge available. The intention of this chapter has been to open up and recognize these possibilities, as well as to understand the constraints they bring with them. Metalanguages, like the basic models with which we started Part I, necessarily abstract only what they are designed to identify; like Lakoff and Johnson's metaphors, they hide as much as they reveal. But this is also what makes them useful: as we have seen, completeness of coverage requires in turn a new layer of analysis to make sense of the resultant detail. If we can accept that the usefulness of our knowledge is contingent upon its very selectivity, we may find ourselves less frustrated with its limitations.

---

[33] Nicholas Cook, *Music, Imagination and Culture* (Oxford, 1990), p. 4.

PART II
Choral Singing and Enculturation[1]

> The only voluntary factor about joining a voluntary choir is the voluntary act of joining. After that, everything is compulsory.[2]

Part II develops the thesis that the rehearsal process is one of enculturation. That is, it teaches choir members the accepted norms and values of the practice of choral singing in order that individuals may fulfil their roles competently within the group. Through a combination of example, instruction and disciplinary sanctions operated both by those in leadership roles and by peer pressure, individuals internalize the appropriate belief systems and forms of behaviour to operate effectively as a choir member.

In this introduction, I will outline the theoretical perspectives that underlie this section of the book. Chapter 5 then discusses how choral practice is constructed as a coherent and stable practice within the discourses of the instructional literature and associated institutions, Chapter 6 analyses the means by which the boundaries of this practice are located, and Chapter 7 examines how they are policed.

The analyses that follow rely on the concept of discourse analysis as developed by critical theorists after Michel Foucault.[3] This contends that our social world is constructed by and within the systems we have to represent it (language, visual codes, mythologies), and that we can gain insight into a culture's values, ideologies and power relations by analysing its cultural products. In this case, the 'text' I shall be examining is the collection of choral conducting manuals I have been referring to as the practitioner literature, combined with data arising from my choir observations, and some promotional and networking material issued by choral organizations. Although these may seem very different forms of evidence, their status as cultural products is equal: as statements made by members of the

---

[1] Some of the material in this Part first appeared in Liz Garnett, 'Choral Singing as Bodily Regime', *International Review of the Aesthetics and Sociology of Music*, 36/2 (2005b): 249–69.

[2] Attributed to Dr Lional Dakers in John Bertalot, *How to be a Successful Choir Director* (Stowmarket, 2002), p. 19.

[3] For an introduction to the work of Foucault, see Paul Rabinow (ed.), *The Foucault Reader: An Introduction to Foucault's Thought* (London, 1991). For a wider overview of this intellectual tradition, see Lucy Burke, Tony Crowley and Alan Girvin (eds), *The Routledge Language and Cultural Theory Reader* (New York, 2000).

choral community, accessible to other members of that community in the first decade of the twenty-first century, they can all act as evidence of that community's world-view.

Of course, discourse is only powerful inasmuch as it shapes what people actually do. Consequently, some theorists focus more on how people act in the world than on the language used to account for these actions. This view suggests that we experience our sense of self in and through the acts we perform day to day, that our identities are generated by our habitual forms and modes of action and interaction.[4] We are, it suggests, what we do.

Discourse and performance are related in that we do not have unlimited choice of action, but are constrained by the ways that our systems of representation lead us to perceive and understand the world. A culture's discourses, that is, will define not only what forms of action are considered appropriate, but also which are even imaginable. At the same time, the ideological imperatives of a particular discourse are not monolithic. Individuals have access to a variety of discourses, which will be variously congruent or competing with one another, and the different discourses themselves are rarely if ever self-consistent. It is in the slippage between world-views and within their internal contradictions that individuals are empowered to make choices about how to act, and concomitantly about whom to be.

Some discourses operate pervasively within a culture, and with limited opportunity for individual choice: gender, for instance, or race. People have a range of options as to how to behave as a woman or a man in Western culture, but they cannot decide to opt out of being either. Other discourses only apply to certain spheres of activity; sociologist Anthony Giddens refers to these different contexts of discourse and action as 'lifestyle sectors'.[5] This term reflects the extent to which many of our social contexts are chosen at least partly voluntarily, and also the way most people will operate within several more or less distinct worlds, each with its own languages and repertoires of behaviours. Choral singing clearly fits into this category, although, as we shall see in Chapter 6, it also intersects with the more pervasive categories of identity.

My analysis of the discourse of choral practitioners has sought both common themes and areas of contradiction or dispute. Imperatives stated as absolutes in one text will be contradicted by conflicting imperatives just as strong in another; views change over time and in different locations. As two pictures of the same

---

[4] Judith Butler developed the idea of the 'performative construction of identity' in *Gender Trouble: Feminism and the Subversion of Identity* (New York, 1990). For musical applications of this idea, see Suzanne Cusick, 'On a Lesbian Relationship with Music: A Serious Attempt not to Think Straight' in Philip Brett, Elizabeth Wood and Gary C. Thomas, *Queering the Pitch: The New Lesbian and Gay Musicology* (New York, 1993), and Liz Garnett, *The British Barbershopper: A Study in Socio-Musical Values* (Aldershot, 2005a), Chapter 8.

[5] Anthony Giddens, *Modernity and Self-Identity: Self and Society in the Late Modern Age* (Cambridge, 1991), p. 83.

object can give the sense of depth to their viewer, so the differences in opinion between writers who think they are discussing the same subject set each other's ideas into relief.

As with the Foucauldian tradition from which it stems, this analysis is not claiming a more privileged explanatory power than the knowledge systems it investigates. By critiquing practitioner discourses, that is, I am not suggesting I could say more about choral practice than the writers and speakers I quote; indeed, as a practitioner I have learned a great deal from them. But I am claiming that the vocabulary and concepts of critical theory can provide a different set of insights into the choral world than is available from within it. In particular, they can make explicit the operations of power that the discourses themselves will tend to suppress. My analyses will show how musical practices can be simultaneously independent from and constructed within the power structures of day-to-day social relations.

The language of this critical tradition can appear loaded or excessively polemical to those unfamiliar with it. It is therefore worth noting that vocabulary that carries a political charge in everyday speech – vocabulary such as ideology, discipline, surveillance – does not necessarily imply any moral judgement in this context. To point out how power operates within a social group is not to suggest that it should not do so, since this theoretical perspective proposes that power structures will be present in any and all social groups. Likewise, 'ideology' can generally be read as a synonym for 'value or belief system', with the proviso that the political connotations of the term remind us that humans are political beings, and that this inevitably shapes the way we structure our social relations.

I have nonetheless chosen to retain the some of the overtly contentious language of this critical tradition, for two reasons. The first is to acknowledge an intellectual debt: by adopting the style and tone of the theorists whose work informs this analysis, I am referring those readers familiar with cultural theory of the late twentieth and early twenty-first centuries to the intellectual milieu that permits me to formulate the arguments presented here. The second is to serve a strategic purpose in the development of my argument: the ideologically charged language has the capacity to make strange practices which may be deeply familiar to readers of this book. Like Bruno Nettl's conceit of the 'ethnomusicologist from Mars', it provides a means for those of us involved in Western choral traditions to stand outside of our week-to-week experience and see them afresh.[6]

Finally, in considering enculturation in this part of the book, I am specifically focusing on the nurture end of the nature/nurture continuum. This, again, is a strategic decision. Later sections will document and theorize instinctive – or at least involuntary – behaviours that appear to be part of our evolutionary heritage. But it is all too easy to slip from examining the instinctual to assuming the habitual; the idea that what we do is 'natural' leads all too easily to the idea that the way we

---

[6] Bruno Nettl, 'Mozart and the Ethnomusicological Study of Western Culture: An Essay in Four Movements', in Philip Bohlman and Katherine Bergeron (eds), *Disciplining Music: Musicology and Its Canons* (Chicago, 1996).

do it is inevitable. Consequently, it is useful to prefigure those discussions with an account that explores not only the extent to which choral music-making consists of arbitrary, socially constituted practices, but also how the very idea of the 'natural' is itself deployed to suppress just how contingent those practices are.

Chapter 5
Defining Choral Culture: What Counts as Choral?

The discourse of choral practice constitutes choral singing as an apparently coherent and self-evident category. It takes a range of different types of groups, performing different repertoires in different social spaces, and embraces them within the overarching definition of choral music-making by positing a basic core of common traits shared by all. The result is a stable category that sees no need to question its field of reference: choral singing is so transparently and straightforwardly choral singing, it would seem, that its practitioners can take its definition for granted.

This chapter will examine how the discourses of choral singing construct this category. It will show that the apparent obviousness of the definition conceals inequalities between the groups that it encompasses, in their power to determine norms of good practice, or even to count as legitimate choirs. My purpose is not to challenge the category; not only would that be futile (it has quite clearly established a robust place in the world), but this book relies on the category for its entire basis. Rather, this chapter aims to demonstrate how things that appear to be 'common sense' are not inevitable, but are negotiated within a social group. The more aware we are of this contingency, the more we can question our assumptions about what constitutes choral singing, and the more we will be able, as practitioners, to make conscious, self-aware decisions about the ways we interact with and deploy our common concepts and practices.

The discussion starts by analysing the way the practitioner literature construes choral singing as a universal practice, and how this disguises differences in the power of different groups to define it. It then considers the various taxonomies that the practitioner literature uses to structure the content of the category, and the way these define what counts as choral singing, and, perhaps more significantly, what does not. It finishes by showing how these definitions have been rationalized over time to create an increasingly internationalized and unified knowledge base.

The Universal and the Particular

'When people wish to express their innermost thoughts and dreams, they sing', asserts Nick Strimple, 'and when they sing together, it is called choral music.'[1] This is a classic example of the way that the choral conducting literature presents choral

---
[1] Nick Strimple, *Choral Music in the Twentieth Century* (Portland, 2002), p. 298.

music as a self-evident category by grounding it in the discourse of the universal, articulated through notions of shared humanity and authentic expression. Such a vision supposes a pre-existent interior state common to all humanity, ready to be externalized through the act of singing. This in turn allows choral music to be defined as any such act occurring in a social setting, making a category as broad as our shared human nature. Hence, the cross-cultural phenomena of human sociality and vocal communication are conflated with the specific set of practices that this literature describes.

Discourses that define a subject area will often seek to hide the conventional and arbitrary operations of the language they depend on in order to maintain control over the field they create. They do this by casting the practices they describe as natural and universal, and thence only to be expected. Such appeals to the inevitable, however, cannot avoid displaying the means of their own construction. Finding the internal contradictions and logical gaps in these discourses can thus provide telling insights into the means by which they are maintained, and in whose interests. In the case of choral music, the fissures appear between these two levels of definition, between the cross-cultural practice of people joining together to sing and the particular instances of this that are organized into groups that they and their peers would recognize as 'choirs'.

James Jordan presents a similar elision between universal and particular in his discussion of repertoire and musical meaning:

> A conductor's responsibility is to search for a universal meaning in each piece that he conducts, a meaning that contains a truth or truths that are applicable to life and living. Whether it be a simple church anthem or a major choral work, it is our responsibility to give meaning to the text so that the meaning derived from the relationship of the text and the music connects in a direct way with the lives of the persons singing the work and those who will hear the work performed.[2]

This rests on a similar vision to that of Strimple in its evocation of a universal set of meanings arising from shared humanity, yet it locates these meanings in a conspicuously circumscribed repertoire. His examples are chosen to mark the extremes of the range of possible sources for these life lessons, but, while they may provide contrast in terms of scale and challenge, they do so within a single, specialist musical tradition.

This rhetorical slippage between part and whole has a more subtle manifestation in texts which address themselves to 'all' choral conductors, and then proceed to list which types of choir are encompassed in their notion of 'all'. For instance, Hill, Parfitt and Ash direct their comments at directors 'of all types of choirs, including those singing in cathedrals or parish churches, colleges or primary schools, large

---

[2] James Jordan, *Evoking Sound: Fundamentals of Choral Conducting and Rehearsing* (Chicago, 1996), p. 175.

choral societies or small local groups.'³ These lists are inevitably selective, however much they attempt to include; they provide, moreover, a useful picture of the range of experiences a particular writer brings to bear on the subject. But the attempt to delineate a global category through enumeration of its constituent parts leads to a definition that is necessarily limited, even while claiming to be inclusive.

The result of this rhetorical strategy is twofold. First, it serves to elevate the particular practices to a level of universal significance. Choral musicians are thereby encouraged to consider what they do to be important. 'Singing', Bob Chilcott told members of the Association of British Choral Directors at their annual convention in 2005, 'can change the world.'

The second result is that any activity that could be embraced by the universal definition of 'people singing together', but is not one of the specific practices used as exemplars, becomes conceptually invisible. There are plenty of ensemble vocal practices that are not usually considered 'choral music', particularly those which use a single voice per part.[4] Moreover, some of these, most notably pop and rock styles, are specifically excluded as acceptable by many writers on choral music: Donald Neuen's distinction between styles of pop vocal production and 'legitimate choral singing' reminds us that the act of definition is legislative as well as descriptive.[5]

To the extent that a marginal practice is acknowledged at all, it is subject to the rules of the dominant discourse by virtue of its inclusion within the universal category. Its exclusion from the range of specific sub-categories, however, prevents it from making any significant contribution to the discourse. It becomes a subject rather than a citizen of the domain, bound by its rules, but unable to vote.

An example of this is John Hylton's critique of barbershop vocal production:

> In the past, there was a tendency on the part of barbershop ensembles (both male and female) to sing with an unnaturally pushed straight tone. Currently, this does not seem to be the case, but barbershoppers should always employ the same kind of natural free sound as other choral singers.[6]

Thus a carefully cultivated form of vocal styling, with a particular aesthetic significance within its own performing tradition, is dismissed as simply 'wrong' from a perspective that sees itself as 'mainstream'. Moreover, as Hylton's reference to changes in approach suggests, this judgement has to an extent been accepted by that tradition itself; there has been a noticeable change in barbershop vocal

---

[3] David Hill, Hilary Parfitt and Elizabth Ash, *Giving Voice: A Handbook for Choir Directors and Trainers* (Rattlesden, 1995), p. 7.

[4] For instance, John Potter (ed.), *The Cambridge Companion to Singing* (Cambridge, 2000) treats choral genres separately from ensembles using one voice per part.

[5] Donald Neuen, *Choral Concepts: A Text for Conductors* (Belmont, 2002), p. 45.

[6] John Hylton, *Comprehensive Choral Music Education* (Englewood Cliffs, 1995), p. 248.

production styles since the early 1990s. The power of definition carries with it the power to affect practices.[7]

The discourse of the universal thus acts as a means to disguise both the contingency of the category of choral singing and – possibly more significantly – the power that accrues to those who define it. The cultural politics involved in this discourse play out in more detail within the taxonomies used to structure and codify the category's contents.

Choral Taxonomies

There are two primary taxonomies used to define choral singing. The first, the taxonomy of type, identifies the types of performing ensemble that count as choral, while the second, the taxonomy of craft, identifies the key elements that comprise the content of the activity. The taxonomy of type is apparent to an extent in the practitioner literature, but becomes more visible in the membership lists of choral organizations and category lists of festivals and contests. The taxonomy of craft is articulated through the chapter headings of conducting manuals, and is enacted through choirs' rehearsal routines. A third taxonomy, that of musical style, is less prominent in the discourse, but is arguably the most powerful, since it draws upon the wider narratives of the Western classical canon.

Taxonomy of Type

The taxonomy of types of choir uses a variety of different parameters to create its categories: age (children's, youth, adult); the social spaces in which choirs perform or from which their members are drawn (church, university, community); gender (male, female, mixed); size (chamber choir, choral society); and typical repertoire (jazz, gospel, contemporary music). None of these parameters are applied systematically, however, and the idiosyncrasies in how they are used to organize choir types reveal a number of assumptions built into the definitions.

The primary categorization is almost always by age and gender. For instance, the membership application form for the American Choral Directors' Association (ACDA) gives six of its nine categories of choir as children, boy, girl, male,

---

[7] This change in vocal approach is one of several shifts in barbershop performance style since the 1950s, and is articulated in the shift from the scoring category of 'sound' to 'singing' in the 1993 revisions to the judging system. It should be added that barbershop's own discourses about appropriate singing style are just as categorical as Hylton's, casting elements that arguably refer to stylistic choices as either 'correct' or 'incorrect'. See my 'Cool Charts or Barbertrash? Barbershop Harmony's Flexible Concept of the Musical Work', *Twentieth-Century Music*, 2 (2005): 245–63.

women, SATB/mixed.[8] The BBC Radio 3 Choir of the Year competition in 2004, meanwhile, just gave three divisions – children's, youth, and adult – having previously distinguished between single (equal) voice and mixed voice adult choirs in previous years.[9] This at first seems both rational and systematic. It makes sense to distinguish between children, teenagers and adults for competitive purposes, since older and more experienced singers can reasonably be expected to bring more sophistication to their performances, and thus have an inherent advantage. They also have rather different vocal and educational needs, so one can see why the ACDA would differentiate for purposes of member development.

However, this builds in an assumption that children and adults do not sing together. Such a categorization excludes not only the cathedral men and boys tradition that has been the training-ground for so many choral professionals in Europe, but also the many church choirs that embrace in their ranks the full age range of their congregations. Admittedly, some listings, such as those of the Missoula International Choral Festival and the CBC/Radio-Canada National Radio Competition for Amateur Choirs, have a separate category for church choirs.[10] But it is worth stopping to consider whether faith communities should have a monopoly on inter-generational singing. Given both the values of social cohesion expressed by so many choral organizations and the difficulties in recruiting younger members that many adult choirs report, we should ask whether age is necessarily the most useful criterion by which to make our primary conceptual divisions.

The categorization by gender likewise appears at first to be a basic and straightforward division by social identity. In adult choirs, the distinction between men's, women's and mixed choirs also carries musical information; it tells us a lot about the range and timbre of voices we should expect to hear, and – partly as a consequence of this – a little about the types of repertoire. For the social category to be musically relevant, however, one has to assume a simple correlation between gender and vocal range. That a few women sing tenor and men alto in mixed choirs does not disturb the categories unduly, although participants sometimes experience a degree of tension between gender and voice roles. For example, the secretary of a mixed choral society I visited was anxious to position a male alto next to the other men in the seating plan for a forthcoming concert; the singer, meanwhile, appeared to experience his voice in solely musical terms with no connection to his gender identity and said he did not mind either way. Assumptions about the 'natural' vocal range for one's sex can also work coercively. In June 2005, a seventeen-year-old

---

[8] See the membership form available online at: http://www.acdaonline.org/mbrform.phtml [accessed 12 February 2008].

[9] In 2006 and 2008, meanwhile, an 'open choir' class was introduced for choirs 'who want to do something a little bit different'; see http://www.choiroftheyear.co.uk/categories.htm [accessed 12 February 2008].

[10] See the competition pages online at http://www.choralfestival.org/pdf/2009ICFApplication.pdf [accessed 12 February 2008] and http://www.cbc.ca/choralconcert/choralcomp/index.html [accessed 2 August 2005].

countertenor was forbidden from auditioning for what reports referred to as a 'traditional girl's part' in the Texas All-State Choir.[11] The relationship between gender and vocal range is sufficiently stable that the category of 'single' or 'equal' voices works well enough at a pragmatic level, but this stability clearly needs to be maintained by a certain amount of ongoing cultural work.

Categories defined by repertoire and/or performance tradition, meanwhile, could be accommodated quite easily by standard divisions by age and gender, but are routinely listed separately. The ACDA's final three categories, for instance, are jazz, ethnic/multicultural and show choir, any of which would fit as easily as any other choir into one of the other six age- and gender-based sections. The Llangollen International Eisteddfod, meanwhile, puts male and female barbershop choruses together in their own class, rather than as members of the classes of male and female choirs.[12] Further specific designations proposed by other organizations include categories of gospel, light entertainment, folklore and 'pancultural tradition', while the ChoralNet choir directory bundles all these together in the category of 'other'.[13]

These 'other' types of choir, then, are all marked terms in relationship to the basic categories.[14] That is, their labels carry extra information that is considered unnecessary for the default taxonomy in place of the standard labels. The implication is therefore that we all know what repertoires choirs sing and how they sing them, and if a choir sings a significantly different repertoire or in a significantly different way, we need to specify what that is, so as not to have them confused with a 'normal' choir. Notably, these generally belong to musical idioms that have either been developed in the last 50 years or have at least started participating in choral organizations within that time-frame. Thus, by declining to include these arrivistes in the general definitions, those types of choir defined by social categories rather than repertoire retain the right to define the content of the choral tradition by default. The assumption of this right is based both on the cultural prestige associated with the Western classical canon and an ostensible continuity of performing tradition associated with it.

---

[11] 'Choir denies boy's bid to sing soprano', available online at http://www.msnbc.msn.com/id/8407763/ [accessed 11 February 2008].

[12] The 2008 syllabus is available online at http://www.international-eisteddfod.co.uk/index3.asp?cat=16&d=1&pageid=864041 [accessed 12 February 2008].

[13] See the ChoralNet choir directory online at http://www.choralnet.org/choirs/index.phtml [accessed 12 February 2008].

[14] The idea of 'markedness' was originally introduced into semiotic theory by Roman Jakobson as a means to articulate the way that contrasted categories are rarely equally weighted; the marked category is often cast, as here, as a more specific variant of a generic term. The concept has received its most developed use in music theory in the work of Robert Hatten. See Robert S. Hatten, *Musical Meaning in Beethoven: Markedness, Correlation, and Interpretation* (Bloomington, 1994).

These 'marked' classes of ensemble overlap considerably with those types excluded by the conflation of universal and particular noted above. There, the conceptual invisibility produced by this exclusion served to bring these choirs into the dominion of choral discourse and practice while preventing them from making any significant reciprocal impact. The separate classification of 'other' choirs serves a similar purpose, insulating them from the 'mainstream'. In one sense, this is a potentially valuable recognition of difference. It would arguably be unfair to judge a show choir by the same criteria as a chamber choir, since they are attempting to achieve rather different ends: the separation of the 'others' guards them against the hegemony of one subset of the choral world. At the same time, however, it also protects the 'mainstream' from having to engage with aesthetics of the 'others'. A segregationist, or 'separate but equal', model may appear to offer a minority group their due recognition, but the equality may be nominal rather than real, as the taxonomies of craft and of style suggest.

Taxonomy of Craft

The taxonomy of choral craft as presented in the practitioner literature centres on a handful of key categories: vocal production (posture, breathing, placement); diction (vowel shape, enunciation of consonants, accent); choral ensemble (blend, intonation, precision); interpretation (style, dynamics, articulation); and performance (visual presentation; stage decorum). Additionally, the director is expected to impart these elements to his or her choir through the crafts of conducting (stance, beat patterns, expressive gesture) and rehearsal (planning, choir training, leadership). Not all writers deal with all of these areas, and their relative emphasis varies between texts, but the spread of these themes is remarkably consistent.[15] The increase in scholarly as well as practical texts has tended to reinforce these categories, moreover, since the literature review function vastly increases cross-reference between texts and the concomitant sense of a rationalized knowledge-base with a common core.

The result is a system of knowledge that is simultaneously all-encompassing and very flexible. The broad terms of debate are so well established as to be inescapable, yet they provide plenty of room within themselves for contention to develop. At one level, the myriad differences in opinion between writers allow contingency to show through between absolute statements: one cannot simultaneously sing with a high larynx to produce the brilliance of sound required by Charles Cleall and obey Sydney Nicholson's dictate that the larynx must remain low at all times.[16]

---

[15] Useful overviews of the American literature can be found in Gerald F. Darrow, *Four Decades of Choral Training* (Metuchen, 1975) and Steven Robert Hart, 'Evolution of Thought and Recurrent Ideas in Choral Conducting Books and Secondary Music Education Texts Published from 1939 to 1995' (Ph.D. Dissertation, University of Colorado, 1996).

[16] Charles Cleall, *Voice Production in Choral Technique* (Sevenoaks, 1970), p. 35; Sydney H. Nicholson, *Practical Methods in Choir Training* (London, n.d.), pp. 6–7.

At another, though, they safeguard the categories of thought. Different authorities may disagree on whether choirs should sing the post-vocalic r, or on the type and degree of vibrato suitable for choral blend, but the debates themselves confirm diction, vocal production and ensemble as primary categories by which to organize one's understanding, and hence one's practice, of choral singing.

This unity of discourse also gives room for the growing historical relativism manifest in more recent texts, both with regard to an awareness of changing choral styles and competing traditions over the past century, and to questions of historical performance practice. Earlier writers such as Coward and Davison assert the superiority of the methods they propound over practices of their immediate predecessors.[17] More recent writers are more willing to acknowledge changes in taste and practice over time as representing different, but nonetheless valid, artistic choices, and encourage the aspiring conductor to develop his/her own concept of the 'ideal' choral sound. The terms in which the reader is invited to hear these shifts in fashion and to imagine his/her own ideal, however, are those of the discipline's basic taxonomy. Hence, Hylton's comparison between the four American 'schools' of St Olaf's Choir, Westminster College Choir, Fred Waring's Glee Club and the Robert Shaw Chorale is couched in terms of their approach to vocal tone.[18] These are not four different practices, it would appear, but four variations on a single theme.

The categories defined by the taxonomy of craft reflect not only a consistency of discourse, but also a consistency of practice: the objectives of rehearsal and the techniques for achieving them discussed in the practitioner literature have also been apparent in the rehearsals I have observed. Again, while not all rehearsals cover all elements, all do engage with a significant proportion of them. Not all directors start rehearsal with a warm-up, for instance, and some will focus their interpretative energies more on dynamics, others on rhythmic qualities. Nearly all, meanwhile, use orthodox conducting patterns at least some of the time, although the extent to which they form the core of a director's technique varies immensely.

While this taxonomy accounts for the whole of some choirs' rehearsals, however, others include activities as integral to the process that the literature does not discuss at all. For example, all the gospel choirs I have visited include significant devotional elements in their rehearsals. These have included a prepared, spoken homily at the start of the rehearsal, a prayer at the end, and a spontaneous act of witnessing at the end of a piece, during which the rest of the choir continued to sing the song's harmonic pattern to a quiet 'oo'. The first two of these might be considered external to the categories of music or singing, but the last could not; none of them, though, are embraced by the category of choral music as defined by the literature. Another example is the characteristic barbershop gestural vocabulary for directing rhythmically free ballads, which is discussed in more detail in Chapter 8.

---

[17] Henry Coward, *Choral Technique and Interpretation* (London, 1914); Archibald T. Davison, *Choral Conducting,* (Cambridge, MA, 1954).

[18] Hylton, pp. 28–9.

Discussion of the principles or methods that govern this style is absent not only from choral texts aimed at 'mainstream' directors, but also from barbershop's own literature and pedagogy, which focuses exclusively on orthodox beat patterns.[19] Indeed, the questions this book asks about how much one can generalize across genres arose in part from my experience in delivering this curriculum and being asked, 'Why do we have to learn patterns, given that we don't use them?'

The most significant element of practice omitted from the taxonomy of craft is physical movement. Elements of dance or movement are integral to many choral styles, whether as individual response to a style's rhythmic character, bodily percussion such as hand-clapping, or explicit choreography. In all cases, an inability to participate fluently in this movement would be seen as a significant skill deficit that has a directly detrimental impact on the performance. Yet principles for good practice in the performance of physical movement and teaching strategies to develop it are markedly absent from the practitioner literature.

Indeed, where movement is mentioned at all, it is explicitly defined as outside and inferior to the core definition of choral performance. Hylton, for example, gives the following advice on show choirs:

> Be sure to create a choir that is choreographed, rather than a group of dancers who also try to sing ...
> Unless you have a strong talent in the area of choreography, engage the services of someone to design and teach the movement. It is important to find a person who understands that the movement should enhance the singing rather than detract from it. People who teach dance for a living often have difficulty with this concept. Perhaps there is an alumnus of the group who is available to assist with the choreography. Initially, it is possible that someone or some group of individuals in the choir may have the interest and experience to do the choreography.[20]

The order of priority between music and movement is articulated both in terms of the group's identity and in terms of the relationship between the two elements, with a quick sideswipe at dance teachers to confirm that this hierarchy obtains also between educational personnel. At the same time, the task of choreography is placed firmly outside the remit of the choral director. The suggestions that the director turn to alumni or current members to fill this gap reveal the way that choral choreography lives in a disciplinary no-man's land. Outside the realm of choral singing per se, it has no claim to the director's expertise, but choral music is reluctant to relinquish artistic control of its content to experts from relevant neighbouring art forms. The task falls to members of the choir to maintain the

---

[19] SPEBSQSA, *Directing a Barbershop Chorus: Method, Techniques and Philosophies* (Kenosha, 1999).

[20] Hylton, p. 245.

performance tradition in what looks – from the perspective of the choral practitioner literature – like a theoretical vacuum.[21]

The exclusion of these various 'extra-choral' elements from the category of choral performance may be defended on the grounds that they relate to matters that are not directly musical. This argument, however, depends on a post-Enlightenment aesthetic taxonomy that both separates the arts from one another and divorces them from social function. So as a rationale for disregarding these elements, it only makes sense from the context of the Western art tradition: after all, it is as problematic for gospel singers to separate the musical from the devotional as it is for an aesthetic of absolute music to conflate the two.[22]

Besides, the lines around the category of choral music are not drawn in exactly the same places as around the aesthetic of music as a fine art. One might expect the barbershop ballad style of directing to count as fully musical, for instance, in the same way that beat patterns and expressive gestures do. Conversely, one might consider some of the matters of choir management that are discussed by the practitioner literature, such as relations with the choir committee and the tidiness of the rehearsal room, to lie outside the strictly musical elements of the job. The distinction appears to be made not on philosophical grounds, therefore, but on grounds of genre.

For it is notable that the elements included in the taxonomy of craft are those relevant to the choirs that, in the taxonomy of type, defined themselves by age or gender profile rather than by repertoire. The elements excluded, meanwhile, are those associated with choirs from the 'other' categories, but not with the 'default' types. The taxonomy of craft thus brings more fully into focus the way that these choirs are subject to the discipline's dominant discourses, but are prevented from contributing to them, as discussed with relation to the discourse of the universal above. They are in one sense more than choral, in that they have these extra elements to their practices. Paradoxically, though, they are also thus less than choral, in that they represent mixed, or impure forms. 'Extra-choral' elements are both additional to and outside a tradition that constitutes itself as complete without them.

Taxonomy of Style

A common theme in the more recent practitioner literature is that it is no longer considered appropriate to approach all music in the same way, and that different repertoires require different performance styles. Steven Hart dates interest in this theme to the 1970s, and illustrates its development through discussion of

---

[21] There is a very small body of literature dealing specifically with choral choreography. See for example John Jacobson, *Riser Choreography: A Director's Guide for Enhancing Choral Performances* (Milwaukee, 1993).

[22] See Mellonnee Burnim, 'The Performance of Black Gospel Music as Transformation', in David Power, Mary Collins and Mellonnee Burnim (eds), *Music and the Experience of God* (Edinburgh, 1989).

successive editions of Garretson's *Conducting Choral Music*.[23] This of course simply reflects changing attitudes in Western art music as a whole, and indeed the discussion of style is usually quite brief since it can point to a much wider general literature. Nonetheless, it is interesting to see how this taxonomy plays out in the choral literature, as it resonates strongly with the patterns of inclusion and exclusion already identified.

Not all practitioner texts discuss style explicitly, but those that do base their discussion on the standard Grand Narrative of the periods of Western art music.[24] These discussions are necessarily brief, as they cover a wide range of styles in a single chapter, and thereby give an unusually focused view of what are considered the essential elements of each. What is striking about them is the way that they structure knowledge about genre and repertoire so as to exclude anything outside the Western art tradition.

They achieve this by using the supposedly neutral axis of time to define the categories, and, by accounting for all periods of history in the last millennium, they purport to account for all music. The continuous narrative leaves no room for the insertion of music from traditions with parallel histories. So, for example, Hylton appends a page and a half on 'African American Spirituals' at the end of his section on twentieth-century music.[25] Interestingly, this gives a brief résumé of the history of the spiritual from the eighteenth century, inadvertently revealing how the seemingly impartial categorization by chronology struggles to admit events happening in other cultures or communities at the same time as those it recounts. Paul Roe, meanwhile, squeezes in his discussion of the performance of swung rhythms in his chapter on rehearsal techniques rather than that on style.[26]

These exclusions testify to the discursive power of the Western classical canon: it is actually rather difficult to see where one would place those 'other' repertoires articulated by the taxonomy of type in this narrative structure. But this structural exclusion also reflects value judgements, as Roe reveals in the introduction to his chapter on style:

> Cheap, trivial literature obviously cannot be used for the teaching of style or for the development of the musical concepts that lead a student to the possession of musical taste and discrimination. Authentic examples of jazz

---

[23] Hart, pp. 11–12.

[24] The distinction between the Grand Narratives that provide totalizing structures to organize knowledge and experience on one hand, and the postmodern proliferation of *petits récits* that represent the world from a myriad of different perspectives on the other, was introduced by Jean-François Lyotard in *The Postmodern Condition: A Report on Knowledge* (Manchester, 1984). A good introduction to his ideas can be found in Richard Kearney, *The Poetics of Imagining* (London, 1991), pp. 170–205.

[25] Hylton, pp. 200–201.

[26] Paul Roe, *Choral Music Education*, 2nd edn (Englewood Cliffs, 1983), p. 271.

and folk music are not ruled out, for the student must be exposed to all important stylistic influences.[27]

Jazz and folk music are accorded a grudging potential respect, but the implication is that even the best examples are to be embraced only as token representatives of their genre, not for their inherent musical value.

Hence, the stylistic flexibility required of the modern choir is proposed by splitting the standard Western canon up into contrasting styles, rather than engaging with repertoires or styles that might change the content of the established canon. The Grand Narrative fragments do give the illusion of *petits récits* without actually allowing more voices into the telling of music history. Thus the taxonomy of style, while less explicitly articulated by practitioner texts than those of type or craft, appears to wield its power to define what counts as legitimate choral music considerably more stringently than either of the other two taxonomies, and the aesthetic values and performing traditions of the genre-based choirs remain almost entirely absent from the instructional literature.

Governmentality

This increased integration with the standard narratives of Western art music is one of several ways in which the literature of choral practice has become progressively rationalized over time. In this chapter and the next two, I take a primarily synchronic perspective, since the texts I examine, although written over the course of nearly a century, form an extant body of knowledge available today. However, it is worth observing a number of features of both the literature and the practice of choral music that show significant changes over time.

The first is their increased sense of historical context. This shows both in the developing interest in style and in the way that recent writers are starting to use the knowledge frameworks they present as a means to organize and account for changing practice over recent generations, as in Hylton's account of the four schools of American choral singing cited above. Second, there is a shift towards a more scholarly mode of presentation, both in the style and tone of language used, and in the inclusion of bibliographies and references to situate this new work in relation to previous texts and performance contexts. Personal practical experience still strongly informs these later texts, but is no longer the sole basis for a writer's authority. This is particularly apparent in the practitioner literature written since the 1990s by authors involved in teaching choral conducting in higher education, such as James Jordan and Colin Durrant.[28] The result is a much greater sense of a systematic, coherent and integrated discourse.

---

[27] Roe, p. 293.

[28] James Jordan built his reputation as a teacher and conductor at Westminster Choir College in Princeton, while Colin Durrant has combined a freelance choral conducting

This standardization of discourse over time in turn parallels the growth of institutional structures that support and promote the practice. Educational and networking organizations such as the American Choral Directors Association (founded 1959), the International Federation for Choral Music (founded 1982) and the Association of British Choral Directors (founded 1986) rely upon the idea of choral singing as an ontologically secure category for their existence, and also serve as mechanisms to extend the consistency and scope of that discourse's reach. Likewise, the development of choral programmes within the academy both promotes a standardized set of concepts and practices and also provides badges of legitimacy that authorize their holders to engage in professional practice.

In this sense, choral singing provides a classic example of Foucault's notion of 'governmentality', that is, the centralization of power through the construction of systematic and/or scientific knowledge.[29] Foucault dates the emergence of this form of power in the political arena to the sixteenth century, with the erosion of the power of the absolute monarch on one hand and the changing relationships with religious doctrine and hierarchies that followed the Reformation and Counter-Reformation on the other. A body of literature on the art of government developed over the following two centuries, which asked 'how to govern oneself, how to be governed, how to govern others, by whom the people will accept being governed, how to become the best possible governor'.[30] This discourse developed in dialogue with changing political institutions, and together they reconstituted political power as rational and systematic rather than arbitrarily imposed by conquest, inheritance or divine right.

The gradual systemization of choral practice's knowledge and institutions over the past century shows an analogous process. The choral leader's authority no longer rests solely on the power of their personality, but is mediated through methodically ordered concepts of good practice. 'Most of the biographical accounts of leading conductors refer to their abilities to inspire', comments Colin Durrant, 'and although it is not within the capacity of any teacher to teach students to develop or generate charisma, it is possible to reflect upon and develop certain behavioural and interpersonal skills and patterns of operation that will be appropriate for getting the best out of singers individually and collectively.'[31] The emergence of the empirical conducting literature starts to look, in this light, as the next stage of rationalization in the development of a systematic science of choral government. An efficient civil service, after all, protects the populace from the vagaries of even their more charismatic elected leaders.

---

career with academic posts in Music Education at the University of Surrey and the Institute of Education in London.

[29] Michel Foucault, 'Governmentality', in Graham Burchill, Colin Gordon and Peter Miller (eds), *The Foucault Effect: Studies in Governmentality* (Chicago, 1991).

[30] Ibid., p. 87.

[31] Colin Durrant, 'Developing a Choral Conducting Curriculum', *British Journal of Music Education* 15/3 (1998): 303–16, p. 304.

The unity of discourse that constructs the category of choral singing generates in turn a unity of praxis that, to a considerable extent, transcends the local. As Howard Swan claimed in 1988, 'Conformity of procedure has now reached the point where one particular exercise, the "yawn-sigh," is known by the same title in every section of the country.'[32] Differences between national traditions remain, but these may be more subtle than the differences between different vocal genres within a single geographical area: the structure of international choral competitions acknowledges that chamber choirs from Norway, Ireland and the United States share a clearer basis for comparison than any of them do with male voice choirs from their own countries. The breadth and consistency of practice in choral music, that is, is not evidence of a universal human nature, but the result of the practice's formalized knowledge base. The role of the choral singer emerges as a supranational identity constituted by this unified international discourse.

Having examined the structure of this discourse, we will now turn our attention to the ways that it shapes participants' behaviours and beliefs in order that they may assume this identity and learn to operate as competent choral singers.

---

[32] Howard Swan, 'The Development of a Choral Instrument', in Harold A. Decker and Julius Herford (eds) *Choral Conducting: A Symposium* (Englewood Cliffs, 1988), p. 59.

Chapter 6
Creating Choral Culture: The Dos and Don'ts

> A choir which is enthusiastic and assiduous, possessed of a lively team-spirit, loyal to its conductor and governing body, regular and punctual in rehearsal and concert, comes well into the category of 'consummations devoutly to be wished'.[1]

The category of choral singing is built through the stipulation of prescribed and proscribed practices: certain forms of behaviour are mandatory, others forbidden. The way that these behaviours are defined, though, draws on realms of experience far wider than the basic taxonomy of choral craft. The actions required from choral singers are not just vocal and musical, but also imaginative and attitudinal, and the ways that these actions are understood refer to discourses from culture at large.

This chapter traces the terms in which choral culture construes the boundaries between acceptable and unacceptable choral behaviour. Again, it draws heavily on the practitioner literature for its analyses, and also cross-references these with examples from rehearsal observations. It starts by looking at the four major themes that emerge from these discourses: those of bodily control, social identity, genre and moral character. It then goes on to examine the relationship between these themes in the ways they are deployed to mark both the extremities of the territory they outline, and the internal divisions within it. This sets up Chapter 7's discussion of the ways in which the compulsory behaviours are enforced.

Building the Boundaries: Themes

Bodily Control and the Un/Natural Voice

The first theme, bodily control, is the most obvious place to observe the production of choral singers. The inexperienced singer has a host of 'natural' faults, and this list of undesirable attributes defines what lies outside the boundaries of acceptable choral behaviour. To counter this, the texts outline a whole host of practices specifically to be desired, relating to stance, breathing and vocal production (the latter including the position of the larynx, soft palate and tongue, and the placement of resonance). That is, the texts provide specific instructions for how singers are to

---

[1] Joseph Lewis, *Conducting without Fears: A Helpful Handbook for the Beginner, Part II: Choral and Orchestral Conducting* (London, 1945), p. 46.

use their bodies; indeed, the singer's body is often referred to as an instrument, an implement to be wielded in service of the conductor's musical ends.

The natural body is simultaneously valued as the self-evident rationale for the practice of choral singing and regarded as the unformed, fault-ridden matter from which choral singers are to be moulded. The shared heritage of biological being is widely represented in anatomical diagrams of the various mechanisms of voice: stance, breath, tone production, resonators. At the same time, the body is regarded as an instrument to be deployed in prescribed ways by the singer's act of will. This contradiction runs throughout the literature as an ever-present conundrum: 'It [the voice] is the most natural musical instrument and one which we all possess. Its use has been evolving for millennia. So why do we have to learn to use it? Why can we not simply sing?'[2]

The singing body is conceived as both born and made, with functions such as breathing both coming naturally and needing to be learned:

> Just as the onset of sound is exactly the same as the natural calls of animals and birds, so the 'belted' sound relates back to the cries of babies, and can be heard in street calls worldwide and in the fold songs of Italy. ... Breathe naturally and don't constrict the airflow, and all will be well.[3]

> Don't assume that it's natural for your singers to know how to breathe. It isn't. If there's one fault above all others that most choirs share (apart from not blending, not singing together, having no sense of rhythm and not watching the conductor) it is shallow breathing.[4]

The simultaneity of nature's and nurture's formation of the voice, and the value to be placed thereon, is articulated through two distinct, but interrelated dichotomies: the voice as trained or untrained, and the voice as authentic or manufactured. Hence, Davison prefers a chorus of untrained voices, on the grounds that 'trained singers find it both difficult and wearisome to adjust their particular "method" to the needs of tonal homogeneity'.[5] Imogen Holst, meanwhile, finds that untrained voices bring with them their own faults:

> Good voices are rare, and if you are lucky enough to have one in your choir you will find that its benign influence will help to convert any soprano who shrieks, or alto who booms, or tenor who bleats, or bass who bellows.[6]

---

[2] David Hill, Hilary Parfitt and Elizabeth Ash, *Giving Voice: A Handbook for Choir Directors and Trainers* (Rattlesden, 1995), p. 12.

[3] Mike Brewer, *Fine-Tune your Choir: The Indispensable Handbook for Choral Directors and Singers* (London, 2004), p. 33.

[4] John Bertalot, *How to be a Successful Choir Director* (Stowmarket, 2002), p. 40.

[5] Archibald Davison, *Choral Conducting* (Cambridge, MA, 1954), pp. 28–9.

[6] Imogen Holst, *Conducting a Choir: A Guide for Amateurs* (Oxford, 1973), p. 52.

For other writers, the voice's naturalness or otherwise rests less on whether or not it is trained, but upon whether it is genuine to the self of the singer. Hence Neuen states that 'To sing, and to conduct singers, is to work with the instrument of nature. There should be nothing unnatural or gimmicky – no "tricks of the trade"', and that 'singers should sing like natural human beings, not like a conductor's conception of how they might be transformed, manipulated, or manufactured into something else!'[7] The authenticity of the singer's emotional expression is often discussed in terms of vibrato, with a common distinction between a 'natural' vibrato which is to be encouraged, and an excessive, undesirable vibrato, dubbed a 'wobble' or 'tremolo'.

Hence, Victor Knight interprets the excessive form as the result of an attempt to fabricate a derivative rather than sincere form of expression:

> The singer who is addicted to these forms of wobbly singing may have started doing it in imitation of someone else, under the mistaken impression that it indicates emotional commitment to the song. If so, he probably can no longer hear himself doing it, which is perhaps fortunate for him but certainly the reverse for everyone else.[8]

Vibrato stands as a metonym for the distinctiveness of an individual's voice, and it is in service of the question of how best to mediate between the uniqueness of individual voices and the corporate sound of choral blend that the discourse of the natural is commonly deployed. Hence, Davison regards the construct of vocal 'method' as an impediment to a unit sound, and Joseph Lewis considers a choir of trained voices to sound as 'a mass of clashing vocal colours – a heterogeneous huddle of warring resonances, each striving to be heard above the rest'.[9] In both of these instances the problem is not merely that the process of training has made voices sound too unlike one another, but that it has fostered an overly individualistic attitude that values this uniqueness above the corporate endeavour of the whole. The natural voice may be faulty, but it is at least not obstructive; it has the potential to be shaped.

Counterpoised to this is the notion that the manufacturing process that removes the voice from its natural state goes on not in singing lessons, but in the very process of melding voices together in a choir:

> Our singers are individuals. They deserve to be respected and treated as individuals. They should not be manipulated into some kind of mass unit that has no individual identity. They are all human beings. They will sound similarly beautiful, and surprisingly uniform, if they sing naturally, freely, energetically, and with sensitivity. They need not be forced to sound like

---

[7] Donald Neuen, *Choral Concepts: A Text for Conductors* (Belmont, 2002), p. 27.
[8] Victor Knight, *Directing Amateur Singers*, (West Kirby, 2000), p. 73.
[9] Joseph Lewis, *Conducting without Fears*, p. 10.

someone else, or manipulated into a 'special sound' for which the conductor wishes to be known.[10]

The idea of the natural voice as authentic expression is thus deployed in direct opposition to that of the natural voice as untrained, although in search of an answer to the same practical and philosophical questions.

The discourse of the natural thus becomes a means to regulate and rationalize the required forms of bodily control appropriate to the act of choral singing. It represents, on one hand, the nasty and brutish Hobbesian state of nature; the untrained voice can escape into the civil society of the choir by signing up to its social contract of correct bodily behaviours and acquiescing to the power of the sovereign conductor. On the other, it represents a vocal noble savage, unfettered by the encumbrances of artificial vocal methods and free to express its innate, unspoiled virtues.

Social Identity

The second theme used to define boundaries of acceptable choral demeanour is that of social identities such as class, educational level, and regionality. This theme emerges most frequently in the literature through the discussion of diction, although other aspects of choral practice such as voice placement are also implicated on occasion. Hylton's assertion that 'no matter which language is sung, the aim is to pronounce words in a universally accepted manner, devoid of regional and colloquial mannerisms', is typical in positing a manner of diction that transcends the particular identities of specific localities, and in doing so contributes to the notion of a universalized choral practice discussed in Chapter 5.[11] The social judgments implied by his casting of regional accents as 'mannered' are underlined by their association with the 'colloquial'. Garretson likewise advocates avoiding 'vocal mannerisms characteristic of particular regional areas', and fleshes out the social implications of this by recommending 'a standardized "general American" approach to pronunciation, as utilized by most radio and television announcers'.[12] Coward makes more explicit still the associations of class indexed by accent by mandating the use of 'the King's English' as a means of dealing with those 'districts in which even educated people have certain peculiarities of pronunciation'.[13] It is worth noting in this context that the idealized 'default' or 'universal' pronunciation promoted by writers is invariably mediated by place: British writers such as Coward, Cleall and Knight warn singers against sounding

---

[10] Neuen, p. 12.

[11] John Hylton, *Comprehensive Choral Music Education* (Englewood Cliffs, 1995), p. 21.

[12] Robert L. Garretson, *Conducting Choral Music*, 3rd edn (Boston, MA, 1970), p. 56.

[13] Henry Coward, *Choral Technique and Interpretation* (London, 1914), pp. 86–7.

too American, while American authors such as Sandra Willetts caution singers that certain vowel shapes may sound 'terribly British'.[14]

While Cleall's discussion of diction makes some reference to regionality ('A dialect such as Scottish, which inverts and exchanges vowels, alters the flow and movement of sounds in an unjustifiable way'),[15] it rests to a greater extent on the axes of class and education:

> It may be said, 'But language is a living thing. Correct pronunciation is established by usage; not by the dictionary'.
>
> Attractive as the argument may seem, it is not used by those who have an ear for language; because usage constantly falls into error by imitating ignorance, supposing ignorance to be fashionable.
>
> Without the guidance of The Oxford English Dictionary, we shall ape the yob or the nob every time we open our mouths: with it, we may learn to pronounce English beautifully, in a way which is neither posh nor common.[16]

Hence the aesthetic quality of beauty is directly linked to a specifically middle-class sensibility that is considered well educated and therefore able to transcend mere fashion. The location of authority over language in the Oxford English Dictionary suggests not only a respect for the written word, but also, by invoking Britain's oldest university, references a particular accent, and, indeed, a particular collegiate choral tradition.

Conductors in rehearsal likewise use references to wider social identities to indicate what is and what is not acceptable in performance. For example, a cathedral choir director working with boy trebles called their insufficiently crisp consonants 'soppy': 10-year-old boys might not have strong musical opinions about articulation, but they are often motivated to avoid behaviour that might be too much like a girl's. He later indexed their shared masculine identity again in referring to the list of repertoire for the service they prepared for as the 'batting order'. The director of a gospel church choir, meanwhile, asked for notes to be sung 'stepped', rather than 'slurred', since in slurred singing, she drawled, 'we really do sound like Southern Americans'. More indirect references to social identities show through the metaphors used within a rehearsal: a director who asks for a 'full-bodied sound – like the best cabernet sauvignon' draws upon a certain set of shared experiences and social habits for the request to be meaningful.

Of course, to use metaphors that resonate with the experience of singers is at one level simply a sensible approach to communication; conductors are only going to be effective if their instructions are intelligible. But such cultural references

---

[14] Coward, p. 44; Charles Cleall, *Voice Production in Choral Technique* (Sevenoaks, 1970), p. 37; Knight, p. 79; Sandra Willetts, *Beyond the Downbeat: Choral Rehearsal Skills and Techniques* (Nashville, 2000), p. 24.

[15] Cleall, p. 33.

[16] Ibid., p. 94.

reveal assumptions about the choir's wider social world. The metaphor helps define what counts as 'people like us'. Not only will teetotallers and the drinkers of alcopops lack the direct experience to make sense of the cabernet sauvignon metaphor, but they will also recognize in it associations of class, belief system and forms of social contact that are similarly foreign. Moreover, in their prescriptions for how choristers shape their word sounds, these cultural politics act directly on audible elements of the singers' social identities, affirming or erasing vocal behaviours that in everyday life carry information about origin and background. However they speak at home, when they come to choir, they need to sing with a choral accent.

Genre

The third theme by which the boundaries of acceptable choral practice are defined is by reference to other genres. Notwithstanding the universalized definition of choral singing as the natural expression of shared humanity, styles of singing associated with some other repertoires are explicitly excluded, especially those associated with pop and rock. So, Willetts attributes tuning problems to 'faulty vocal production' arising from 'male changing voices and with females who have sung only pop or country music in a chesty register', while Hylton asserts that 'the current pop vocal sound of many female singers is not a desirable model for choral singing, since it is breathy, lacking in focus, and dependent on electronic amplification for projection'.[17]

Related to the marking of boundaries by genre is the overwhelming assumption of literacy: choral music is conceived in the literature almost exclusively in terms of the notated works that constitute the classical canon. Hence, the ability to sight-read is demanded by those writers discussing audition criteria, and promoted by those writing for conductors working in an educational context. It also shows through in the discourses of rehearsal. One conductor I observed made frequent and varied references to harmonic context, with terms such as 'modulation', 'dominant', and 'E flat major chord', all of which make assumptions about the level and type of prior education and experience. Interestingly, though, the choir's committee was taking orders for learning CDs for those members who could not read music, suggesting a possibly problematic disjunction between the genre markers in the conductor's discourse and the actual background of at least some of the singers.

Steven Demorest places music literacy so firmly in the heart of choral music that he entitles his book dedicated to developing this skill *Building Choral*

---

[17] Willetts, p. 31; Hylton, p. 73. Objections to pop styles are not limited to female singers: Hylton continues: 'Many male pop singers also produce a sound that is an inappropriate model for most choral situations, although a positive point is their use of falsetto.'

Excellence.[18] His discussion of vocal traditions that rely on orality rather than literacy show that 'choral' here refers to the specific rather than the universalized practice:

> The influx of world music into choral repertoire over the last ten years has been a welcome and very positive addition to choral music education. ... However, many of the singing cultures represented do not rely on standard notation for either the transmission or performance of their music. In fact, notated editions of some cultures' music can conceal more than they reveal about authentic performance practice. Consequently, there is often a greater reliance on rote procedures for learning this music, and the skill of reading traditional notation is less important.[19]

Hence, repertoires that arise from oral traditions are seen as inherently outside the category of choral music, since their recent inclusion is seen as an 'influx' brought about by their transformation into notated scores. The contrast here between 'rote procedures' and 'traditional notation' is telling: oral transmission is cast as a set of concrete operations devoid of understanding, while literacy takes on the associations of a valued continuity of practice carried by the term 'tradition'. 'World music' is also (as ever) a problematic term; its discussion here solely in terms of non-notated idioms invites a connection with the term 'ethnic music', which often appears as either implicit or explicit euphemism for music from African American traditions. For example, Samuel Adler states that:

> There are many instances when we wish to perform authentic ethnic music, or 'composed' music with an ethnic flavor. 'Hold On' by James Furman gives us an opportunity to look at a work that attempts to notate the Gospel singing style. James Furman is one of our foremost authorities on black Gospel music, and in this, as in some of his other works, he has given us as close an approximation as possible of all the rhythmic, melodic, and harmonic nuances of the style.[20]

The repeated use of 'we' and 'us' in this passage, and the way this is counterpointed against the mysteries of a black idiom requiring the intercession of an 'authority' to make it performable, signal that the choir of Adler's imagination is predominantly white. Notation marks the boundaries of choral music not only by repertoire, that is, but also by race.

At the same time, the musics of the African Diaspora are often invoked from within the classical tradition as a kind of pre-cultural, universalized music accessible to all. With their origins in the continent where humanity first evolved,

---

[18] Steven M. Demorest, *Building Choral Excellence: Teaching Sight-Singing in the Choral Rehearsal* (Oxford, 2001).
[19] Ibid., p. 17.
[20] Samuel Adler, *Choral Conducting: An Anthology* (Fort Worth, 1971), p. 540.

black musics are treated as the songs of nature: authentic in expression, closely tied to the body (in contrast to the cerebral world of art music), and simple both to learn and understand. Accordingly, African, African American and Caribbean songs are used as warm-up and workshop materials by classical practitioners, but find their way into the performing repertoire much less frequently.[21]

For example, at a large, all-white choral society I visited, a vocal coach taught a calypso song as part of her vocal warm-up. It included reference to singing calypso in the lyrics so as to make the genre association absolutely clear, and also included the instruction to 'shake a little', for which the coach demonstrated an associated hip movement. Nobody in the choir performed the hip movement when they sang it back, so she added to her demonstration an explicit instruction to do so, whereupon a few of the women joined in. This gives a telling demonstration of the way that acts of cultural appropriation may not be purposeful, but result from the appropriating group applying their own definitions and understandings to cultural products from other traditions. Hence, not only did this classical choir sing this song with their default style of vocal production and accents from middle-class Middle England, but they erased the 'extra-choral' element of body movement as not applying to them, even though it was directly referenced within the song.

This is not to say that these types of song do not bring useful skills to notation-based choirs; they can help develop both aural memory and bodily connection with the voice. At the same time, though, they trivialize the traditions from which they borrow, since they engage with them at such a very basic level. Anyone can sing this primitive, African stuff, they imply, but it takes dedication to sing Brahms. Black musics are thus reduced to a single, homogenous tradition requiring about the same degree of connoisseurship as a nursery rhyme. They are embraced by high art traditions to the extent that they can be understood to represent a lingua franca of human brotherhood, but at the same time relegated to functions that do not require their users to engage with genre-specific elements either of technique or style.

Moral Character

The final category used to mark the boundaries of choral practice is that of the moral attributes of a singer's character. We have already seen how the trained voice and/or the voice with excessive vibrato can be regarded as evincing an overly individualistic attitude and a concomitant refusal to commit to the corporate endeavour. A singer at a male voice choir I visited articulated this as the problem of 'people who think they should be soloists', and gave as examples of their egotism their habits of hanging on to notes too long at the ends of phrases and of singing too loudly.

---

[21] I am grateful to Jonathan Smith for this insight.

Discussion of choral blend consequently focuses on attitudes and relationships within the group as much as on the technical elements of voice production and word sounds. Thus, Lewis states that:

> Team-work or what we call ensemble is more to be desired than outstanding voices, and the only possible way to obtain this 'togetherness' is by the part being subservient to the whole, ... being content to be a strand in the rope, and not the whole rope, but all the while handing his or her contribution up to the conductor.[22]

Likewise, Leslie Woodgate asserts: 'No one should feel that he is a leader, but each should be an integral part of the whole.'[23]

John Potter views the choral society movement in Victorian Britain as a means to enforce the moral values of the dominant classes, and these pronouncements certainly seem to paint a picture of a world order in which the lower classes know their place and are content to remain in it.[24] It is interesting to note in this context that debates over the competing claims of voice teachers and choral conductors to dictate how student singers use their voices and the increasing interest in the study of acoustics as a means to achieve choral blend are both developments of the late twentieth century.[25] It could be that, as dominant ideologies in wider culture have become more overtly individualistic and meritocratic, it has become less socially acceptable simply to dictate along with Garretson that voices of 'unusual and distinct tone quality' should be 'subdued'.[26]

Equally threatening to choral unity, however, is the other commonly identified moral failing of singers, that of laziness, and this is apparently as reprehensible in the early twenty-first century as it was in Coward's day. Diction is a common area to be singled out for disapproval: Garretson and Cleall both decry 'slovenly' articulation, while Woodgate complains that 'so many of us are lip-lazy'.[27] Phillips, meanwhile, links these problems with issues of pronunciation in wider social life: 'Singers bring lazy speech habits to choral singing; plosives (bursts of air) are

---

[22] Joseph Lewis, *Conducting without Fears*, p. 10.
[23] Leslie Woodgate, *The Chorus Master* (London, 1944), p. 6.
[24] John Potter, *Vocal Authority: Singing Style and Ideology* (Cambridge, 1998), pp. 81–2.
[25] See, for example, James F. Daugherty, 'Choir Spacing and Formation: Choral Sound Preferences in Random, Synergistic, and Gender-Specific Chamber Choir Placements', *International Journal of Research in Choral Singing*, 1/1 (2003): 48–59; and Elizabeth Ekholm, 'The Effect of Singing Mode and Seating Arrangement on Choral Blend and Overall Choral Sound', *Journal of Research in Music Education*, 48/2 (2000): 123–35.
[26] Garretson, p. 136.
[27] Ibid., p. 56; Cleall, p. 55; Woodgate, *The Chorus Master*, p. 11.

imploded, voiced consonants are sung under pitch, and lack of energy prevails.'[28] Incorrect pronunciation is a moral as well as a social failing, it seems.

Laziness also shows up as a more general fault, in both physical and mental terms. Roe gives a long list of potential causes for fatigue in singers, from 'poor physical condition', through 'muscle tension', 'shallow breathing' and 'unsuitable tessitura' to the final possibility of 'laziness'.[29] William Ehmann likewise links character to physical ailment when he claims that '"mouth breathers" are often lazy people, and one associates them with the dull people who suffer from chronic catarrh'.[30] A conductor I observed in rehearsal, meanwhile, on hearing the tonal centre drop, told his singers that 'tuning is mostly psychological' and 'it's mostly just laziness'.

Sometimes the moral disapproval hints not only at idleness, but also elements of depravity. Cleall, for instance, considers 'the conventionally fat and feverish tone' employed by choirs as 'not only thriftless of energy, but musically ineffective'.[31] Holst distinguishes between faults due to inexperience and those of 'self-indulgence' and 'sentimentality'.[32] As with the singer who likes the sound of their own vibrato, it is not just that singers lack application, but they are positively wallowing in the behaviours the conductor would like to eliminate. Coward, meanwhile, proposes that a taste for 'rhythmless music':

> ... arises from the hyper-sensitive taste of a limited class of musicians who prefer the nebulous, dreamy and inconclusive, rather than the clear and well defined. Whether this is an indication of superior judgement or merely depraved taste is a debatable point which need not now be discussed.[33]

Given the adjectives he has used to describe this aesthetic, discussion is hardly needed. Particularly telling is his use of the word 'limited' to imply both a simple subset of the musical world and to suggest a judgement as to their musical, intellectual and/or moral capacities.

Deploying the Boundaries

I should like to make two overall observations about the way that these themes are deployed to mark the limits of acceptable choral conduct. The first is that the boundaries are strongly overdetermined. That is, any one form of behaviour to

---

[28] Kenneth H. Phillips, *Directing the Choral Music Program* (New York, 2004), p. 237.
[29] Paul Roe, *Choral Music Education*, 2nd edn (Englewood Cliffs, 1983), p. 114.
[30] William Ehmann, *Choral Directing*, trans. G. Wiebe (Minneapolis, 1968) p. 22.
[31] Cleall, pp. 55, 35.
[32] Holst, p. 47.
[33] Coward, p. 96.

be included or excluded is defined in terms of more than one of these discourses. We have already seen how music literacy (or the lack of it) accrues associations with different styles or idioms, and thereby can index race or ethnicity. Likewise, 'scooping' up to a note might be labelled as simply a fault due to lack of training, as the result of an indolent and complacent character, or as an attribute of other, inappropriate, styles of singing such as crooning.[34] Knight conflates the discourses of genre, bodily dysfunction and regionality in his assertion that:

> Singers whose singing or listening experience has been limited to pop music present serious problems when they join choirs. Some of them may have excellent voices if they sing properly, but seem to be under the impression that, in order to sing at all, they should sound as though they suffered with their adenoids and came from Tennessee.[35]

As a result, it is not possible to separate out those behaviours that are conceived in terms of cultural political axes of identity (race, class, education level, regionality), from those that are 'purely' technical or musical. The bodily, the moral, the social and the generic are inextricably intertwined in defining what constitutes choral singing, and ostensibly pragmatic statements of good practice, when placed in their broader intertextual web of reference, are rarely neutral with reference to the operations of power in wider culture.

This is not to say that, at an artistic level, these requirements for behaviour are wrong. Matched word sounds, deep-seated breathing and a clean onset of sound are all clearly skills that are important to the choral craft. What I do wish to highlight, however, is that the ways in which these are understood and articulated by choral culture draw on connotations of value systems and social norms from beyond the choral sphere. So, when we ask someone to relinquish a mode of vocal production developed in dialogue with a different style, we are also asking them to put aside those cultural and aesthetic allegiances; we are asking them, for the duration of the choral rehearsal at least, to become a somewhat different person.

The second observation is that the catalogue of desirable and undesirable habits, whether physical, social or moral, is used not only to build the boundaries between acceptable and unacceptable choral behaviour, but also to delineate different roles and identities within the broad category of choral singer. Hence, Holst defined the voice parts of a classical choir in terms of their typical vocal deficiencies: shrieking, hooting, bleating and bellowing. Gordon Reynolds, meanwhile, develops the same stereotypes using social attributes:

> The opportunity knocking at your door may turn out to be nothing more exciting than an evening class containing three sopranos over fifty, five altos occupying

---

[34] Roe, p. 120; Holst, p. 47; Knight, p. 106.
[35] Knight, p. 6.

more than one seat each, one tenor who has to go early because of his train, and two basses, one seventeen and the other seventy.[36]

These intra-choral categories are articulated in both positive and negative terms at the same time, since their purpose is to define rather than to exclude. The stereotypes can be deployed to praise or to deride, and can be applied from the outside or assumed from within. Hence, Neuen can reinterpret the sopranos' tendency to shrillness and inappropriate girlishness as 'youthful freshness with great clarity, flexibility, and warmth', and recast the altos' relative obscurity as a function of their neglect: 'They are often the best musicians, so the conductor seemingly has less to worry about with them.'[37]

Part stereotypes are also developed in dialogue with the musical characteristics of the music they sing. So, Willetts links the idea of high pitch to high altitude in order to account for a vocal flaw: 'There are also those who vibrate on the top side of the pitch. I've come across this characteristic only with high sopranos. Don't ask me why. It probably has something to do with rarefied air.'[38] Vance George, meanwhile, manages to knit together the ideas of musicianship, anonymity and ripeness of figure in his discussion of rehearsing a Bach chorale: 'Make them [the altos] feel special by impressing upon them how important they are to the harmonic structure, since they get all the left-over notes in a triad and are usually cast in opera as witches, mothers or handmaids.'[39]

As a result of this, part stereotypes are quite genre-specific. Within a genre, the primary differentiator will usually be conceived as the 'natural' attribute of vocal range, but the meaning of that range will be quite different in different musical worlds. The female barbershop baritone has some characteristics in common with the classical alto, but these arise more from analogous musical roles (musicianship, getting the 'left-over notes') than from occupying the same vocal range. She has far more in common, though, with the male barbershop baritone, who takes the same musical and social role in a lower-pitched and differently gendered ensemble.[40] Moreover, the ostensibly inborn trait of vocal range develops within the context of the musical demands of the genre and the discursive meanings attached to them. The size of a singer's larynx will define the outer limits of their range in an absolute sense, but different choral traditions use different subsets of the complete possible range, and thus both develop voices differently and give them different meanings.

---

[36] Gordon Reynolds, *The Choirmaster in Action* (London, 1972), p. 11.
[37] Neuen, pp. 41, 43.
[38] Willetts, p.41.
[39] Vance George, 'Choral Conducting', in José Bowen (ed.), *The Cambridge Companion to Conducting* (Cambridge, 2003), p. 50.
[40] For a discussion of the barbershop part stereotype of the baritone, see Liz Garnett, *The British Barbershopper: A Study in Socio-Musical Values* (Aldershot, 2005a), pp. 170–72. See also pp. 93–4 for a discussion of how expectations about gender and vocal range differ between the barbershop and classical traditions.

This is one reason, I hypothesize, why SATB choirs sometimes struggle to find tenors, while male voice choirs drawing their membership from the same geographical area can find plenty. The male voice choir tradition appears not to construe tenors as rare, delicate and temperamental in the same way the classical tradition does.

These discourses, then, provide the framework that defines what a choral singer must do, and therefore, to an extent, whom they must be, in order to count as a competent member of the culture. The behaviours are relatively stable, and correlate well with the taxonomy of craft outlined in Chapter 5. The ways these behaviours are understood, meanwhile, gives the practice of choral singing multiple and tangled ties to categories and belief systems in wider social life. The musical and the extra-musical interpenetrate, and both are inscribed upon the singers' bodies as they create their choral identities in negotiation with social values and cultural associations derived from wider communities of meaning. Chapter 7 will examine this process of inscription, as it traces the means by which the borders around the choral terrain are policed, and the mechanisms by which the required behaviours are enforced.

Chapter 7

Maintaining Choral Culture: Policing the Boundaries

At the beginning of a practice you have before you a collection of individuals. It's your job, within the first ten seconds of the practice, to weld them together into a choir – and a choir is a body of singers which feels a corporate sense of identity. That implies a strong sense of self-discipline – which means listening to every word that their director says. So make sure that everything you say is worth listening to.[1]

John Bertalot's vignette of the start of a choir rehearsal captures many of the key issues that surface repeatedly in discussions of how to transform a more or less random group of people into a coherent and effective choral ensemble. These include questions of group identity, of discipline (and particularly self-discipline) and the director's own obligations to the choir. While the boundaries that define choral practice are constituted through discourse, their enforcement relies on a range of disciplinary mechanisms operated by both conductors and by the singers themselves. These entail both the literal exclusion of individuals who display inappropriate forms of behaviour and the imposition of practices intended to transform participants' behaviours into more appropriate forms. The transformation is effected on one hand through processes of surveillance and coercion and on the other through the internalization of values. These values also underpin the conductor's craft; the right to command the ensemble is rooted in the director's willingness to subordinate themselves to higher artistic and/or moral principles.

Exclusion versus Transformation

All choirs have filters of some sort to identify whether and to what extent potential members display the attributes they seek, although how formal the filtering process is, and how explicitly it articulates its criteria, varies enormously. Audition procedures represent the most systematic end of the spectrum, and will nearly always present their desiderata in primarily musical terms. An amateur choral society, for instance, tells newcomers that 'the most important thing is whether

---

[1] John Bertalot, *How to be a Successful Choir Director* (Stowmarket, 2002), p. 28.

you can sing in tune, can hold your part and will blend in. Good sight-reading is helpful but not essential.'[2]

Other choirs demand attributes that are more personal or attitudinal than musical, either instead of or in addition to skill-based audition criteria. Some ask for moral qualities such as 'commitment' or 'loyalty' – which will presumably be apparent through the investment of time and attention in the choir[3] – while others ask for a more emotional investment in opening membership to anyone who 'loves singing'.[4] Faith choirs, meanwhile, may prioritize religious devotion over musical skill. The processes for deciding who qualifies under these more subjective criteria are generally less systematized than the audition process. Choirs may define attendance policies overtly, requiring members to meet certain standards of behaviour on an ongoing basis in order to qualify for continued membership, but perceived deficiencies in enthusiasm or cooperativeness are more likely to be dealt with informally, with a senior member of the group – either director or committee member – negotiating with the problematic individual.

Of course, as we saw in Chapter 6, the musical and the moral are at least partly related to one another. Hence, for example, the conductors I observed who promoted a more soloistic (as opposed to blended) ethos in their choirs were almost always working with auditioned singers: they had less need to change their singers' vocal behaviours since they had already selected singers who displayed the behaviours they sought. The relationship between musical and social selection criteria, however, is not necessarily simple, as Coward points out:

> As to the social qualifications, I am convinced that, other things being equal, the better a singer has been educated the more refined are the results obtainable. But while admitting, with pleasure, that some of the most energetic and enthusiastic singers I have ever met are high in the social scale, it would be fatal to a high standard of performance to elect members upon social position alone, because so many would join and then refuse to work. ... The best plan, therefore, is to insist on vocal and reading ability as being the basis of admission to a choir.[5]

---

[2] Solihull Choral Society, 'Membership Information', available online at: http://www.solihullchoral.org.uk/index.php?module=pagemaster&PAGE_user_op=view_page&PAGE_id=4&MMN_position=4:4 [accessed 19 February 2008].

[3] See, for example, the application form for the Hallé Youth Choir, which asks for 'passionate and committed singers open to new challenges'; available online at: http://www.halle.co.uk/publishedSite/sitefiles/resources/youthchoir_form.pdf [accessed 28 February 2008].

[4] For example, the community choir Bristol Voices states that 'you don't need an audition to join. You don't need to read music or have experience. All you need is a love of singing and a desire to learn songs from all traditions, cultures and times.' See their website at: http://www.bristolvoices.org.uk/page3.htm [accessed 28 February 2008].

[5] Henry Coward, *Choral Technique and Interpretation* (London, 1914), pp. 258–9.

Few modern writers would feel comfortable displaying their class prejudices quite so overtly. Given the way that the definitions of required attributes are overdetermined, however, such assumptions may still lurk within ostensibly purely musical requirements. Music literacy again provides a telling example: regarded as a fundamental criterion for selection by authors such as Neuen, it immediately excludes those who have learned to sing in traditions that work primarily by ear.[6] This is not to deny the importance of sight-reading skill for the performance of notated repertoire, of course. But it does highlight the way that eliding the cross-cultural phenomenon of ensemble singing with the more limited set of practices usually listed in the practitioner literature can hide exclusions on social grounds within musical and vocal expectations.

To maintain the boundaries by literal exclusion, however, is less important than to do so by the modification of participants' conduct. Many writers assume that the director will have to craft a choir out of whoever presents themselves as volunteers, and even those writers who do discuss audition procedures and requirements spend far less time discussing selection than detailing the means by which to promote desired behaviours and to prevent those deemed unsuitable. Moreover, the notion that the choral singer is made rather than born betrays an egalitarian ideal that to an extent counter-balances the ideological investments of the behavioural ideals themselves. Hence, Reynolds advises aspiring choral conductors that:

> It is necessary to learn how to include in one conversation people of widely differing mental attainments. A choir may include labourers, doctors, teachers, office workers, all manner of people – and the choirmaster is usually the best person to ensure that they all feel wanted.[7]

So, while the boundaries that delimit the identity of the choral singer may be located with reference to wider social categories, it is by the execution of correct practices, rather than by the possession of congenital attributes, that the individual can have access to that identity. Whatever one's previous musical experience and regional or class accent, one merely needs to learn the accepted styles of vocal production and diction to become a choir member. In this sense, the practice has some claim to its supposed universality: choral singing may be a narrower and more culturally contingent activity than it would like to imagine, but it is one that has well-developed techniques for transforming disparate individuals to suit its needs. These techniques fall into the Foucauldian categories of technologies of power and technologies of the self, and are represented in the choral conducting literature

---

[6] Donald Neuen, *Choral Concepts: A Text for Conductors,* (Belmont, 2002), p. 182.
[7] Gordon Reynolds, *The Choirmaster in Action* (London, 1972), p. 49.

and practice by the range of training methods and disciplinary frameworks by which a choir director can generate choral singers.[8]

Technologies of Power

The technologies of power provide the surveillance mechanisms by which the choral director enforces required behaviour. Most if not all choral conducting texts devote far less space to the discussion of the conducting techniques of beat pattern and gesture than to furnishing a repertoire of techniques for the regulation of appropriate choral behaviour in rehearsal. Indeed, the entire rehearsal is framed as a process of monitoring what the singers are doing, identifying what is faulty or lacking and then altering it. 'Even if the change is not for the better and has to be modified later', claims Abraham Kaplan, 'the essence of a good instruction is that it is understood by the chorus and requires that they *change something* in their performance.'[9]

The diagnostic phase of this process, the detail of perception brought to the director's aural and visual surveillance of choral behaviour, is key to the success of the enforcement mechanisms: there is a clear correlation between the attainment levels of choirs and the precision with which their directors can identify the source of problems. Contrast, for example, 'There's something wrong in the harmony' with, 'Tenors, that should be an A natural, not flat'; or, 'I can hear voices, I can hear soloists in the sound' with 'that ee vowel is too forward-placed; it will blend better placed further back.'

It is not enough that directors should observe their choirs, however; the singers must also be aware of being observed. Instructions such as 'I need to see your teeth' thus serve not only to define the required behaviour, but also to remind the choir that their compliance is being monitored. Furthermore, the more individualized the surveillance is, the more control it affords the director. Not only does it help with precise diagnosis, but it also makes each singer feel individually subject to the director's power. Rehearsal techniques that break down the musical texture into individual parts are a standard method for more selective aural surveillance. Gospel directors routinely rehearse by walking up to their choirs to listen to and work with individuals within the flow of the music. I have also seen a director break down the choir by row, then down into groups of four singers in order to identify which singer needed correcting. This practice goes beyond the coercive effects of individual scrutiny to the punitive effect of public shaming.

---

[8] Michel Foucault, 'Technologies of the Self', in Luther H. Martin, Huck Gutman and Patrick H. Hutton (eds), *Technologies of the Self: A Seminar with Michel Foucault* (Amherst, 1988).

[9] Abraham Kaplan, *Choral Conducting* (New York, 1985), p. 188, emphasis in original.

An extreme version of this tactic occurred in an open rehearsal just prior to a contest performance at the Barbershop Harmony Society's annual International Convention, when a director stopped his chorus, looked at an individual on the second row, and said, 'Twelve thousand people just heard that mistake.' Here the director not only paraded his aural prowess in singing out one singer from a chorus of 80, but also magnified the humiliation by invoking the entire convention audience as witness to the transgression as well as the people actually in the room.

The signs of this supervision are apparent not just in the director's instructions, but also through their gestures within the flow of the music. This regulatory function may relate to musical or to vocal issues – dynamic level, balance, tuning, support or vowel shapes – and will often be directed towards specific subsets of the choir or at individual singers. The gesture will usually be the 'didactic' type, to be discussed in Chapter 9; that is, it will be corrective or instructional rather than interpretative or expressive. The pointed finger is an important part of this disciplinary aspect of conducting technique, both for selecting and identifying the participants towards whom the gestures are directed and for demanding attention to the particular issue the director wishes to focus upon.

As the appropriate behaviours were construed in extra-musical as well as musical/vocal terms, so the director's superintendence of his or her singers extends beyond their specifically musical and vocal behaviours to control their affective, psychological and moral states as well. This is evinced in concerns with the maintenance of orderly habits in the rehearsal and performance environment; laxness in putting away the choir's robes, it is suggested, fosters a general moral decline that will infect not just choral technique but the entire spirit of the choir.[10] Appropriate attire, whether choir robes, stagewear or polo shirts bearing the choir's logo can thus come under the director's purview: 'Uniform appearance in any organization', states Garretson, 'places emphasis upon the group rather than the individual. It helps to develop pride and a feeling of belonging – a feeling so essential to the success of any organization.'[11]

This concern with the singer's internal states also extends to their state of being outside rehearsal. Hence, the director of a church choir I observed spent some time explaining to new members that they should not leave the performance area during services because that was 'disrespectful', and that therefore they should therefore avoid doing so if at all possible during rehearsals, since 'what we practise is what we do'. It is not surprising that questions of performance etiquette leech back into the rehearsal room, since the performance is where the activities developed in rehearsal come to fruition. But the director's jurisdiction can also include non-musical activities: the same director also asked the choir to offer their full support to a planned choir social event, since 'community makes unity'.

---

[10] Bertalot, p. 19; Neuen, p. 15.

[11] Robert L. Garretson, *Conducting Choral Music*, 3rd edn (Boston, MA, 1970), p. 211.

The interest in a singer's subjective experience also relates to the understanding of the voice as both site and expression of individual self-identity: 'I begin with the conviction', states Swan, 'that we must know our singers as persons before we can help to build their voices.'[12] This statement mediates between the multiple meanings of 'natural' discussed in Chapter 6: the natural, authentic self must be respected if the natural, unformed body is to be successfully transformed into a choral singer.

A key element of this process of enforcing choral discipline through the surveillance of the whole person is the development and maintenance of eye contact. At one level, close visual attention to the chorus complements the aural monitoring of their vocal behaviour, providing information about how singers are managing their vocal equipment. At another, this is a means for the director to exert power over the singers, as Bertalot suggests when he instructs the director: 'Always make sure, when you give an order, that you are standing up straight, like an officer in front of his troops, and looking everyone in the eye.'[13] While eye contact between individuals can be an intimate and reciprocal experience, as the practitioners' accounts of the interaction model attest, there is an imbalance of power in the director's command of their singers' visual attention. The conductor cannot look at all singers at once, but expects to be able to meet the eye of any singer whenever they look their way. Choral rehearsals resound with exhortations for the singers to look at the director: 'You're not together because you're not watching me. Please watch'; 'Watch me and I'll give you a clue when to sing.'

The technologies of power are particularly evident in choirs that include a spread of age groups, where the younger members have yet to fully learn the standard disciplines of the choir's culture. For instance, in a gospel church choir, there was a group of new singers in their early teens who had not yet learned the forms of bodily engagement with the music and vocal styling displayed by more experienced members of the choir. The director repeatedly had to ask them to stand tall and to open their mouths up wider. Likewise, in the rehearsal of a cathedral men and boys choir, the director had to work hard to keep the boys' eyes on him, particularly in the later stages of the rehearsal as they tired. Watching them, it was clear that the boys were generally quite well engaged with the music, but this could often involve drifting off into their own thoughts with it; the conductor was perpetually having to pull them back into the present to get them to respond to his directions for dynamics and balance. That is, the problem was not in getting them to pay attention, but in training them in the type of conscious, alert attention that the intensive and detailed rehearsal style required.

Most of the time, though, the enforcement can proceed with a lighter touch because the majority of the singers have internalized the norms and values expected of them. Paul Attinello claims that the structure of a choir is 'highly authoritarian', but my observations suggest that despotic power is often both softened and

---

[12] Howard Swan, *Conscience of a Profession* (Chapel Hill, 1987), p. 96.
[13] Bertalot, p. 18.

strengthened into the form of power that Gramsci referred to as 'hegemonic', that is, rules that are enforced by those who are subject to them.[14] We see this, for instance, when choir members hush each other as the conductor waits for their attention. Even this behaviour, though, is considered less ideal than that of the self-disciplined ensemble in which chattering never breaks out in the first place. The model choir is one in which the choir members enforce the rules not only on each other, but also on themselves. The technologies of power succeed most fully when they prompt the singers into operating the technologies of the self.

Technologies of the Self

'Singers', asserts Bertalot, 'need to correct their own faults.'[15] Colin Durrant makes a more developed statement of the same principle:

> By far the most valuable feedback for choral singers is that perceived by the singers themselves. As singers learn how to detect their own feedback, intrinsic reward is increased with that self-mastery, conductor feedback becomes less necessary (rehearsal time is saved), and emotional attachment to singing is intensified.[16]

These pronouncements give a good account of the rationale and the processes of the technologies of the self. Foucault defined these as methods by which individuals 'effect by their own means or with the help of others a certain number of operations on their own bodies and souls, thoughts, conduct, and way of being, so as to transform themselves in order to attain a certain state of happiness, purity, wisdom, perfection, or immortality'.[17] That is, they provide a means not only for the singers to take over the monitoring and modification of their own behaviour, but in so doing they are rewarded by attaining the state of grace of becoming a competent and emotionally committed choir member.

These technologies are operated both by the self being transformed and by others: the choral trainer provides instruction and demonstration, but the

---

[14] Paul Attinello, 'Authority and Freedom: Toward a Sociology of the Gay Choruses', in Philip Brett, Elizabeth Wood and Gary Thomas (eds), *Queering the Pitch: The New Lesbian and Gay Musicology*, 2nd edn (New York, 1993), p. 321. John Potter analyses the nineteenth-century choral society movement in terms of the 'hegemonic fraction', as 'enabling all classes to have access to sufficient of the system to keep them happy while denying them any real power'; Potter, *Vocal Authority: Singing Style and Ideology* (Cambridge, 1998), p. 82.

[15] Bertalot, p. 46.

[16] Colin Durrant, *Choral Conducting: Philosophy and Practice* (London, 2003), p. 33.

[17] Foucault, 'Technologies of the Self', p. 17.

individual enacts the practices thus prescribed. The cooperative nature of this endeavour is apparent whenever directors use direct modelling to promote desired behaviour. We see this particularly in warm-ups, where directors will routinely participate in the physical stretching or limbering exercises they give the choir, but also within the flow of the rehearsal as they demonstrate aspects of vocal technique such as stance, vowel shape or facial expression. The message is: be as I am. Likewise, rehearsal strategies that involve the singers in gesture or physical movement as a way to understand a vocal or musical point not only make them more available to surveillance (since it is very clear whether and how successfully singers are participating in the exercise), but also blurs the role between conductor and singer.

The joint involvement of director and singers also shows through the literature in an ambiguity as to whether instructions are addressed to the choir trainer or the singers in his or her care. Hence, Cleall delivers his comments directly to the singer: 'Stand, or sit, like a soldier at attention, but without his rigidity: head up, chin in, shoulders loosely back and down, chest up, abdomen in.'[18] Willetts, meanwhile, talks about the singers' experience to their leader: 'They must memorize what it feels like to sing in the dome or mask, and humming is nature's way of achieving that automatically.'[19] Roe attempts to encompass both by presenting notional monologues that the director might present to the chorus: 'One of the very first things a director must tell a new choir is, "Hold up your music".'[20]

Like the technologies of power, those of the self relate both to individuals' bodily experiences and to their interior states; 'Good singing', says Lloyd Pfautsch, 'is always more of a mental than a physical effort.'[21] The 'self' on whom the technologies operate is thus an integrated psychophysical unit, and the techniques for transforming it involve both instructions for actions and for ways to imagine and experience those actions. Cleall's instruction above, then, invites the singer to identify with a particular role or persona as a means to learn how to hold the body, while Willetts links the act of humming with both bodily sensation and memory. Singers' affective states are also invoked as a means to achieve appropriate bodily disposition: two of the techniques that Roe provides to establish 'a firm, open throat and relaxed neck muscles' are to 'feel suddenly amazed' and to 'feel ecstasy'.[22] The frequent use of medical metaphors signals that the process of change operates more deeply on the singer's experience of him or herself than simply following instructions. Hence Lewis writes of individual instruction being required to 'cure'

---

[18] Charles Cleall, *Voice Production in Choral Technique* (Sevenoaks, 1970), p. 11.

[19] Sandra Willetts, *Beyond the Downbeat: Choral Rehearsal Skills and Techniques* (Nashville, 2000), p. 12.

[20] Paul Roe, *Choral Music Education*, 2nd edn (Englewood Cliffs, 1983), p. 73.

[21] Lloyd Pfautsch, 'The Choral Conductor and the Rehearsal', in Harold A. Decker and Julius Herford (eds), *Choral Conducting: A Symposium* (Englewood Cliffs, 1988), p. 99.

[22] Roe, p. 77.

the 'defects' of problem voices, and Garretson suggests that 'it might be well for the choir director or voice teacher to think of various vocal exercises as a physician might think of a prescription or a form of therapy'.[23] Several directors I observed in rehearsal, meanwhile, asked for singers to align their interior selves with the music they sang: 'Believe the sound you're making'; 'Sing from the heart'; 'And this time with attitude'. It is not enough simply to follow the music's instructions; the singer must also participate emotionally in the music's agenda.

There can be a degree of slippage between external actions and internal states, as an example from one of my rehearsal observations shows. During a vocal warm-up, the director instructed the choir to 'take a resonant breath', which, he explained, meant 'taking a breath so that it coats your teeth'. The next instruction was likewise expressed in physical terms, but was actually physically impossible: he asked the choir to inhale the breath up over their cheeks to the backs of their heads. Hence, a direct physical instruction that allowed the singers to self-monitor by bodily sensation developed into a breathing technique that relied for its success on the singers' creation of imaginative constructs of their physical selves.

The technologies of the self are in evidence wherever singers engage in behaviours without being directly asked to. A good example is those choirs that have a culture of bringing pencils to rehearsal to annotate the music: here the singers take responsibility for writing instructions to themselves, that they will thereafter be expected to follow without further reminder. An extension of this is those choirs in which members who cannot sing for whatever reason still attend rehearsal to hear what the choir works on and to mark up their own copies accordingly. The more artistically ambitious the choir is, the more sophisticated are the behaviours that singers engage in upon their own behalf. For instance, when the director of a professional choir I observed asked the sopranos for a trill in a contrapuntal piece, all the other parts added the trill when they had the same musical material. And one of the means by which cathedral choirs manage the large quantity of music they need to rehearse is the convention whereby singers raise their hands when they make a mistake in order to signal that the director need not spend rehearsal time correcting them.[24]

Conversations with choir members at rehearsal, moreover, show them typically to be quite self-aware about their choir's strengths and weaknesses, and at times to have quite strong opinions about what they have achieved to date and what they need to work on. At the same time, the particular aspects of choral craft they bring up invariably correlate strongly with the rehearsal focus of their director. A member of a choral society I visited told me that their director was 'good at getting us note

---

[23] Joseph Lewis, *Conducting without Fears: A Helpful Handbook for the Beginner, Part II: Choral and Orchestral Conducting* (London, 1945), p. 24; Garretson, p. 41.

[24] John Potter aligns this practice with coercive power, calling it a 'ritual humiliation' (see Potter (1998), p. 84). While it can share the quality of individual blame associated with the technologies of power, however, the transfer to the singers of the responsibility for monitoring accuracy marks it as a technology of the self.

and rhythm perfect, and produces quite a good sound'; the rehearsal itself focused primarily on accuracy, with subsidiary themes of blend and vocal support. This shows not only the degree to which singers internalize the values of their choir, but also the power the director has to determine what those values might be.

In the rehearsal situation, the director shunts back and forth between deploying the technologies of power and asking the singers to engage the technologies of the self. A good example of this flexibility was displayed by a director of a chamber choir who was trying to deal with a persistent slipping of the tonal centre. He started off by simply asking the singers not to drop in pitch, and made his ongoing monitoring of this issue clear both by a pointed finger twisting upwards in a corrective gesture, and then, more punitively, leaving them to sing a cappella, then coming in with the piano after a few phrases to demonstrate the pitch drop. Next, he started to make more explicit interventions. He addressed their interior state, saying, 'You're feeling this as too lugubrious', and followed this by enrolling them in physical action, asking them to stand up, and to copy an exercise to improve vocal support that he demonstrated. This was the most successful tactic so far, and he followed it up with a direction to think of any repeated note as slightly higher than the one before. Hence, he combined surveillance and punishment with helping the singers act upon their own bodies, thoughts and feelings, and shifted his focus between all these elements until they succeeded in attaining the desired state of singing in tune.

The Limitations of Power

If the technologies of power represent the overt enforcement mechanisms directors have at their disposal, the technologies of self are brought into play as their singers internalize the knowledge, skills and values of the choral world into which they have entered. Hence, the latter present a more sophisticated form of control, and as we have seen, are strongly correlated with more ambitious levels of artistic and technical achievement. The technologies of the self are thus integrally related to the notion of governmentality discussed in Chapter 5, in that they are associated both with a shift from absolute to rationalized power, and with the development of a more mature and complex knowledge base. High-level choirs attain their results not just by the power of their conductor's personality, but by their constituent singers' participation in the ensemble's artistic order. This artistic order is constituted through the discourses that define the techniques and values that shape the ensemble's activities, and each singer signals their personal investment in it by schooling themselves into observably correct ways of being. Hence, both meanings of the word 'discipline' – as a field of endeavour or expertise, and as the enforcement of required modes of behaviour – come into play at the same time: each relies on the other for its existence.

Governmentality thus increases the effectiveness of power, first, by developing systems and techniques that those who are subject to that power can apply for themselves, and, second, by engaging their willingness to do so. The cost of this increase in effectiveness is the limitation of the power wielded by any one leader. The enlightened prince was one who ruled rationally, whose subjects could see a clear reasoning behind his decisions. Likewise, there is a strong emphasis within the choral conducting literature on avoiding the abuse of one's position of authority: 'Be wary of your power', cautions Brewer, 'and use it for good.'[25]

Those that enforce the rules are expected to discipline themselves as much as their choristers. Hence, Kaplan's chapter on 'Discipline' refers to the director's control over their technique, both gestural and instructional, not to their control over their singers.[26] The idea that directors should limit how much they speak, meanwhile, is not only a recurrent refrain throughout the literature, but often receives especial emphasis, either typographically or through punctuation. So, Holst tells us that 'a golden rule for all conductors is DON'T TALK TOO MUCH'. Others suggest what to do instead: 'Do not talk too much – communicate musically!' states Adler, while Davison adds, '*Sing whenever you feel the inclination to talk.*'[27] And as we have seen, many texts also require conductors to shape their choirs' behaviours from a position of responsiveness to and empathy with them; Reynolds, for instance, asserts that the choir 'will only function properly, and with that degree of unanimity which a first-class team must have, if there is complete understanding between the choir-master and each individual singer'.[28]

Directors, like singers, are expected to monitor and correct themselves. Indeed, the act of monitoring the choral sound is connected with this self-supervision in the idea that lies behind this book's central research questions, that is, the prevailing assumption that choral sound automatically reflects the qualities of a conductor's gestures. Gunther Schuller describes this relationship as follows:

> I like to think of that listening ear as the 'third ear', an ear which 'sits' well outside the conductor's body and listens not only to the totality of what the orchestra is producing but also to the effect the *conductor's* conducting is having on that orchestra and on the music. It is therefore a highly critical, a highly discriminating ear; it is a regulatory ear. But it must also be a *self-regulatory* ear. It must be as much directed at one's self (the conductor) as at the orchestra. Thus the 'third ear' is an ear which critically assesses whether how and what someone is conducting corresponds in fact to what is intended by the composer in his score.[29]

---

[25] Mike Brewer, *Kick-Start Your Choir* (London, 1997), p. 14.
[26] Kaplan, p. 90ff.
[27] Imogen Holst, *Conducting a Choir: A Guide for Amateurs* (Oxford, 1973), p. 46; Samuel Adler, *Choral Conducting: An Anthology* (Fort Worth, 1971), p. 12; Archibald Davison, *Choral Conducting* (Cambridge, MA, 1954), p. 40; emphasis in the originals.
[28] Reynolds, p. 6.
[29] Gunther Schuller, *The Compleat Conductor* (Oxford, 1997), p. 17, emphasis in original.

Although this passage focuses on orchestral rather than choral conducting, it is worth quoting for its detailed exposition of the way that the surveillance mechanisms involved in the conductor's control over the ensemble interact with their own technologies of the self. It also draws attention to the way that conductors are themselves subject to higher authority. They may command the ensemble, but this power is both legitimated and constrained by moral obligations not only to the ensemble but also to a more fundamental set of principles or guiding values.

The higher power in whose service the conductor acts may be conceived in terms of communication with or impact on an audience, or of worship or ministry in the case of faith choirs, but is most commonly characterized as service to 'the music'. This may be expressed, as in Schuller's case, in terms of fidelity to text of the composer's score, or may be presented more abstractly as an obligation to the 'music itself', or, as Lewis puts it, to 'the Divine Art'.[30] In all cases, the purpose of this higher power is to place limits on the conductor's egotism; 'Honoring the composer's structural design', says George, 'will keep your music honest by getting inside the piece and allowing it sound, which guards against the temptation to "interpret".'[31] Just as choristers are enjoined to 'sing from the heart', conductors are required to subordinate their subjective experience to the cognitive and affective structures encoded in the music they direct. An 'aesthetically satisfying interpretation', claims Roe, comes from 'empathy with the words and music'.[32]

Choral conducting itself can thus be seen as a disciplinary regime in its own right, distinct from but related to that of the choral singer. Directors, like singers, are required to act hegemonically, enforcing rules to which they themselves are also subject. And it is to the craft of the director that we shall now turn, to investigate two key elements of this regime. Part III will explore the process of personal alignment between director and music to try to understand what is going on when a conductor 'gets inside' a piece. Part IV will focus in turn on the relationship between conductor and choir, and attempt to unpick the processes that allow conductors' surveillance of their singers to double as a means to monitor their own performance.

---

[30] William Ehmann, *Choral Directing*, trans. G. Wiebe (Minneapolis, 1968), p. 92; Joseph Lewis (1945), p. 2.

[31] Vance George, 'Choral Conducting', in José Bowen (ed.), *The Cambridge Companion to Conducting* (Cambridge, 2003), p. 46.

[32] Roe, p. 70.

PART III
Conducting Gesture and Musical Thought

A really successful conductor *becomes the music itself.*[1]

The idea that the conductor should 'look like the music' runs through the literature of both choral and orchestral conducting.[2] From the time when the conductor first emerged as a specialist musical role in the early nineteenth century, this ability to 'become the embodiment of the composition'[3] has been a key criterion by which to tell the true artist from the 'mere time-beater'.[4] But how does this happen? What are the processes by which the imagination can become visible, and how do physical motions become musically meaningful?

Part III focuses in on the conductor in order to explore this connection between the musical imagination and physical gesture. It argues that conducting gesture is integral to the way that conductors understand and conceptualize musical content, and that different gestural traditions are both the visible traces of and the means to maintain and develop distinct communities of meaning.

---

[1] Donald Neuen, *Choral Concepts: A Text for Conductors* (Belmont, 2002), p. 204 (emphasis in the original).

[2] Robert Garretson, *Conducting Choral Music*, 3rd edn (Boston, MA, 1970), p. 12.

[3] Robert Schumann, quoted in Elliott Galkin, *A History of Orchestral Conducting in Theory and Practice* (New York, 1988), p. 241.

[4] The 'mere time-beater' is a stock phrase that runs through conducting discourse. Introduced by Berlioz, it drew invective from Wagner and Weingartner before becoming enshrined in the most widely used English-language conducting manual of the twentieth century, Max Rudolph's *The Grammar of Conducting*. It continues to appear in the discourse of conductors of the early twenty-first century as a term that seems to require little or no explanation, and has even provided the basic categories around which to devise empirical studies of conducting. See Hector Berlioz, *Treatise on Instrumentation, Including Berlioz's Essay on Conducting*, enlarged and revised by Richard Strauss, trans. Theodore Front (New York, 1948), p. 410; Felix Weingartner, *Weingartner on Music and Conducting: Three Essays by Felix Weingartner*, trans. Ernest Newman, Jessie Crosland and H.M. Schott (New York, 1969), p. 224–5; Richard Wagner, *On Conducting: A Treatise on Style in the Execution of Classical Music*, trans. Edward Dannreuther (London, 1897), pp. 98–9; and Max Rudolph, *The Grammar of Conducting: A Comprehensive Guide to Baton Technique and Interpretation*, 3rd edn (New York, 1995), p. xiii.

Chapter 8 examines the distinct gestural traditions represented by the four conductors on the accompanying DVD. Making detailed reference to the rehearsal footage presented, it discusses distinctive elements of gestural vocabulary in three specific choral traditions – British cathedral, gospel and barbershop – and explores the common ground between choral and orchestral conducting gestures in the conductor of a symphony chorus. These examples have been chosen for their clearly identifiable profiles of posture, gesture and vocal styling, and so allow a discussion of the relationship between these directing styles and the characteristic performance styles of the different traditions.

Chapter 9 examines points of contact between these genres, documenting elements of conducting technique in relation to 'textbook' good practice and exploring how these function within the rehearsal process. It outlines a variety of elements that are found across choral genres, but which either contradict 'good practice' or are simply not documented by written authorities. Chapters 8 and 9, then, explore choral conducting as an interlocking set of practices that both share a common fund of procedures and include aspects that are developed in relation to specialized musical contexts. They not only provide material for the theoretical chapters that follow, but will also be of a directly practical interest to conductors who find themselves working in a variety of stylistic contexts.

Chapters 10 and 11 examine these practical examples through the lens of two interrelated theories in an attempt to explain the relationship between conductor gesture and musical thought. The first is Lakoff and Johnson's theory of metaphor as cross-domain mapping. This will be useful for several reasons. First, it can account for the process of 'translation' between musical content, conductor gesture and verbal gloss that occurs as a matter of course during rehearsal. Second, the idea that such mapping is selective in the features to which it draws attention captures very nicely the way that the act of musical interpretation is both analytical and creative. Third, the emphasis on an embodied understanding gives these concepts an obvious and direct relationship to conducting as an explicitly physical expression of musical meaning. I will explore this theory by applying it to two core elements of conducting technique, dynamic shaping and pattern.

The second theory is David McNeill's account of the relationship between gesture and thought in spoken language. While there are always obstacles in applying theories about language to music, McNeill develops ideas that can provide illuminating explanations for the ways that conductors generate expressive gestures spontaneously in response to musical needs that arise in rehearsal. As we have seen, the so-called 'left-hand function' gets very little attention in most conducting manuals, with readers advised to figure out for themselves what to do to express their ideas. And it has been clear from my rehearsal observations that conductors do this successfully and unselfconsciously as a matter of course. McNeill's theories can help us understand how we convert imagination into gesture, while Lakoff and Johnson's can help us understand how those gestures carry musical meaning.

One final issue that needs addressing before embarking on the detail of Part III is the relationship between choral and orchestral conducting. The practitioner literature sees a recurrent debate as to whether these should be seen as a single or two separate disciplines. The argument in favour of a single discipline points out that a significant quantity of core repertoire combines choir and orchestra, whether a symphony with a choral finale or a mass with orchestral accompaniment, and so a conductor has to be competent to conduct both.[5] The argument for two separate disciplines points out that conducting voices requires a different style of gesture from conducting instruments, since the physical operations the performers undertake to make music are quite different.[6]

Certainly, in practice, there are gestural 'dialects' that differ between choral and orchestral conductors, just as there are characteristic gestural styles associated with different choral genres. The most obvious difference is that choral conductors use batons relatively rarely except when working with both choir and orchestra, while orchestral conductors rarely do without. Musical exigencies also play their part; the varied texture of orchestral music involves conductors more in cueing gestures and balancing volume relationships between sections, while choral conductors concern themselves more with projection of text and vocal line. But the different dialects also reflect the way that even those conductors who have received formal training (and many may not have) formed their basic understanding of the gestural vocabulary as performers in ensembles watching other conductors. A central part of this book's thesis is that gestural style is deeply embedded within musical cultures, and this section intends to show how integral it can be to the way musicians understand their praxis.

Nonetheless, there is a broad agreement of approach in both the formal grammar of beat patterns and the means by which these are inflected for expressive purposes. There may be considerable variation in manner of presentation, but the basic topology remains constant. Indeed, two of the principal texts on orchestral conducting in use in the US – those of Max Rudolph and Elizabeth Green – are also recommended by choral conductors,[7] and the influence of Rudolph's taxonomy of articulation styles is apparent throughout the American choral literature.[8]

---

[5] Leonard Davis, *Practical Guidelines for Orchestral and Choral Conducting: For those Wishing to Build on their Existing Experience rather than for Complete Beginners* (London, n.d.), p. 3; Frederick Goldbeck, *The Perfect Conductor: An Introduction to his Skill and Art for Musicians and Music Lovers*, (London, 1960), p. 91.

[6] William Ehmann, *Choral Directing*, trans. George D. Wiebe (Minneapolis, 1968), p. 115; Lewis Gordon, *Choral Director's Rehearsal and Performance Guide* (West Nyack, 1989), p. 83.

[7] See for examples the threads discussing textbook recommendations for college conducting classes archived in the ChoralNet Resources, available online at: http://choralnet.org/resources/viewResource.phtml?id=12&category=5 [accessed 11 December 2007].

[8] See for example Harold A. Decker and Colleen J. Kirk, *Choral Conducting: Focus on Communication*, (Englewood Cliffs, 1988), pp. 12–15; Garretson, p. 24; James Jordan,

For the purposes of the discussion presented here, it will be clear that many of the gestures discussed in Chapters 8 and 9 are specific not only to choral conducting, but often to particular subsets of the choral world. On the other hand, the processes by which these gestures become meaningful, as discussed in Chapters 10 and 11, do transfer effectively to conductors of other types of ensemble.[9]

Evoking Sound: Fundamentals of Choral Conducting and Rehearsing (Chicago, 1996), p. 119.

[9] Wind band conducting is another genre that has its own specialist literature, albeit considerably less extensive than either choral or orchestral conducting.

Chapter 8
Different Styles, Different Gestures

This chapter explores distinctive gestural traditions through the exemplars of four individual directors, as presented on the accompanying DVD. It will introduce each in turn, giving some background information about each director and the choir they are working with, as well the specific context of the rehearsal occasion itself. It will then go on to discuss various aspects of their conducting technique, pinpointing particular moments chronologically through the extracts shown. This structure of presentation is intended to make it easy for the reader to work through the chapter and the DVD in parallel. Some will prefer to view the material before reading about it, others vice versa, but in either case each section will work as a unit, without requiring too much interruption on the way through. The comparative discussions in subsequent chapters will then make more sense, as the reader will already have a basic familiarity with the examples.

As I explained in Chapter 3, each director was chosen because their personal directing styles showed a strong affiliation with a specific musical genre or style. Hence my discussion in this chapter will focus on those elements which are recognizably shared with other directors working in the same area. That is, it will highlight those features that operate at the level of 'dialect' rather than 'idiolect'. All directors do things that are typical as well as those that are uniquely theirs, and, while it is the latter that make them interesting as artists, it is the former that will help us understand the relationship between gesture and style. The clips were chosen, however, with all four chapters of Part III in mind, so those that receive less discussion in this chapter will often include examples that receive more attention later on. The editing decisions for all four rehearsals were thus undertaken together, in order to provide appropriate points of comparison and contrast as well as points of interest specific to each conductor.

Adrian Lucas and the Worcester Cathedral Choir

Worcester Cathedral Choir is a traditional men and boys choir, consisting of boy trebles and adult men singing alto, tenor and bass. The boys are pupils at the King's School, Worcester, which offers scholarships to choristers from the age of seven upwards, while the men are lay clerks, that is, they are engaged to sing on part-time salaried posts that they will typically combine with other freelance work and/or teaching in the school. The cathedral has evensong six days a week, plus a sung Eucharist on Sundays, and while the main choir does not sing for every service (there is also a voluntary choir, and visiting choirs sing during the school holidays), it has a heavy and regular workload.[1] The discipline of rehearsing and performing large quantities of music on a daily basis requires the boys to develop fluent sight-singing skills, and the depth and rigour of this musicianship training is the basis upon which many of Britain's professional musicians have built their careers.

Adrian Lucas was appointed Master of the Choristers at Worcester in 1996, having previously worked at a number of other cathedrals around the country. He combines his work at the cathedral with a variety of other musical activities: organ recitals and recordings, composition, orchestral conducting, work with a number of choral societies, and directing a major annual festival. This profile demonstrates clearly how cathedral work can underpin a broader professional musical life not just as a training ground but as part of a portfolio career. This choral tradition is thus simultaneously very specialized and very well integrated into Britain's wider musical life.

The rehearsal featured on the DVD was filmed on Saturday 22 December 2007. It took place from 5.30 p.m in preparation for a Christmas carol service starting at 7.30 p.m. The first part of the rehearsal took place in the choir school with the boys only, and then they moved into the cathedral, where they were joined by the men. As the cathedral started to fill up with people arriving for the service, all moved back into the choir school. The rehearsal finished at 7.15 p.m, which just gave time for the choristers to put on their surplices before returning for the cathedral for the service. Figure 8.1 shows the layout of the choir for the service. Although they were singing in front of the chancel steps rather than in the choir for this service, they used the traditional antiphonal layout, with cantoris and decani sides of the choir facing each other; the rehearsal room in the choir school also uses this layout.

Figure 8.1   Worcester Cathedral Choir

---

[1] Details of the choir's musical programme can be found at http://www.cofe-worcester.org.uk/cathedral/services.php [accessed 7 January 2008].

The first clip on the DVD shows Lucas rehearsing the boys in his own arrangement of the Coventry Carol. He directs from the piano here, and uses a combination of hand gestures and movements of his head and upper body to coordinate the singing. The other three clips are from the full rehearsal in the cathedral, and feature Jim Clements's 'Awake, glad heart!' which was to receive its premiere in the carol service that evening, plus some fragments of other carols at the end of the final clip.

Lucas's technique is clearly based on traditional conducting patterns, but these also undergo considerable variation in their form and use. When he directs from the piano in clip 1.1, of course, his hands are not continuously available for this function, so his gestures focus on onset and release of sound and some dynamic shaping and phrasing. His upper body, meanwhile moves subtly to the metre, and his head gets involved in marking cross-rhythms and breath points. At the start of the clip 1.2, he presents a clear two-pattern, but as he starts to work on the detail of the piece, the gestures relating to melodic rhythm become much stronger than those relating to metre. At one point the pattern disappears completely for a couple of bars as Lucas focuses his attention on his eye contact with the choir, and in a legato passage shortly thereafter, metre is reduced briefly to a circular pulse.

The third and fourth clips show a more continuous use of pattern, although it remains varied in execution. The default level of the ictus is around sternum level, but it moves lower for accents or loud dynamics, and higher for quieter moments. The higher ictus, particularly when it moves closer into the body, also seems to be associated with moments when the singers need less guidance, such as in the solo passage at the start of clip 1.3, or even with moments when attention is more on listening than on directing. The elbow is the primary joint involved in the pattern; wrist and shoulder are flexible but move much less.

Distinctive variants of pattern that are shared with other directors working in this genre include the following:

- Forming the ictus by opening the hand rather than by tapping on an imaginary plane. This occurs throughout all four clips, in a variety of expressive contexts. Thirty seconds into clip 1.1, it emerges out of a preparatory beat executed with thumb and forefinger held together as a means of focusing the choristers' attention. A contrasting example is 20 seconds into clip 1.4, where we see the fingers gathered together on the upbeat, then springing apart in a rebound that blossoms gently upwards; this gesture appears to configure the alternation of upbeat and downbeat as a collection and releasing of the sound.
- The forward, 'shovel' downbeat. This appears several times, most clearly at the first big accent in clip 1.3. This is a 'downbeat' that comes not downwards, but forwards and slightly upwards from hip to waist level (although it may be prepared from higher, so that it travels down to hip level, then up and forward to the ictus). The hand is gently closed, with the extended thumb uppermost as if holding a small trowel. The head and upper

- body dip forwards in the preparation to this downbeat, and then straighten up again as it arrives.
- The 'twisting' downbeat. This appears most clearly about 1 minute and 20 seconds into clip 1.3. Again, this is a downbeat that comes forward, though it will also usually be approached from above. It is characterized by a twisting motion that circles in on the ictus, and may be executed either with a closed hand or a pointed finger. In either case, it often has something reminiscent of wielding a rapier. The example here gives a vigorous dynamic accent; it can also be used for softer agogic accents in quieter dynamic contexts.
- The 'breath elbow'. This is where an upbeat is executed not just from the elbow joint, but with a subtle lifting of the upper arm from the shoulder as well. The name indicates that this is often used as a preparatory beat to signal a breath point, and as such it is a good example of an ergotic, or work-associated gesture, since it is associated with the expansion of the ribcage; a good example of this use can be seen 1 minute 30 seconds into clip 1.3. This gesture can serve musical as well as vocal purposes, however, such as 45–50 seconds into clip 1.4, where it is used to mark two off-beat changes of harmony.

There are also a number of characteristic hand shapes that are found much more frequently in directors from this liturgical background than in other genres:

- The 'bullhorn' hand. This is where the middle fingers fold inwards, leaving the thumb and little finger extended. The name refers to the resultant shape, but is something of a misnomer for either its expressive use or type of movement. At the start of clip 1.1, for example, we can see it emerging from an open-handed gesture as a way to 'stroke' the sound.
- Closed hand, with extended thumb on top. This has already been mentioned as part of the 'shovel' downbeat, but it is not restricted to this context. It carries the pattern for a bar a minute and half into clip 1.3, and returns 20 seconds later, this time with the forefinger extended, a common variant of this hand position. Gestures in this hand position are often subtly led by the wrist, resulting in the quality Laban analysis would identify as 'floating', that is, light, flexible and sustained.
- The 'Sistine wrist'. This is probably the most archetypal hand position of the British cathedral/collegiate tradition, and although it only ever appears fleetingly in its pure form in the footage on the DVD, it infiltrates many of Lucas's gestures, especially in legato passages; watch his left hand at the start of clip 1.3, for instance. Michelangelo's depiction of the hands of God and Adam presents its key elements. Adam's hand, on the left, presents the more exaggerated version, with its lifted wrist and fingers that are relaxed but long. God's hand, on the right, gives a straighter profile, but still leaves the wrist open and flexible, with a clear sense that the extended

forefinger connects to and acts as a unit with the forearm, without any muscular tension intervening. At least some directors in this tradition are consciously aware of the importance of this gestural world for their praxis; as one conductor told me, 'all the music is in the wrist'.

Finally, it is worth noting how the antiphonal layout of the choir inflects Lucas's gestures. Chapter 9 will consider symmetrical gestures in more detail, as they are relevant across genres, but in the situation of a conductors whose choir is either side of them, symmetrical gestures make a different kind of sense from when a choir is in front of the director. For instance, the cut-off and 'ready' gestures during the rehearsal of 'Adam Lay y-Bounden' in clip 1.4 clearly maintain a connection between director and both halves of the choir.

Sally McLean and the White Rosettes

The White Rosettes is a ladies' barbershop chorus based in Leeds, UK. Formed in 1977, they have consistently been one of the most successful barbershop choruses in the country, with a strong track record in both barbershop contests and wider choral competitions. This focus on contest is typical of the genre, and provides a strong structure for the group's rehearsal goals. Other performance activities include guest appearances on shows and at events organized by other groups, and hosting their own Christmas show.

The chorus has just over 50 members, and all are amateurs. There is, however, a strong national and international training infrastructure within barbershop, of which they take full advantage; on the night I was there filming, for instance, they announced an impending coaching visit from the director of the 2007 men's International Chorus champions. Not all members read music, and many will learn repertoire from recordings ('teach tapes' or 'learning tracks'). All music is performed from memory, and sheet music is used in rehearsal only at the early stages of learning a song.

Sally McLean has been directing the White Rosettes since 1998, having previously been singing with them since 1982. She had established a track record for musical leadership within the chorus during the 1980s and 1990s via three national gold medals in quartet, and as a section leader and then assistant director prior to the founder-director's retirement in 1998. Her musical background prior to barbershop included learning violin at school and performing in rock bands.

This footage was filmed on 5 December 2007, on a regular Wednesday evening rehearsal. The main event of the chorus's performance calendar, the Ladies Association of British Barbershop Singers annual convention, had taken place about five weeks before this rehearsal and the chorus was now into a phase of working on skills and new repertoire. There was a consistent focus throughout the evening on breath management techniques, and it was clear that this was building on coaching they had had earlier in the year. They also spent a considerable proportion of the time rehearsing a new song – a medley of gospel songs arranged in the barbershop style. This was at the point where the notes and words were mostly memorized, and the focus of the rehearsal was on characterizing the different parts of the medley and bringing out details of the arrangement.

The DVD includes four clips. The first is from early in the rehearsal, where they are transferring the breathing technique from vocal exercises into their repertoire. It shows a partial run-through of the song 'Do I Love You' sung to an 'ah' vowel, and is chosen as a classic example of barbershop 'ballad' style, both in terms of the phrasing and delivery of the performance, and the characteristic gestural style. The second is an extract from the rehearsal process of the gospel medley, and the third is a run-through of the whole piece. These show a wider range of gestural worlds, as well some features of gesture in rehearsal that will be discussed in later chapters. The final extract shows a run-through of an arrangement of 'I'm Beginning to See the Light' to show another style of body language. Figure 8.2 shows the chorus on the risers, on which they remained standing all evening.

Figure 8.2   The White Rosettes

Barbershop ballad style, as clip 2.1 shows, uses a very free, rubato phrasing. It is not entirely non-metrical – the accent points still largely coincide with the written downbeats – but it is driven by a poetic more than musical concept of metre, and feels absolutely no obligation for the beats to be of equal duration.[2] Likewise, the associated directing style has only a very attenuated relationship to conventional conducting patterns.

---

[2] For a more detailed discussion of this style of interpretation/phrasing, see Liz Garnett, *The British Barbershopper: A Study in Socio-Musical Values* (Aldershot, 2005a), Chapter 6.

There are basic elements comparable to textbook technique, however. The ictus retains its function as a pulse-point that marks musical events, although this is likely to be less frequent than in conventional patterns (sometimes only once a bar), and is as likely to articulate melodic rhythm as underlying metre. There is also a general sense in which the ictus is likely to see a change of direction for the gesture, although this is more likely to come in response to harmonic or melodic shape than underlying rhythmic structure. Hence, we often see an alternation between gestures that move upwards to mark less stable harmonies and those that move outwards for points of rest, such as at 1 minute 15 seconds in, where the II minor chord on which the melody initially settles at the phrase end is stroked upwards, and the harmonic shift to a more solid V7 sees the hands moving outwards at waist level.

These gestures are defined much more by their departure from than their approach to the ictus: there is a sense of pulling, or stretching the sound away from the pulse point that correlates with the prevailing legato delivery style. The ictus is created not by arrival at a location, but by the change in direction of the hands. Of course, logically this is true for conventional beat patterns too: the beat location is identifiable at the moment where preparatory beat turns into rebound. But it becomes a much more defining element of the technique where the musical focus is so strongly on the rebound rather than the approach to the beat, and where the location of that beat is not predetermined. It is the speed of the hands' motion that makes the pulse point predictable in this context: the more energy there is in the stretch, the faster the acceleration into the next ictus. Ictus height is also correlated with dynamic level; stronger sounds see lower gestures, and lighter sounds see the hands nearer the face. The ictus point is also often accompanied by a marked muscular engagement, from a slight opening of the hand at softer moments, to the involvement of arms, back and lower body where more vocal support is needed.

Indeed, the involvement of the lower body marks larger-scale musical shape. Major points of arrival in the phrase structure are prepared by a significant bending of the knees, and marked by a straightening and strengthening of the whole body. Smaller versions of this move sometimes see the weight shifting from leg to leg in tandem with the metre. The knee-bends are inflected with a sideways and/or backwards and forward movement at phrase breaks, and the sound of creaking from the risers indicates that the singers are joining in with this motion to release and 'reset' their stance for the new phrase.

The hand gestures are largely led by the right hand, which only rarely departs from its role of guiding the pace of delivery. The left is the more likely to give cautionary or reminding gestures, but is also often involved in the shaping of phrases. The sense of 'stretching' the sound is enhanced by the frequent use of gestures in which the hands start close together and move apart. Some barbershop coaches use the metaphor of the sound as a ball of energy that can be manipulated as a method to help singers develop vocal resonance; this metaphor also seems evocative of many of McLean's two-handed gestures here.[3]

Clip 2.2 starts in this same gestural world, and includes some rehearsal that makes the connection between gestural style and legato delivery explicit. It then moves into a more rhythmic section using a figure-of-eight in-out pattern for the duple metre. The next clip then shows a run-through of the whole 'Gospel Medley', and a gives a very good picture of the relationship between metrical and ballad-style directing as the piece moves through a succession of different tempi, often with transitions that require the rhythm to be broken. In rhythmic sections, the gestures stay with the pulse rather than melodic rhythm except at a couple of moments of strong syncopation or where particular words need articulating. Some of the time this is in a conventional up-down two-pattern, sometimes in an in-out alternation and sometimes reduced to a simple pulse. The location of the ictus is much more consistent here, mostly at diaphragm level, but moving up to sternum level when there is need to draw attention to it. However, the pattern is still defined more by departure than by arrival, even when beat locations are much more predictable. The different rhythmic characters of the different sections of the medley are articulated by different levels of muscular engagement, but even at its punchiest, the rebound continues to 'pull' the sound out of each pulse point and into the next. The lower body also gets involved in the metre; a slight bend of the knee on the off-beat allows a straightening of the whole body on the pulse point. Hand gestures and body movement are both therefore made out of the same elements, whether free-style or metrical.

Despite the variety of tempi in the Gospel Medley, it shows a basic three-way distinction in body language between the loose-limbed ballad style in which both arm gestures and lower body bending and straightening move quite expansively, the tighter up-tempo style in which knee-bends are smaller but more regular, and arms stay closer to the body, and a strong declarative style used in transitions and tags that sees the body very erect and both hands low, 'holding' the sound.[4] Clip 2.4 adds a fourth style of body language to this in response to the 'jazz' style of the arrangement.[5] This combines the regular rhythmic involvement of lower body of the up-tempo style with the freer, larger gestures of ballad style, and results in a

---

[3] I am grateful to Toby Balsley for this insight.

[4] The tag is the final section, or coda, to a barbershop arrangement, and has its own distinctive conventions; see Garnett, *The British Barbershopper*, Chapter 7. This is the equivalent of the 'tail' that gospel musicians refer to (see below), but has a quite different set of typical procedures for approaching musical closure.

[5] This arrangement is clearly barbershop in its basic approach to voicing, but the treatment of this swing-era song, with strong syncopations, and the prominent use of the added-sixth chord mark it as 'jazzy' as opposed to classic barbershop. For a discussion of the cultural politics of style in barbershop, see Liz Garnett, 'Cool Charts or Barbertrash?: Barbershop Harmony's Flexible Concept of the Musical Work', *Twentieth-Century Music*, 2 (2005c): 245–63.

posture that sits slightly lower into the hips than in the more orthodox barbershop repertoire. A forward pulsing motion in the head also signals the swing feel. As with the ballad style, the larger knee-bends prepare more significant places in the phrase structure; here the release after the straightening on the downbeat may also see the right foot lift backwards. These different styles of body language are shared not only between barbershop directors, but also with quartet singers. This is partly because many directors, like McLean, also sing in quartet, but also because both the contest and training infrastructures of barbershop posit a strong continuity of style and tradition between the two types of ensemble.

Maxine Brooks and the Birmingham Community Gospel Choir

The Birmingham Community Gospel Choir was formed in 2005 to promote gospel music in Birmingham, and to act as a training ground for members of other local choirs. It usually rehearses twice a month, and most of its members also belong to their own church choirs. Consequently, it both draws upon and intends to contribute to a considerable fund of experience. This structure leads to a quite fluid membership. At full strength they have around 50 members, but they also perform in much smaller groupings; on the morning of the rehearsal I filmed, a group of seven singers had appeared on local radio. The rehearsal featured here involved between 15 and 20 singers – the number varied as some arrived part-way through, and others had to leave before the end.

Maxine Brooks is the choir's founder director, and has been directing since the age of 14, starting with her church choir. She has had some formal musical tuition, but as a songwriter and director is largely self-taught. Many gospel directors combine interests in directing with composition and solo singing and/or piano-playing, and there is a clear affinity of musical focus between these activities: the genre values both harmonic richness in the piano and a creative approach to singing the lead line.

The rehearsal presented here took place on 19 December 2007 in the Recital Hall at Birmingham Conservatoire, where the choir was due to give a concert the following night. The purpose of the rehearsal was therefore mostly minor troubleshooting, polishing details and ironing out any uncertainties. Much of the rehearsing process was undertaken within the flow of the music over large stretches of musical time, with relatively few stops and starts. The musical structures of this style are well suited to this style of rehearsing: gaps between the short phrases give room to focus in on detailed points, while the larger-scale forms are made up of a series of sections, each of which can be repeated until the director is satisfied it has been rehearsed enough. Given that the choir works entirely by ear, moreover, maintaining musical continuity in rehearsal will be important for helping the singers build up their longer-range musical memory.

The clips chosen start with one of the shorter continuous passages of the evening, which nonetheless shows a number of typical gestures. The next clip presents the start of a longer rehearsal process, and cuts when the director walks out of the shot to go and work closely with individual singers and sections, listening to them and correcting what they were singing. The next clip shows them rehearsing just the end section of the same song. The last section gives a complete run-through of the song 'God of a Second Chance'. The choir stood for the whole rehearsal in a single, slightly curved row, most of which is visible in Figure 8.3.

Figure 8.3   Birmingham Community Gospel Choir

The gospel directing style often preserves a strong division of musical labour between body and hands. Tempo and metre are maintained by the regular side-to-side step-and-sway, while the hands are involved much more in articulating the sung content rather than presenting the rhythmic framework. The director may click her fingers or give an in-out figure-of-eight shaped beat during instrumental introductions or solo passages, but we see much less of this kind of metrical work in the hands while the choir is singing.

Both types of movement are shared between director and singers. The body sway is enforced as part of the performance; indeed, Brooks sometimes requires the singers to maintain it during brief spoken instructions, maintaining at least the outline of musical continuity between separate runs-through of a song. The hand gestures do not have this kind of formal status, but singers often choose to gesture as they sing, and there is a clear consistency between gestures used by directors to invite singing and gestures used while singing. Choir members will often echo the director's movements, especially when learning notes or troubleshooting specific passages, and these gestures may stay in singers' performances in a subtler, sketchier form, as a mnemonic aid. Lead singers, meanwhile, will often accompany their solos with gestures that trace the shape of the music. We see this clearly at the start of clip 3.1, where Brooks starts off singing the lead line, then brings the choir in for the choral parts. The gestural vocabulary in both modes is very similar, except that the gestures that accompany her singing are lower down and closer in towards her body, while those directed at the choir move up and out, opening her arms a little to turn her palms towards the singers.

The hand gestures trace the musical content of the vocal lines as a holistic entity that includes elements of melodic rhythm, pitch-patterning, dynamic shaping and prosody. If singers are struggling with notes, teaching gestures may be reduced to simple outlines of relative pitch level, but the directing gestures are usually more complex than this. For example, in clip 3.2 the first appearance of the cadential phrase 'Holy is thy name' is shaped by a gesture that not only joins the phrase up in the first significant departure from the previous staccato articulation, but combines elements both of melodic and dynamic contour. The following a cappella verse is interesting in the way it gives insight into the relationship between gesture and word sounds. The initial detached statements of 'Holy' are sung each time on repeated notes, yet Brooks's gestures are quite different for the two syllables: the first is higher, and directed upwards, the second lower and directed outwards. This suggests that she is directing pitch contour only to the extent that it rises and falls in tandem with other musical elements. We can also hear in this verse a correlation between brightness of vowel sound and how much of Brooks's palms are visible to the choir on the last note of the phrase: compare, for example, the first and second iterations of 'Holy' in the second phrase at two minutes into the clip.

Gestures for musical content are mostly symmetrical, although one hand may sometimes be removed from this musical flow to add particular instructions to a sub-set of the choir, such as the left hand's explicit pitch patterning for the altos at the end of the first verse of 'Holy' in clip 3.2. The symmetrical gestures are typically directed up, out and/or forward from the director's body. Metrical downbeats may pulse downwards, but the onset of singing is very rarely indicated with a downwards gesture. Even exceptions, such as the words 'the way' at the very end of clip 3.1, combine a forward flick with the downward motion. Likewise, gestures that invite the choir to sing will often move from a resting position with the palms down and facing in towards the body to lift the palms up and towards the choir. This change of palm direction also appears in the figure-of-eight beat, glossing duple metre as an alternation of open and closed.

Many gestures have the quick, light and directionally varied quality Laban analysis would identify as 'flicking'. The impetus comes from both the wrist and the first knuckle, and the resultant sense of 'throwing' the hand forward, up or out correlates with the style's short, front-accented phrases. The fingers remain long whether the hands are outstretched, bent at the knuckle to form a right angle, or folded down over the heel of the hand; there is very little bend in the top knuckle at any time. A characteristic gesture for more sustained singing is to hold the hands outstretched and wiggle the fingers in quick, light motions to keep the sound alive; we see this in both clip 3.2 and clip 3.4.

Finally, it is worth mentioning some more or less conventionalized gestures. The first is the cut-off, which takes the form of the two hands moving outwards with thumb and forefinger together, as if pulling a piece of string tight, and the second is the 'repeat this section' gesture, which involves the hands in a forwards rolling-over gesture. These are conventionalized inasmuch as they have meanings that can also be stated in words, although they also both have some metaphorical/ iconic resemblance to their literal meanings, and the cut-off in particular can be integrated into more complex musical gestures (as in the hook line to 'God of Second Chance'). The 'go to the tail' gesture (taking the form of a capital T between the hands) is fully conventionalized, that is, its meaning is not only translatable into words, but cannot be inferred from its form without prior knowledge. Indeed, shortly before its use in clip 3.4, a singer had needed to have it explained, since they were more familiar with the other standard gesture in use in this tradition. This is a thumb cocked over the shoulder as if hitching a lift, and Brooks glossed this in the discussion as 'take me home'.

Simon Halsey and the City of Birmingham Symphony Chorus

The City of Birmingham Symphony Chorus was founded in 1974, and describes itself as a 'body of unpaid professionals'. That is, it works at a professional level in its concert and recording programmes, and has professional administration and musical leadership, but all the singers are volunteers. Many of these volunteers are committed amateurs: people whose working lives are in other arenas, but who are able and willing to organize their other commitments around a rehearsal schedule that can make significant inroads into their evenings and weekends. There are also a number of members who work in various branches of the music profession in the area – teachers, arts administrators and freelance conductors of other local choirs and choral societies – so the chorus acts as something of a focal point for the classical choral life of the region, not just because of its artistic status, but also as an important hub in local networks. As this profile implies, the expectations for standards of music-reading are high, and the culture of annotating scores with performance instructions is thoroughly embedded.

Simon Halsey's choral background lies in the British collegiate/cathedral tradition: he sang in the choirs of New College, Oxford and King's College Cambridge. He is particularly known for his work with choirs in the UK and across Europe, although he has also worked extensively with orchestras. In his role as chorus-master for a symphony chorus, he inhabits the intersection between these two worlds, working with singers, but preparing them for performances that will usually be accompanied by an orchestra.

The filming took place on Wednesday 14 November 2007 at the CBSO Centre in central Birmingham. The chorus was preparing for a concert performance of *The Rake's Progress* on 5 December, which was to be conducted by guest conductor Jac van Steen as part of the City of Birmingham Symphony Orchestra's ongoing festival of Stravinsky's music, *IgorFest*. The next rehearsal was to be the first with the guest conductor, so the focus of the rehearsal was on ensuring that the singers were secure and confident throughout. The rehearsal lasted two and half hours (with a short break in the middle), and covered all the music for chorus in the opera. It was a very focused rehearsal, with little if any interpenetration of the social and the musical; this is another sense in which the choir can be considered 'professional'. It was a nice touch of rehearsal planning, however, that the evening finished with a section that entailed the choir singing 'Hurrah!'

The first three extracts on the DVD involve detailed rehearsal of compact passages of music. In complete contrast to the gospel technique of keeping the musical flow and correcting from within, this process involves frequent stops and starts, sometimes extracting phrases as short as two notes for attention. This reflects the culture of music literacy: with musical content stored in the notation rather than in memory, it becomes possible to abstract these small moments without danger to the coherence of the whole. The last clip shows a run-through of a passage where the rehearsal focus shifts from precision of detail to musical characterization, and shows a significant change in gestural world to match. Figure 8.4 shows the choir layout, with chairs on stepped risers arranged as three sides of a rectangle, and conductor and accompanist occupying the fourth side. The choir remained seated for much of the rehearsal, standing only for vocal warm-ups and to run through longer sections. Again, this is congruent with the culture of musical literacy: it is easier to make the required frequent annotations on one's score when sitting down.

Figure 8.4   City of Birmingham Symphony Chorus

The directing style here is the closest to 'textbook' technique of any of the conductors shown. Conventional beat patterns are used consistently, and with relatively few variations of their form; the ictus is placed at sternum level almost invariably. It is often quite a 'loopy' style, with generously curved rebounds to encourage vocal smoothness, but the beat locations are always unambiguous and placed where one would expect. There are several reasons why Halsey might choose such an orthodox approach for this rehearsal. First, the nature of the repertoire is such that careful counting is required; moreover, since there is a lot of music to be covered in a short time, and the singers will probably not therefore have enough time to fully internalize the rhythms, they will need to rely on metrical clarity from their conductor. Second, the final rehearsals and performance of this music were to be taken by a different guest conductor, so maintaining a gestural style that draws on the acknowledged lingua franca of international conducting minimizes the chance that the singers might be confused when directed by someone else. Third – and related to this – orchestral conducting, for all its scope to display personal style and imagination, tends to preserve the literal form of beat patterns, particularly the clear direction of upbeat and downbeat, more religiously than purely choral genres, so this is the gestural world in which a symphony chorus is going to spend most of its time. This insistence on the integrity of the downbeat in orchestral conducting is a product both of the internationalization of the profession, with its need for guest conductors to produce performances with relatively little rehearsal, and of the nature of orchestral scores: choral singers rarely face the oboist's regular challenge of keeping track of many bars' rest between entries.

The way these various imperatives towards metrical clarity impact on Halsey's gestural choices can be inferred from changes in gestural vocabulary through the rehearsal process. Initial runs-through of individual sections will usually contain nothing to distract from the intelligibility of the pattern. The gestural vocabulary then becomes more varied, and less overtly metrical, for working through the detail, but returns to a simpler outline when putting sections back together again, with just occasional reminiscences of gestures used in the analytical rehearsal process. For instance, about a minute into clip 4.1 sees Halsey helping the basses with the vocal management of a phrase with a number of shaping gestures used in tandem both with his vocal demonstrations and the basses' subsequent attempts at the phrase; however, as soon as they reinsert the text, he returns to directing in pattern. Likewise, 1 minute and 15 seconds before the end of this clip, he brings his ictus up into the same visual field as his face as he works on diction, then returns it to its usual level when this phrase slots back into its musical context.

Clip 4.2 is very short, but chosen specifically to show the gesture at the words 'he loves her still'. This full-armed legato gesture from the shoulder (used here with both arms in parallel) is one that I hypothesize is borrowed from orchestral conducting. It is to be found reasonably frequently in conductors working in the Western classical tradition, particularly those with large choirs or choral societies, but I have only ever observed it used by directors who either moved into choral directing from a background with instrumental ensembles, or who work regularly in both worlds.

Clip 4.3, by contrast, shows a couple of characteristic gestures associated more with the cathedral/collegiate tradition. A minute into this clip, for example, we see the a left hand gesture using the 'bull-horn' shape of long thumb and little finger, with the middle fingers folded over at the knuckle. Shortly after this, when demonstrating the shape of the phrase 'mourn for Adonis', Halsey gives a classic, closed-hand, 'shovel' ictus to mark the accent. When he puts this back into context, he restores the orthodox downwards direction of the downbeat, but retains some of the expressive qualities of this type of ictus in the way he leans into the conducting space during its preparation, and straightens out of it again as the beat arrives. The ictus is also approached not just from above, but slightly from the side, giving a sense of 'gathering' the beat. The final sung 'weep' of this clip is cued by a 'breath elbow'. In addition, the shaping gestures to help the basses in clip 4.1 mentioned above bear a strong resemblance to the 'Sistine wrist'.

The final clip somewhat breaks down the distinction between strict pattern for musical continuity versus gestural variety for analytical rehearsal. This passage counterpoises the male and female choruses, ending with a joint 'toast to Venus and to Mars'. As Halsey characterizes it, there is a clear division in body languages to evoke the masculine and feminine stereotypes the passage dramatizes. He starts off with the clear, orthodox beat and precise cueing that has featured in these contexts throughout the rehearsal, but with the entry of the sopranos and altos, he develops a more loose-limbed and playful demeanour. After a few bars, he stands up to allow his lower body to participate in the characterization. The two-pattern shifts here briefly from its up-down orientation in front of his body to a side-to-side movement coordinated with the sway of hips and shoulders. The second men's entry is once again seated, with no further involvement of his lower body, although the gestures are clearly more swashbuckling than the first time through. This departure from orthodox pattern is possible both because of the relative rhythmic simplicity of the passage and the choir's familiarity with it. However, while the pattern might deviate in form here, and be embellished by the involvement of much more of the body, it remains present throughout.

Chapter 9
Different Styles, Common Ground

In the movie *The Blues Brothers*, the protagonists' blues band turns up at Bob's Country Bunker to play a gig. Somewhat uncertain about the social world they face on arrival, they ask a waitress what kind of music they play there. 'Both kinds', she replies, 'Country *and* Western.' Choral practitioners who optimistically proclaim their conducting manuals as suitable for 'all types of choir' might be suffering from an analogous, if milder, form of musical myopia. As the examples in Chapter 8 make vividly clear, choral conducting is not a homogenous category.

On the other hand, these very disparate musical and gestural traditions do have common problems to solve, common rehearsal processes and at times even common gestures. This chapter explores some of these shared issues, drawing on the material from my rehearsal observations to identify themes, and illustrating the discussion with examples from the DVD. They fall into two main areas. The first is a constellation of issues surrounding the somewhat vexed relationship between 'textbook' good practice and what conductors actually do. In the spirit of the discipline of performance studies, I make no assumption about which is 'right', but rather seek to understand the tensions between theory and practice in the context of the musical circumstances in which they arise. The second area relates to how gestures work within the rehearsal process, a theme on which the practitioner literature is largely silent. This will start to open up questions of the relationship between a conductor's gestures and their thought processes, and provide concrete examples on which theoretical enterprises in Chapters 10 and 11 can build.

Textbook versus Practice

Use of Pattern

Conducting manuals, whether they focus on choral or orchestral music, are unanimous on the importance of traditional beat patterns. Nicholson, for example, considers conducting to be 'useless' unless it is 'clear and correct', while Adler sees 'stick technique' as 'indispensable'.[1] In practice, however, choral conductors vary considerably in the extent to which they use pattern, and the extent to which they preserve its conventional form. Even the most consistently 'textbook' conductor shown in Chapter 8 varied the form of the beat patterns occasionally.

---

[1] Sydney Nicholson, *Practical Methods in Choir Training* (London, n.d.), p. 24; Samuel Adler, *Choral Conducting: An Anthology* (Fort Worth, 1971), p. xvi.

The primary purpose of conducting patterns is to enable all members of an ensemble to perform together in a synchronized fashion: what one might call the 'sheepdog function'.[2] Hence, we find a strong inverse correlation between the use of pattern and the presence of other factors that serve this unifying function. The first of these is body movement in the choir and/or director. The most obvious example is the gospel step-and-sway, which embeds the metrical flow in the participation of all singers, leaving the director's hands free for other purposes, and rendering pattern almost (though not quite) redundant. But even where the choir does not get physically involved in the rhythm, lower body movement in the director is often accompanied by a de-emphasis of the pattern; it may get smaller, or move from the front/central conducting space to a lower position nearer the conductor's side (as in clip 4.4), or it may be reduced to a simple pulse.

The second factor that is inversely related to a reliance on pattern is singing from memory. Traditional patterns encode information not just about the timing of beats, but also their location in the bar, and this information will be useful to singers working from notation for two reasons. The first is because they are sharing their gaze between score and conductor, and so will glean more information at a glance from pattern than from simple pulse, and the second is because they will often be less familiar with the music than singers working from memory, since one of the amenities notation offers is the means to process large volumes of music without having to internalize it fully. In contrast, singers working from memory will be both more familiar with the musical content of what they are singing, and able to look at their director much more continuously, and so will have less direct need for pattern's encoding of beat locations.

On the other hand, both body movement and singing from memory tend to be positively correlated with the use of figural rather than metrical gestures, that is, gestures that outline the shape of the singers' lines rather than the rhythmic framework in which they fit.[3] Body movement makes this possible by taking over the metrical function, while the reliance on memory makes it necessary, since the singers do not have the notation to rely on. One also sees this relationship between figural gestures and learning by ear in choirs that work from notation, but that include a mixture of music-readers and ear-singers. Here the directors will tend to use pattern when conducting whole passages, but move into pitch-patterning when breaking a piece down into parts to learn the individual lines.

Even where pattern is present – and virtually all the directors I have observed use it in some form at least some of the time – its form can vary significantly.

---

[2] See Adler, p. 3, William Ehmann, *Choral Directing*, trans. G. Wiebe (Minneapolis, 1968) p. 14, and Abraham Kaplan, *Choral Conducting* (New York, 1985), p. xiv.

[3] This use of the term 'figural' is adopted from Jeanne Bamberger's account of two contrasting modes of musical thought, the formal, which conceives music as an abstract, symbolic structure, and the figural, which conceives it iconically, chunking events into local groups. See Jeanne Bamberger, *The Mind Behind the Musical Ear: How Children Develop Musical Intelligence* (Cambridge, MA, 1995).

In particular, the downbeat could often be better described as an *in*beat: the pulse point is placed in the same general area as the textbooks show (central to the body, at around diaphragm level) but may be approached from the side, from underneath, or even from behind, as in the 'shovel' ictus, as often as it is approached from above. Sometimes this is used for a particular expressive effect – a grand accent reminiscent of crash cymbals, for example – and the rest of the pattern reverts to its conventional shape. At other times, the up-down orientation of strong and weak beats is turned on its side to turn into a figure-of-eight alternation between in and out beats; both Sally McLean and Maxine Brooks use this gesture in the extracts on the DVD.

This variation of the downbeat's direction runs directly counter to textbook orthodoxy; Brian Busch, for instance, instructs: 'REMEMBER: THE DOWNBEAT IS ALWAYS DOWN'.[4] It is also probably one of the main causes of the orchestral or generalist conductor's disdain for the choral specialist's technique: 'You'd never get away with that with an orchestra', said one conductor with whom I discussed these observations.[5] However, it also solves the problem that Ehmann identifies as 'beating the music to pieces'.[6] That is, sideways motions are often found to be more conducive to vocal freedom than vertical motions, particularly where legato singing is required. Ehmann proposes to solve this problem by the use of the left hand ('What the right hand destroys (with its beats) the left hand must constantly sustain and support.'[7]), but varying the direction of the downbeat mitigates its disruptive accent without needing such compensatory left-hand gestures.

An in-out alternation also gives an ergotic aspect to the pattern, promoting the experience of the lungs as bellows. A pattern than moves the arms in towards the body encourages a contraction of the ribs, pushing air out, whereas the arms moving away from the body lift and open the ribs to allow air in. This is experienced literally with the 'breath elbow' type of preparatory beat, but the binary in-out of the breath also gives an intuitively meaningful metaphor through which to understand metre.

Symmetrical Gestures

Another element of technique on which there is near unanimity in the practitioner literature is the redundancy of symmetrical gestures.[8] The occasional mirroring of

---

[4] Brian R. Busch, *The Complete Choral Conductor: Gesture and Method* (New York, 1984), p. 15; emphasis in original.

[5] The literature is rife with disparaging comments about the idiosyncrasies of choral conductors; see for example Archibald Davison, *Choral Conducting* (Cambridge, MA, 1954), p. 3 and Leslie Woodgate, *The Choral Conductor* (London, 1949), p. 3.

[6] Ehmann, p. 110.

[7] Ehmann, p. 115.

[8] See, for example, Harold A. Decker and Colleen J. Kirk, *Choral Conducting: Focus on Communication*, (Englewood Cliffs, 1988), p. 12; Paul Roe, *Choral Music Education*,

the right hand's gestures with the left is a useful device for particular emphasis, the argument goes, but to do this all the time is a waste of the conductor's energy, and/or a waste of the opportunity to use the left hand to give different information. However, all four of the directors shown on the DVD use symmetrical gestures, as do virtually all the directors I have observed, whatever their genre or their level of experience. This ubiquity suggests that mirrored gestures serve a function that is under-appreciated by the writers of textbooks.

We have seen one useful context for symmetrical gestures in the antiphonal arrangement of the cathedral choir: they allow the director to make direct contact with both sides of the choir. This may apply in a milder form to any director whose choir layout extends round either side of him or her. In these situations, directors will often use symmetrical gestures as a means to transfer the pattern from one hand to another: the right hand carries the pattern, the left hand joins in for a couple of bars, then the right hand stops while the left hand carries on, allowing them to direct their primary gesture towards singers on their left hand side for a cue or just to offer support.

A second context in which symmetrical gestures have an advantage over single-handed gestures is in the ergotic function identified above whereby arm movements connect to the breath. James Jordan, one of a very small minority of practitioner-writers to advocate mirrored gestures, cites this as his rationale:

> Many introductory conducting books begin instruction with only the right arm. This approach advocates the use of both arms, in many texts referred to as mirroring. This is done so that conducting students, from the beginning of their study, become accustomed to breathing with and for the choir with a balanced gesture that will, in turn, encourage a deep-seated breath from the choir.[9]

Injunctions against mirroring are of course rooted in a general expectation about the function of the two hands: that the right hand beats time, and the left hand is 'the hand of the heart'.[10] Thus, to use both hands for pattern would by implication be to conduct without emotion. However, as Schuller points out, this expectation coexists with the apparently contradictory idea that the right hand's gestures should embody all the nuances of musical flow and shape within the execution of the pattern, thus rendering the left hand theoretically redundant.[11] Moreover, the left hand's role in activities such as cueing relates far more to technical than artistic

---

2nd edn (Englewood Cliffs, 1983) p. 221; and Max Rudolph, *The Grammar of Conducting: A Comprehensive Guide to Baton Technique and Interpretation*, 3rd edn (New York, 1995) pp. 309–10.

[9] James Jordan, *Evoking Sound: Fundamentals of Choral Conducting and Rehearsing* (Chicago, 1996), p. 80.

[10] Ehmann, p. 126

[11] Gunther Schuller, *The Compleat Conductor* (Oxford 1997), p. 59.

elements of the music. So, symmetrical gesture is not necessarily preventing engagement with expression as the stereotypes of hand function would suggest.

However, this standard expectation does have an interesting basis in neuroscience. The two hemispheres of the brain have different functions: the left hemisphere deals with analytical, symbolic aspects of thought, while the right deals with the holistic and the spatial. Moreover, each hemisphere is generally thought to control the opposite side of the body. Hence, it makes sense for the analytical element of time-beating to be controlled by the left hemisphere of the brain, and the synthetic, global gestures to be controlled by the right.[12] However, this general picture needs to be inflected. According to Axel Mulder:

> As far as cortico-spinal systems are concerned, arm, hand and finger movements are controlled contralaterally [that is, from the opposite side of the brain], while arm and shoulder movements may also be controlled ipsilaterally [that is, from the same side of the brain], ie. proximal movements can be controlled contra- as well as ipsilaterally, while distal movements are only controlled contralaterally. … Consequently, movements involving identical commands to the two limbs, i.e. motor commands resulting in mirror image movements, whether they are temporally coinciding or not, are more frequent in natural gestural communication. In contrast, different, simultaneously expressed hand postures occur frequently due to the more disparate control of the distal musculature.[13]

That is, the hands are controlled by the opposite sides of the brains, but the arms and shoulders can be controlled by either hemisphere as they are closer to the centre of the body. This would lead us to expect more mirrored gestures at the level of the limb, but different gestures at the level of the hand. And we can see a good example of this in clip 4.3, where both of Halsey's arms are involved in the metrical shape of the pattern, but his right hand is holding a pencil as a baton, and his left hand moves from tracing the pattern with a pointed finger to forming the 'bull-horn' shape before withdrawing from the metre between cues.

This in turn opens up the question of how hand functions relate to a conductor's thought processes. One sometimes sees a conductor use mirroring as a means to pass pattern from one hand to another when there is no externally apparent reason, such as a cue, for doing so. These moments are typically deep into the flow of a passage, and the conductor may appear more focused on listening to the choir than making explicit signals to them. It is as if the director needs to involve the left hand to help them access the right hemisphere of their brain. Indeed, one

---

[12] See Teresa Marrin Nakra, 'Inside the Conductor's Jacket: Analysis, Interpretation and Musical Synthesis of Musical Gesture' (Ph.D. Dissertation, Massachusetts Institute of Technology, 2000), p. 76.

[13] Axel Mulder, 'Hand gestures for HCI', Hand Centred Studies of Human Movement Project, Technical Report 96-1 (1996), available online at http://www.xspasm.com/x/sfu/vmi/HCI-gestures.htm [accessed 22 January 2008].

wonders whether the damping effect that Ehmann claims results from single-handed conducting is as much an imaginative as a physical deficit:

> The various beat patterns and all other conducting motions should be learned and practiced with both hands. Occasionally one meets a director who believes in conducting with one hand only. This has the effect of 'laming' the side of the inactive hand and this inertness of one side of the body greatly minimizes the animation and vitality of the choir.[14]

This is not to deny that gestural richness is a good thing, and as such, the hands will often be involved in different gestures. But is to suggest that symmetrical gestures are not as inherently reprehensible as many writers suggest, and may indeed have positive functions both in helping directors to think musically and in helping choirs to sing well.

Rhythmic Structure and the Body

The prevailing focus on pattern in conducting manuals encourages a concept of musical structure that focuses on metre. Bars, beats and occasionally subdivisions of beats are the rhythmic levels that standard technique, with its focus on hand and arm, caters for. Conductors in action, though, sometimes seem to maintain an awareness of rhythmic levels at both larger and smaller scales than this, and to experience them in other parts of the body as well as arms and hands. Gospel may be unusual in how systematically it assigns different rhythmic functions to lower and upper parts of the body, but similar processes can also be observed in less overt and more intermittent forms in genres that are more closely related to 'textbook' conducting.

Rhythmic structure is often portrayed as a kind of tree diagram. Beginners' guides to notation show a semibreve branching out to two minims, which branch in turn, each level having more, smaller units than the last. Cooper and Meyer's method of rhythmic analysis, meanwhile, starts with the smallest elements, and groups them into progressively larger units that go beyond metre to hypermetre, phrase and even form.[15] Our basic mental structures for rhythm thus see slower-moving units as both larger and more fundamental than faster elements. Indeed, the bone structure of our limbs also works like this, with the solitary humerus closest to our bodies leading to the double-boned forearm, and then the cluster of bones that forms the hand. Whilst we might not experience the duality of radius and ulna as distinct contributors to directing technique, we certainly do experience the way that fast movement is easier from joints further away from the body,

---

[14] Ehmann, pp. 125–6.

[15] Grosvenor Cooper and Leonard B. Meyer, *The Rhythmic Structure of Music* (Chicago, 1960).

both because of the progressively shorter length of lever and the commensurately lighter weight to move.[16]

This would lead us to expect the joints closest to the body to be involved in the higher-level rhythmic units, and those farther away in the smaller. Nakra's study of orchestral conductors found exactly this, a phenomenon she referred to as 'gestural polyphony':

> The level of structure in which these muscle groups respond seems to have a direct relationship with their size and distance from the torso. For example, the *trapezius* muscle of the shoulder seemed to be activated every two or four bars, roughly on the level of the phrase, whereas the biceps muscle is active every beat, and the forearm *extensor* muscle gives the internal structure of notes within that beat (such as articulation and sustain), and the hand gives occasional, spikey, indications of small accents and energy.[17]

Interestingly, this relationship between length of lever and rhythmic level explains why it is virtually impossible to tap one's foot in time with one's conducting gestures: not only is the foot much shorter than the forearm, but the ankle has much less flexibility than the elbow, and so the toe invariably reaches the floor before the hand reaches its ictus. The only director I have observed who managed to coordinate his foot with his pattern did so by tapping subdivisions of the beats he was directing.

It is not just the different parts of the arm that participate in these different rhythmic levels, however. In clip 1.1, where Lucas's hands are only intermittently available to direct, we see a subtle rhythmic counterpoint between his upper body's movement with metre and his head's involvement in details of melodic rhythm. Three minutes into clip 4.1, meanwhile, Halsey accompanies a traditional four-pattern with a very slight side-to-side sway on the half bar. McLean also shows a significant involvement of the lower body, with small cycles of bending and straightening at the level of the bar, and much larger ones at phrase breaks and significant points of arrival.

The visible presence of these different levels of articulation varies, I would suggest, with the nature of the director's attention to musical content. That is, it is an intuitive part of their relationship with the music, part of their practical consciousness, rather than a self-aware element of technique. This suggestion is

---

[16] Indeed, Adrian Boult proposes that a primary purpose of the baton is to provide an extra, lighter lever, and so allow the conductor to make less use of the shoulder joint, although he places his analysis of the joints of the arm in service of dynamic shaping rather than rhythmic structure; indeed, he expressly warns against the participation of the lower body in the conductor's gesture. See *A Handbook on the Technique of Conducting*, 7th edn (London, 1949), pp. 16–17 and 13.

[17] Nakra, p. 108.

based partly on the scarcity of reference in the literature[18] (indeed, most writers advocate a stable frame with much less movement than many directors use in practice[19]), but also on the basis of observation. One conductor I observed presented a combination of four different levels of rhythmic involvement during the rehearsal of a piece in a slow 12/8 metre. The shifts between a four-pattern that involved the whole arm and a subdivided pattern from the elbow were probably effected with a degree of conscious intention, but at the same time he also shifted his weight slightly from foot to foot over the period of two bars, and also had a continuous minute bounce in knees and ankles at the speed of flowing semiquavers. To try and maintain all these motions consciously would leave very little room for attention to anything else; they were clearly simply a visible trace of his musical awareness.

Gesture in the Rehearsal Process

Musical versus Didactic Gestures

A key distinction to emerge during my rehearsal observations was the difference in function between those gestures intended to correct or instruct, and those intended to evoke musical understanding. I have called these didactic and musical gestures respectively. The musical gesture represents an ideal articulated by virtually every writer on conducting, the imperative to 'look like the music' with which I introduced Part III. It is a gesture enlivened by a vision of the music's entire expressive world: style, colour, flow, character. Indeed, to call it a gesture is possibly misleading, since it involves the conductor's entire bodily demeanour. It is the musical imagination made visible.

The didactic gesture abstracts from this totality a single element that needs attention in rehearsal. Because it is specific, the didactic gesture is commensurately more monodimensional than the musical gesture; the expressive whole is pared down to the single element that needs work. See, for example, Brooks's left-hand pitch-patterning for the altos in clip 3.2: the hand shape becomes clearer, with fingers held together, and the motions are very clear and stepped. The composite, qualitatively nuanced vision of musical content disappears from her hand while she makes sure the choir sings the right notes.

---

[18] James Jordan proposes a practice method for learning repertoire that involves simultaneous walking, gesturing and singing; it locates the music's macro-rhythm in the feet, its micro-rhythm in the hands and its melodic rhythm in the voice. He does not propose to transfer either the macro or melodic levels into actual conducting technique, but he is clearly promoting this kind of multilevel, embodied musical understanding. See *Evoking Sound*, p. 52.

[19] See for example Roe, p. 211 and Joseph Lewis, *Conducting Without Fears: A Helpful Handbook for Beginners, Part I: Conducting – a General Survey* (London, 1942), p. 16.

On first glance, the distinction between musical and didactic gestures might seem to align itself with the expressive conducting/mere time-beating dichotomy that runs through the conducting literature since Berlioz. Certainly, the category of musical gesture resonates well with that of expressive conducting, as movements fully vested with imaginative content. And didactic gesture is narrower, more focused, and might seem to align itself with 'mere' time-beating. But I think this does didactic gesture a disservice. It may be analytic rather than synthetic, but it can nonetheless be both spontaneous and responsive – if this is what an ensemble needs right at the moment, it is not 'merely' anything.

Didactic gestures are defined by both their relatively monodimensional quality, and from their placement relative to the general gestural flow. They will often be both separated in space and distinct in form from the gestures that direct and regulate musical continuity. For example, shortly before the end of clip 1.2, Lucas turns towards the cantoris side of the choir with a static pointed finger, and a clear change in demeanour. As the entry he wanted to secure arrives on time, his body straightens up again and his left hand recedes back into the musical flow.

Didactic gestures may also refer back to previous learning activities, and serve as explicit triggers to recall, especially if they are similar in form to gestures used during those learning phases. A good, extended example of this is in the 'I'll Fly Away' section of the White Rosettes' gospel medley in clip 2.3, where McLean makes a lot of very clear deictic gestures, pointing to different sections of the chorus; some of these gestures are then extended into pitch-patterning. This relates directly back to an earlier section of the rehearsal in which they had systematically worked through and identified each embellishment of the basic homophonic texture.

The shift between musical and didactic gestures is effected intuitively. It reflects the conductor's constant shifting of focus during rehearsal between technique and artistry, between the holistic and the diagnostic. My observations suggest, though, that the pace of improvement in rehearsal is at its best when didactic gestures are used just long enough to achieve the desired change, and no longer. When a director maintains the didactic gesture as a 'reminder' longer than is necessary, he or she effectively denies the singers access to the richer complexity of the musical whole, since it is the complexity that is stripped out to make the learning point clear. As we saw in Chapter 7, the technologies of power are a blunter and more basic form of regulatory power than the technologies of the self; engaging singers' imaginative participation is conversely a more sophisticated form of control than micromanaging their moment-to-moment behaviour.

Depictive versus Musicotopographic Gestures

As we saw in Chapter 4, David Efron's influential system of gesture classification made its primary distinction between gestures that referred to an external object and those that referred to the gesturer's thought processes. While there are problems in making this the fundamental division by which to classify all other gesture types, it remains a useful analytical category. Gesture theorists, with their overwhelming assumption of speech as the context for gestures, call gestures that sketch the logical shape of the gesturer's thoughts 'logicotopographic' gestures. My rehearsal observations suggest that musical thought is likewise facilitated by such inwards-referring gestures, for which I propose the term 'musicotopographic'.

Musicotopographic gestures are most easily observed when the director is involved in some kind of problem-solving, such as mentally trying out alternative ways of shaping a phrase, or working out where to place a breath point. The gestures will usually be quite small and close in to the body, and the director's gaze will avoid contact with the choir. The musical content in these cases will often be speeded up. A good example of this can be seen at the start of clip 3.3, where Brooks is about to restart the song just before the end, and turns her attention inwards, accessing the song's structure in her memory to locate an appropriate start point.

Musicotopographic gestures can also be observed during the flow of the music, although here they lack the 'fast-forward' character that makes them so distinctive in the diagnostic, problem-solving mode. The shift between singing and directing at the start of clip 3.1 discussed in the last chapter gives a good example. The gestures with which Brooks accompanies her own singing are relatively closer to and more directed towards her own body than the directing gestures which open outwards towards the choir.

Likewise, the passage in clip 1.3 where Lucas accompanies the tenor solo alternates between gestures directed outwards and those that are more internally focused. The shifts between them are revealed not only by the changes in size and position of gesture, but also by gaze behaviour: depictive gestures are invariably preceded by eye contact. Indeed, the contrast between 'marking time' between entries and inviting the choir to sing is probably the commonest occurrence of this internal–external shift of focus in choral rehearsals.

What is interesting in this last example is smoothness of the slippage between musicotopographic and depictive gestures. There are two reasonably distinguishable regions in which gestures occur, but the transitions between them are sufficiently gradual that there are moments at which it would be difficult to say definitively whether the focus was inwards or outwards. And, of course, in the midst of the musical flow, it is possible for it to be both at once in a way that is impossible with speech: the performed sound is an external reality shared with the other musicians, while it is the internal imaginative engagement that strings these sounds together to make sense as music. Musicotopographic and depictive gestures start to look less like opposed categories and more like a continuum along which a conductor's attention shunts back and forth between the inner reality of the internalized music and the external reality of the choir's sound. One could posit a 'sweet spot' along this continuum where the director is both focused enough on their imaginative world to 'become the music, both physically and emotionally' and responsive enough to the choir to feel 'at one' with it.[20]

---

[20] Decker and Kirk, p. 3; Ehmann, p. 112.

Emergent Gestures

The term musicotopographic is intended as a corrective to the prevailing assumption in much of the literature on gesticulation that all thought involves verbal language. To differentiate it from the logicotopographic, however, implies that the two are fundamentally different kinds of activity. But my rehearsal observations revealed a remarkable continuity between gestures used to accompany speech, to accompany sung demonstrations and to direct. Conducting gestures routinely emerge from the speech-accompanying gestures directors use as they explain what they want the choir to do.

A good example is the passage in clip 4.1 where Halsey works with the basses on a low G. He tells them, 'Don't dig for it, just let it happen', and with the last word opens out his arms downwards in a smooth, expansive motion. He then uses this same gesture to cue the basses to sing the note in isolation, and again when he demonstrates the whole phrase and the basses it sing it back to him. Something of the spacious quality remains in the right-hand gesture when the rehearsal focus moves on, but the left hand drops out, and the right hand moves back into his default conducting plane. Here we see a gesture emerging in speech in response to rehearsal needs, transferring into conducting gesture, then disappearing again as the need it responded to is met.

A couple of minutes later in the same clip, we see a similar process with the upwards legato gesture Halsey uses to rehearse the phrase 'if true', only this time the gesture occurs first in tandem with vocal demonstration. The gesture then develops into an up-and-down motion as he invents a short exercise to address the vocal challenge of the phrase, and the lower fragment of it is repeated near his diaphragm as he tells them, 'don't lose the connection', suggesting that 'connection' here refers both to the legato line and the voice's connection to its support. Again, some qualities of this gesture infiltrate his pattern for a short while thereafter.

These are both examples of musical gestures emerging through rehearsal: although used as part of an analytical rehearsal process, they remained engaged with the musical and vocal needs of the passages in a holistic way, and were reintegrated into the prevailing conducting gesture. In clip 2.2 we see the emergence of a didactic gesture as McLean traces a wavy line as part of the verbal description of the legato, continuous sound she seeks. This reappears in the full run-through of the piece in clip 2.3 as an explicit reminder, abstracted from the general gestural flow; in real time, moreover, these two occurrences of the gesture were about an hour apart.

Beyond their interest for conductors, these emergent gestures raise two interesting theoretical issues. The first is for gesture studies, in which there has been some disagreement about whether and to what extent spontaneous gestures are culturally learned activities. On one hand, cross-cultural studies have shown different repertoires and habits of gesture in different ethnic groups, but on the other, standard gesture taxonomies, as we saw in Chapter 4, tend to classify speech-accompanying gestures as idiosyncratic and non-conventionalized, as opposed to the more arbitrary and culture-bound speech-replacing gestures.[21] Given the way that directors move fluidly from spontaneous gesticulation with speech and singing to conducting using the same gestural vocabulary, and given the strength and distinctness of the gestural traditions in different musical worlds, then we have to conclude that directors draw on their style-specific gestural vocabulary when they talk about music. This suggests in turn both that there is a significant cultural component to spontaneous gesticulation, and that the gestural vocabularies of a musical style are built into the way that directors in that style think about music.

The second point of theoretical interest is the interpenetration of verbal and musical communication that occurs during the rehearsal process: the common gestural vocabulary across the two modes binds them together into a coherent conceptual world that belies our anxieties about the betrayal of music by words. Gestures emerge in the context of linguistic, declarative meanings, and when they transfer into music, they carry the memory of those words with them. At the same time, though, the gestures are not themselves linguistic, but synthetic and global; they do not attempt to translate musical experience into the categories of language. Gestures seem to mediate between language and music, and the theoretical explorations in Chapter 11 will help explain how.

The Pointed Finger

My final example of gestures in rehearsal is a case study of a particular gestural usage: the pointed finger. Every director I have observed uses it, and there is a strong consistency in its associations across genres. Its very prevalence might make it appear too obvious a gesture to require discussion; on the other hand, its flexibility and variety of contextual meanings makes it an excellent example to set up the theoretical endeavours of Chapter 10.

One would expect the most common use of a pointed finger to be in deictic gestures; after all, this category of gesture is defined as the act of pointing. And this use is routine, both in cueing and didactic gestures; all four of the directors on the DVD give multiple examples of this usage. However, these instances are significantly outnumbered by metaphoric uses. These may still be indexical, in that the finger acts to direct attention, but instead of indicating something external, the finger commands attention to itself and its behaviour in the conceptual space of the conductor's gesture.

Metaphorical uses of the pointed finger can serve either musical or didactic purposes, that is, they can form part of the gestural flow, or they can be superimposed upon it to highlight a specific point; again, the DVD contains plentiful examples of each. Didactic usage will either be corrective, asking for more accuracy, whether of pitch content, intonation or rhythm, or cautionary, asking for greater attention;

---

[21] For an overview of this debate, see Adam Kendon, 'An Agenda for Gesture Studies', *Semiotic Review of Books*, 7/3 (1997): 8–12.

indeed, these two functions are sometimes elided. Musical gestures will focus on adjusting qualitative elements, asking for more brightness or focus in the tone, or for crispness in articulation. These meanings are understood by singers largely through musical and gestural context, although linguistic utterances associated with emergent gestures also clarify the specific meanings in a particular instance. For example, in clip 1.2 Lucas uses a pointed finger to draw attention to rhythmic accuracy. He gives a demonstration of the delivery he wants, then dabs his pointed finger downwards as he says, 'I want you make sure that you [*points*] pass that bar-line at the same time.' Halsey, meanwhile, uses a fleeting pointed gesture three minutes into clip 4.1, to accompany his request that a phrase start 'in the *middle* of an F, not below it'.

Unfolded into these separate linguistic categories, the pointed finger appears to suffer from an unhelpfully diffuse range of meanings: the same basic form can be used to refer to tuning, tone colour, articulation and recollection of previous rehearsal goals. In practice, however, it is not experienced as ambiguous. This is partly because the shared musical experience of singers and conductor constrains the range of possible meanings at that moment: McLean's pointed finger from a lowered left hand in the sustained chords at 'How great thou art' in clip 2.2 is clearly not to do with articulation. But there is also a sense in which all these linguistic glosses – accuracy, focus, attention – are all metaphorically linked through the idea of pointedness. The different elements of pitch, rhythm, tone or mindfulness are analytical categories that a director may disaggregate from the whole as part of a diagnostic process, but do not substitute for the overall expressive idea encapsulated in the pointed finger. A director could ask a choir to pay attention to singing a note in tune, precisely together and with a forward placement; or, they could ask their singers, as one did in a rehearsal I observed, to 'stick a dagger in that note'.

Chapter 10
Metaphoric Gesture and Embodied Musical Meaning

Chapters 8 and 9 presented a number of examples of 'metaphoric gestures', that is, gestures that bear an iconic resemblance to an abstract concept. A wavy line modelled the barbershop ideal of 'continuous sound', for example, and figural gestures in gospel songs outlined a concept of musical shape that encompassed pitch contour, dynamic shape and textual emphasis. The most developed example, of course, was the pointed finger, which appeared across genres and in diverse musical contexts, but was always employed to make some kind of *point*.

These observations, though, remain ad hoc. They abstract fleeting moments that emerge from the gestural flow, but leave that flow itself untheorized. What are the processes by which routine gestures carry meaning? Do gestures for musical structure work differently from gestures for expression? To what extent are conducting gestures codes that need to be learned, and to what extent are they intuitively, inherently evocative?[1]

This chapter returns to Lakoff and Johnson's theory of metaphor to understand how it is that conducting gestures become meaningful. It focuses on two elements of technique – pattern and dynamic shaping – that are archetypically associated with the conventional and the expressive respectively, and explores them in relation both to their presentation in conducting manuals and the ways that they can be observed in practice. Just as Lakoff and Johnson's theories suggest that abstract linguistic (and indeed formal logical) systems have an experiential basis, my analysis will suggest that the formal elements of conducting draw upon the same sorts of metaphorical processes as those that underlie those gestures commonly thought of as more 'subjective'. This analysis in turn will lay the foundations for Chapter 11's investigations of the relationship between gesture and thought.

---

[1] Richard House cites studies that suggest that conducting gestures are not understood universally, while Timothy Benge reaches the opposite conclusion in his doctoral thesis. Richard E. House, 'Effects of Expressive and Nonexpressive Conducting on the Performance and Attitudes of Advanced Instrumentalists' (DMA dissertation, Arizona State University, 1998), p. 29; Timothy Benge, 'Movements Utilized by Conductors in the Stimulation of Expression and Musicianship' (DMA dissertation, University of Southern California, 1996), p. 57.

Theoretical Context

We first encountered Lakoff and Johnson's theory of metaphor in Chapter 4 in the context of metalanguages of conducting. There it provided a theoretical rationale for describing conducting gestures in terms of manipulating the sound as if it were a physical object, a usage that proved effective in Chapter 8 in such cases as the 'shovel' ictus and the 'energy ball'. This chapter moves further into this conceptual world with Johnson's 1987 development of this theory in *The Body in the Mind*.[2]

This book introduces the idea of the image schema as way to organize the process of cross-domain mapping. A potential problem with the idea of metaphorical mapping – of understanding something in terms of something else – is that it could result in a profusion of connections between unrelated domains of experience, with meanings proliferating chaotically. In fact, Lakoff and Johnson's original formulation inhibits this possibility by its claim that these mappings occur in the context of our lived experience. The concept of the image schema formalizes this process by introducing a level of preconceptual orientational structures that underlie the processes of metaphorical mapping, both facilitating them and constraining them. Our physical experiences of living in the world – such as distance, weight, front–back structures or verticality – provide our basic imaginative structures, from which linguistic metaphors and abstract thought can develop figuratively. This grounding of metaphors in interactional experience provides a basic coherence to our conceptual structures that might be lost if all domains could be mapped onto one another willy-nilly. On the other hand, we should not think of image schemata as pre-cultural as well as preconceptual; as Johnson points out, 'these embodied patterns do not remain private or peculiar to the person who experiences them. Our community helps us interpret and codify many of our felt patterns. They become shared cultural modes of experience and help to determine the nature of our meaningful, coherent understanding of our "world".'[3]

The first musical applications of Lakoff and Johnson's ideas were concerned with musical meaning, and how it is that abstract sounding structures can be construed in terms of motion, space or colour. Janna Saslaw and Laurence Zbikowski have both used image schemata as a way to theorize how it is that we understand musical sounds in terms of spatial orientation; Zbikowski, for example, discusses how different cultures construe pitch relations in terms of verticality (high/low), size (small/large) and age (young/old).[4] Maxine Brooks's use of

---

[2] Mark Johnson, *The Body in the Mind: The Bodily Basis of Meaning, Imagination, and Reason* (Chicago, 1987).

[3] Ibid., p. 14.

[4] Janna Saslaw, 'Forces, Containers, and Paths: The Role of Body-Derived Image Schemas in the Conceptualization of Music', *Journal of Music Theory*, 40/2 (1996): 217–43; Laurence Zbikowski, 'Conceptual Models and Cross-Domain Mapping: New Perspectives on Theories of Music and Hierarchy', *Journal of Music Theory*, 41/2 (1997): 193–225.

pitch-patterning in clip 3.2 thus draws on the first of these metaphors to outline the shape of the altos' line, as does Simon Halsey's demonstration of his devised exercise for the phrase 'if true'.

Michael Spitzer continues in this tradition with an extended study of music and metaphor that integrates the cognitive science tradition that produced Lakoff and Johnson's work with literary and philosophical concepts of metaphor, with results that are rich both historically and theoretically.[5] He identifies three foundational metaphors for Western musical thought: harmony as distance from a centre point, rhythm as part-whole or tree-like structures, and melody as a path.[6] He derives these from discourses about music, from the terms that theorists and teachers use to describe it, though we can also see them in the examples discussed in Chapter 9. For example, Spitzer posits the articulation of limbs as a basic element of bodily experience that organizes our comprehension of rhythmic units; as we have seen, it also participates as an integral part of conductors' music-making. Both McLean and Halsey, meanwhile, trace melodies in their emergent gestures as paths through space.

Interestingly, all these studies, like the majority of contributions to Anthony Gritten and Elaine King's collection *Music and Gesture*,[7] tend to see gesture itself as a metaphor, a feature of sounding music that is attributed to or inferred from the work by the listener. Bräm and Bräm's use of metaphor theory to identify a metaphorical function enacted by the conductor's 'non-dominant' or 'expressive' hand is therefore both unusual and significant, since it explores that space at the heart of Lakoff and Johnson's theories where concept and action interact.[8]

Insightful as their study is, Bräm and Bräm make two central assumptions about the nature of conducting that limit the extent to which they can theorize beyond the list of gestures that they catalogue. While both assumptions have a clear, common-sense origin in conducting practice, neither survives detailed scrutiny entirely intact, and putting them aside allows processes to show that otherwise would remain difficult to see.

First is the question of hand function. Bräm and Bräm assume that the right (or dominant) hand gives 'structure', and the left (or non-dominant) hand gives 'expression'. As we saw in Chapter 9, this is a reasonable generalization at a global level, but both hands get involved in both metrical and shaping functions sufficiently often that we should see cross-over between them as routine rather than aberrational. The roles of the hands are only ever intermittently separated. Contained in the assumption of separated hand function is the notion that pattern is conventional whereas qualitative elements are 'subjective'. In this context,

---

[5] Michael Spitzer, *Metaphor and Musical Thought* (Chicago, 2004).
[6] Ibid., pp. 57–8.
[7] Anthony Gritten and Elaine King (eds), *Music and Gesture* (Aldershot, 2006).
[8] Penny Boyes Bräm and Thüring Bräm, 'Expressive Gestures Used by Classical Orchestra Conductors', in Cornelia Müller and Roland Posner (eds), *The Semantics and Pragmatics of Everyday Gestures* (Berlin, 2004).

'subjective' usually implies not only individual to the conductor, but also natural and unconscious. It is certainly the case that left-hand gestures are discussed in a much more ad hoc way in pedagogical texts than the systematic accounts of pattern are. Nonetheless, comparing these ad hoc descriptions and watching conductors in action shows that there are clearly common expressive vocabularies in practice. The nature of these roles is also less differentiated than commonly supposed. Hence, when I analyse dynamic shaping and pattern, I am not assuming that these represent a clear distinction either between right- and left-hand functions or between structural and expressive elements. Rather, I aim to show that one of the reasons these distinctions keep breaking down is because they share many of the same processes.

Bräm and Bräm's second central assumption is that conducting is based on the signalling model discussed in Chapter 2, that it is, as they express it, an act of 'gestural theater'.[9] As my earlier discussion showed, this idea of conducting as a form of visual communication that 'translates' information from the score and 'transmits' it to the performers captures an important part of the process, but is only partially embraced by practitioners. Moreover, it obscures the extent to which conducting gestures circulate as embodied traditions of musical meaning shared among instrumentalists and singers as well as the conductors themselves. We saw this in Chapter 8, where Brooks moved fluidly from gesturing as a singer to directing, and where McLean's body language for a swing style referenced that of quartet performance. We can also infer such shared traditions from the history of conducting gestures and from the role of beat patterns in the training of young musicians.

While the conductor as a specialized role only emerged during the nineteenth century, gesture has been used to coordinate musical performances for hundreds of years. Steve Plank discusses a late-fifteenth-century illumination in which a group of singers all appear to be involved in the gestural keeping of time.[10] Elliott Galkin, meanwhile, documents the proliferation of different patterns advocated by theorists of the sixteenth to the eighteenth centuries, and George Houle traces how these emerged from the gestures associated with *tactus* (the basic pulse that provided the primary rhythmic organization for earlier music) in tandem with modern concepts of metre.[11]

The standardization of modern conducting patterns is commonly dated to Louis Spohr's *Violinschule* of 1832.[12] However, while Spohr was a significant figure in the development of the specialist conductor (he claimed to be the first

---

[9] Bräm and Bräm, p. 130.

[10] Steven Plank, *Choral Performance: A Guide to Historical Practice* (Oxford, 2004), p. 76.

[11] Elliott Galkin, *A History of Orchestral Conducting in Theory and Practice* (New York, 1988); George Houle, *Meter in Music, 1600–1800* (Bloomington, 1987).

[12] Louis Spohr, *Grand Violin School*, trans. C. Rudolphus (London, n.d.).

to use a baton in London, for example[13]), the context in which he presents the patterns is not the technique of conducting, but as a means to teach the novice violinist to understand metre.[14] Time-keeping by gesture was still something to be done rather than simply watched.[15] The use of beat patterns in basic musicianship training continued right through the twentieth century. It remained, for instance, in the syllabus for early grades aural tests issued by the Associated Board of the Royal Schools of Music (the primary provider of graded music examinations in the UK) until the mid-1990s.

Thus, when orchestral players watch a conductor's gestures, they share the spatial/orientational meaning encoded in the standard patterns as a direct part of their musical experience and understanding, and not merely as a visually transmitted code. The iconic value of the patterns lies not only in their reference to musical shapes but also in their reference to how musicians have been taught to understand them. Choral singers will vary rather more in the extent to which they share this background, depending on the degree of formal training they have received. Indeed, we have seen a commensurate variety in how much and how strictly choral conductors rely on patterns, with a reasonably strong correlation between musical literacy in singers and prevalence of pattern in their director's technique.

To put these two assumptions aside, then, offers two advantages. First, it allows us to move beyond the useful, but rather informal approach of naming gestures as a catalogue of observed elements, to an understanding of the means by which formal as well as idiosyncratic aspects of conducting technique acquire their meaning. Conductors in practice are clearly not constrained by rules about the separation either of the hands or their structural or expressive functions, so there is no compelling reason why theorists attempting to understand what they do should be either. Second, it allows us to understand how it is that ensemble performers make sense of these gestures. If, as Lakoff and Johnson assert, metaphors have their basis in our embodied experience of living in the world, then it seems sensible to consider the lived experience of the recipients as well as the makers of the gestures.

---

[13] The veracity of this claim is open to doubt, but that Spohr was able to make it plausibly itself testifies to his involvement in the changing directing practices of the 1820s. See Louis Spohr, *Louis Spohr's Autobiography*, Vol. II (London, 1865), pp. 81–2 and Arthur Jacobs, 'Spohr and the Baton', *Music and Letters* 31/4 (1950): 307–17.

[14] Spohr, *Grand Violin School*, p. 26.

[15] The invective of some of the pioneering specialist conductors against 'mere time-beating' can thus be read as defending the interpretative and leadership skills of a conductor in a world where anyone with a basic musical training would have been drilled in what conductors use as a primary element of technique.

Dynamic Shaping

Dynamics are central to the shaping of musical performance, and are the archetypal 'expressive' as opposed to 'structural' element of music. They appear in musical notation as 'extras' layered over the pitches and rhythms that tell us what to play, in the form of verbal instructions (or their abbreviations) and graphic symbols that instruct us how to play. They are commonly defined as referring to relative loudness or quietness in performance.[16]

A useful starting-point might therefore be to compare the techniques conductors use to indicate dynamic shaping with the means by which the meaning of non-musical gestures can be modulated. In both cases, some kind of syntactic structure is modified in a way that leaves its analysable structure intact, but significantly inflects its communicative impact. Table 10.1 maps Axel Mulder's summary of the ways that emotion can affect the gestures of sign-language users onto a list of devices for dynamic change culled from conducting instruction manuals.[17] (We can note that only the last gesture is specifically associated with left-hand function, and several of the others are explicitly linked with the ostensibly 'structural' conducting pattern.)

Table 10.1 How emotion modulates gesture in sign-language and dynamics modulate gesture in conducting

Means to modulate meaning (Mulder)	Conducting gesture element	References in conducting literature
Size of gesture space	Distance of gestures from body	Rudolph 1995, 85 Decker and Kirk 1988, 11 Reynolds 1972, 26
Size of gesture space	Size of pattern	Rudolph 1995, 71 Roe 1970, 235 Garretson 1970, 73 Woodgate 1944, 27 Holst 1973, 21 Kahn 1975, 86
Size of gesture space	Primary joint driving the gestures (shoulder, elbow, wrist, knuckle)	Boult 1949, 29 Kahn 1975, 9

---

[16] See Robert Donington, 'Dynamics', in Stanley Sadie (ed.), *The New Grove Dictionary of Music and Musicians*, Vol. 5 (London, 1980), p. 795; Don Michael Randel, *The New Harvard Dictionary of Music* (Cambridge, MA, 1986), p. 247; and Percy A. Scholes, *The Oxford Companion to Music*, 10th edn (London, 1970), p. 310.

[17] Axel Mulder, 'Hand Gestures for HCI', Hand Centred Studies of Human Movement Project, Technical Report 96-1 (1996), available online at: http://www.xspasm.com/x/sfu/vmi/HCI-gestures.htm [accessed 22 January 2008]. For full bibliographical details of these citations, see the Bibliography.

Means to modulate meaning (Mulder)	Conducting gesture element	References in conducting literature
Tension of gesturing	Muscular tension	Roe 1970, 235 Busch 1984, 73–4
Speed of gesturing	Speed of movement	Green 1997, 73
Facial expressions		
Number of repetitions (not more than 4 or 5) or duration		
Hold-time of a posture while signing		
	'Weight' of ictus (= acceleration into pulse point)	Roe 1970, 235 Woodgate 1944, 27
	Raising/lowering LH	Rudolph 1995, 74 Gordon 1989, 79 Green 1997, 93 Kahn 1975, 86 Busch 1984, 86

Hence, there are clear correlations between the way that meaning is inflected emotionally in musical and non-musical contexts. Speed, size and tension all correlate directly across these two domains, and even among those items that do not map directly there are some connections. One occasionally sees a conductor rapidly repeating a gesture for emphasis, although the technique is not commonly discussed in conducting manuals. The classic orchestral left-hand modelling of vibrato to ask for more intensity from the strings would fall in this category, and we also see an example in clip 1.3 at the end of the Clements piece where Lucas attempts to restrain a rather piercing treble who is in danger of overbalancing the chord. Hold time of a gesture is somewhat complicated in a musical context since it risks interfering with tempo; however, agogic (that is, durational) accents are an established means to provide musical emphasis, as is abundantly clear from the endings of both the medley and the swing song performed by the White Rosettes. And while conducting texts do not mention facial expression as a specific technique by which to control dynamics, they all emphasize the involvement of the face as part of the general expressive purpose of which dynamics are just a part. So, at first glance it seems that the 'subjective' or 'emotional' elements of both musical and linguistic gesture share a repertoire of methods to inflect the meaning of the semiotic content with which they are associated.

However, just as the distinction between structure and expression in conducting technique is less clear-cut than it might seem, we also need to interrogate the idea that dynamics represent an expressive element that is radically separate from musical structure. In older musical styles, dynamic markings may be notated relatively sparsely, but it is clear from the writings of contemporaneous music theorists that changes in volume should be inferred from musical shape.[18] That is, dynamics are not applied to a structure to change its meaning, but represent implicit meaning in that structure all along. Many composers of the twentieth century, meanwhile, included dynamics as an integral and explicit part of their musical structures. And, at a level of practice, there are some conductors who de-prioritize dynamics in rehearsal, believing that if other interpretative matters are properly understood, the dynamics will 'look after themselves'. The *what* and the *how* seem to be more closely integrated than their notational presentation might imply.

Moreover, the common definition of dynamics as amplitude of sound is remarkably monodimensional compared to the terms in which musicians understand (and perform) dynamics in practice. Even the standard Italian terms of *piano* and *forte* for soft and loud include qualitative associations beyond volume; *piano* can imply gentle, soft, calm, even, little and even slow, depending on context, while *forte* has senses equivalent to strong, heavy, large, deep and robust, as well as loud. For both voices and instruments, volume interacts with pitch register and tone colour such that the 'same' dynamic level may have very different expressive effects in different contexts; a *forte* dynamic may come over as bold or harsh, triumphant or piercing, depending on how these factors combine. When musicians say a performance suffers from a limited dynamic range, it is not merely the gradient between the loudest and softest moments that is the problem; it is the lack of expressive variety that arises from the interaction of amplitude with other performance elements.

Table 10.2 addresses both of these criticisms. It takes the gestures identified from the conducting literature from Table 10.1 and reinterprets them not just as emotional intensifiers but as having their own metaphorical content. Hence, the third column suggests a metaphor for each gesture, while the fourth attributes an underlying image schema to each.

Table 10.2   Gestures for dynamic shaping and their metaphorical associations

Gesture element	References	Metaphor	Image schema
Distance of gestures from body	Rudolph 1995, 85 Decker and Kirk 1988, 11 Reynolds 1972, 26	Louder sounds can be heard further away	DISTANCE or CENTRE-PERIPHERY
Size of pattern	Rudolph 1995, 71 Roe 1970, 235 Garretson 1970, 73 Woodgate 1944, 27 Holst 1973, 21 Kahn 1975, 86	Bigger is louder	SIZE

---

[18] See Matthias Thiemal, 'Dynamics', in L. Macy (ed.), *Grove Music Online*, available online at www.grovemusic.com [accessed 22 January 2008].

Gesture element	References	Metaphor	Image schema
Primary joint driving the gestures (shoulder, elbow, wrist, knuckle)	Boult 1949, 29 Kahn 1975, 9	Delicate work uses digits while heavy work needs limbs.	FORCE and/or SIZE
Muscular tension	Roe 1970, 235 Busch 1984, 73-4	It takes more effort to make louder sounds	FORCE
Speed of movement	Green 1997, 73	Faster is louder	SPEED
'Weight' of ictus (= acceleration into pulse point)	Roe 1970, 235 Woodgate 1944, 27	Heavier objects emit louder sounds	WEIGHT
Raising/lowering LH	Rudolph 1995, 74 Gordon 1989, 79 Green 1997, 93 Kahn 1975, 86 Busch 1984, 86	Up is more	VERTICALITY

The first thing to note is that this gestural vocabulary is far from monodimensional in its metaphorical associations. Just as the amplitude of performed music interacts with register and tone colour to create expressive effect, the idea of amplitude is mapped here onto a wide range of other domains. Table 10.2 also shows us how gestural indications of dynamic contrast draw on similar metaphorical associations to linguistic references. We would talk about raising and lowering the volume, while the last gesture listed involves raising and lowering the hand. 'Volume' itself is a metaphor that maps loudness onto three-dimensional space; as the first gesture suggests, this rests on our experience that louder sounds travel further, and we use it linguistically when we talk about 'projecting our sound to fill the hall' or ask a player to 'back off'. This makes sense of the way that emergent gestures can transfer so easily between accompanying speech, accompanying song and conducting gestures.

While I have listed these as separate elements, in practice they often occur in tandem. For instance, size and speed of gesture are intimately related in the context of conducting pattern. As Elizabeth Green points out, given an invariant tempo, increasing the size of the pattern necessarily increases the speed the baton travels between pulse points.[19] She argues that the louder volume elicited by a larger pattern is the consequence of this faster speed, and not of the increase in size as most other writers would contend. I would argue that, notwithstanding this correlation, they remain as two separable metaphors, since one also sees conductors use large holding gestures to invite loud playing outside of the context of pattern. McLean's gestures in loud block chords come to mind once again. Moreover, size is also generally correlated with distance from body and the joint

---

[19] Elizabeth Green, *The Modern Conductor: A College Text on Conducting based on the Technical Principles of Conductor Nicolai Malko as set forth in his 'The Conductor and his Baton'*, 6th edn (Englewood Cliffs, 1997), p. 73.

from which the gesture is driven, but these elements are also both logically and to an extent practically separable. One can make a small gesture with the finger at arm's length, for instance. Green's insight will nonetheless prove important in the discussion of pattern below.

The DISTANCE image schema deserves particular comment, as it plays out in conducting gesture in two apparently contradictory ways. The first indicates loudness with gestures that are further from the conductor's body. The second involves the conductor 'drawing' the sound towards him or herself to indicate a crescendo, and 'pushing it away' to indicate a diminuendo. In fact, these are visually quite distinct and would not in practice be confused. There are three factors that ensure this distinctness: the differentiation of hands, the interaction with other metaphors, and the constitution of musical subject position.

The first version of the DISTANCE image schema is associated with the right hand conducting patterns; if the left hand is also in use, it will also participate in the near/far indication, but it is not required. The gesture itself is strongly overdetermined – as it moves further from the conductor's body, it will typically also increase in size (and thus speed), and start to involve the joints closer to the body. It will also require more physical exertion, although the degree of muscular tension involved is separable to a considerable degree. The gesture as a whole places conductors in the centre of the sound; it aligns them with the ensemble, and invites a sense producing a sound that fills a space extending further beyond them. The second version is associated with left-hand function, that is, a gesture that operates independently of the metrical pattern, and is effectively a variant of the up-down gesture, inflecting it with near-far. This one places the conductor outside the ensemble; in 'drawing out' or 'pushing back' the sound, the message is 'expand the area your sound fills towards me' or 'keep your sound closer to yourself'. We see both of these versions of in clip 1.3. During the tenor solo, Lucas's pattern varies considerably and fluidly in size with the ebb and flow of the local dynamic climaxes, involving both hands at the louder moments, while the choir's entry at the end of the clip is controlled by a left-handed 'pushing-back' gesture, first to the cantoris side, then the decani. Conductor gesture thus carries information not just about the terms in which to imagine musical shaping but also about the nature of the relationship between conductor and choir.

Hence, while the meaning of the expressive gestures associated with dynamics has a strong relationship with the visible signs of emotionality and subjective state seen in other gestural contexts, this is not the whole story. There is also a complex of metaphorical associations that the conductor can draw on to give a multidimensional interpretation of the dynamic shape of a piece. These metaphors are organized by the same kinds of image schemata that Lakoff and Johnson claim undergird our conceptual structures, and operate by the same processes of cross-domain mapping as our linguistic structures. These gestures, then, do not merely modulate meaning, but participate in the creation of meaning. And, as we shall see next, the same processes underlie the primary structural element of conducting technique, metrical pattern.

Pattern

As discussed in Chapter 9, the primary purpose of beating time is the 'sheepdog' function of keeping the ensemble rhythmically together. Pulse alone can indicate tempo (and may often do so in practice), but patterns indicate not only when a beat occurs in time, but also which beat in the bar it is. This grouping of beats into larger metrical units is thus a means to measure out musical time; indeed, the American usage refers to each group as a measure. In doing so, patterns tell us about the quality as well as the pacing of pulse; they acknowledge that all pulses are not equal. That is, the groupings suggest that all downbeats have something in common that is different from all upbeats. So, when novice conductors get beats two and three in a four-pattern reversed, this tells us that they have yet to internalize the qualitative difference encoded in the beat locations.[20]

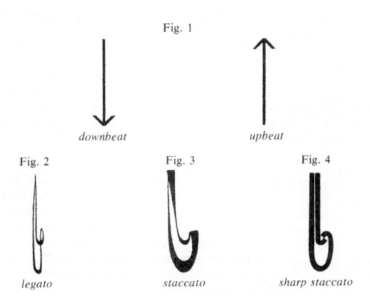

Figure 10.1   Basic elements of the two-pattern and three styles of execution

---

[20]   Interestingly, according to Berlioz, some mid-nineteenth-century German conductors brought their second beat in a three-pattern across their body rather than outwards. One wonders whether this gestural convention was also associated with a different way of articulating music in a triple metre from the French, and whether, in turn, there is scope for the study of historical treatises on beat patterns as a route to understanding qualitative aspects of associated performance styles. Hector Berlioz, *Treatise on Instrumentation, Including Berlioz's Essay on Conducting*, rev. Richard Strauss, trans. Theodore Front (New York, 1948), p. 412.

I will start by considering the two-pattern, as it is both historically and logically prior to the others. Its basic topography, as in Figure 10.1, is a downbeat followed by an upbeat; this is also how early theorists describe the beating of the *tactus*.[21] This clearly and directly draws on image-schemata of VERTICALITY and of WEIGHT to differentiate between pulses, and characterizes them in terms of our bodily experience of gravity, alternating falling and lifting. This is usually glossed in language as an alternation of strong and weak, or accented and unaccented beats, which is in turn a metaphorical mapping of the domain of verticality onto that of strength via the common attribute of gravity's force.

As we saw in Chapter 9, however, verticality is only one of the directions that organize this binary alternation: strong beats are as often in-beats as downbeats, especially when the pattern is mirrored. The first beat in the bar is always directed clearly into the space in front of the conductor's torso, but in addition to the textbook execution of straight down in front of the body, it may involve one or more other directions: forward and down from beside the conductor's head in a whipping motion; in from both sides as if playing crash cymbals; or forward and up from hip level as in the 'shovel' ictus. That these can be effectively described in terms of handling imaginary objects suggests that Bräm and Bräm's description of the area in which the conductor gestures as a 'metaphorical container in which there are objects which one can manipulate' applies as much to the dominant as to the non-dominant hand.[22]

The 'downbeat' that comes in from the side deserves particular mention. As we saw in Chapter 9, this develops a relationship between pattern and the act of breathing that gives an ergotic function to the gesture, especially when associated with that other ostensible faux pas, the mirrored beat. The contrast between the arms closing across the body self-protectively and opening out generously also resonates with our experiences of body language in interpersonal interaction. Contrast, for example, Brooks's gesture in clip 3.4 when she talks about the 'penitent' nature of the song with Halsey's outgoing and uninhibited demonstration to the tenors nearly two minutes into clip 4.3. Symmetrical lateral conducting motions thus have the potential to map the domain of interpersonal confidence onto the rhythmic qualities of beats.

Even this simplest of beat patterns, then, draws on multiple metaphors, and the built-in qualitative associations become richer still when the two-pattern is elaborated out into four. There are two ways to think of the transformation of duple to quadruple metre, as shown in Figure 10.2.

---

[21] From Emil Kahn, *Elements of Conducting*, 2nd edn (New York, 1975), p. 8.
[22] Bräm and Bräm, p. 130.

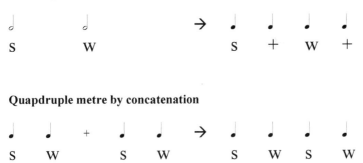

Figure 10.2   Transformation of duple into quadruple metre

The first is by subdivision: each beat is divided into two, producing an accent pattern I have characterized as Strong-and Weak-and. In gestural terms, this separates out the VERTICALITY and INHALATION/EXHALATION schemata of the two-pattern, to produce falling-protecting for the first half of the bar and opening-lifting for the second half. The second is by concatenation: two sets of two are placed one after another, producing an alternating pattern of strong–weak–strong–weak. In gestural terms, this construes the pattern in terms of the relationship between speed and distance travelled noted by Elizabeth Green. If we consider the diagrams in Figure 10.3, we will note that the baton has further to travel to beats one and three than to two and four.[23] This means it will have to travel faster to cover the distance within a steady pulse, and it will thus produce a relative accent via the 'faster is louder' metaphor.

---

[23]   From Adrian Boult, *A Handbook on the Technique of Conducting*, 7th edn (Oxford, 1949), p. 20.

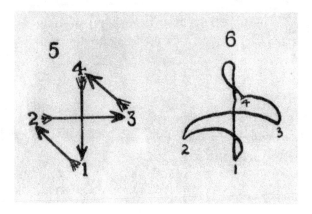

Figure 10.3   Basic topography of the four-pattern and its execution

We thus see that beat three has a dual role as both strong and weak, depending on which orientational perspective we take. Such multiple rhythmic meanings are the sort of thing that Cooper and Meyer would analyse as different levels of accent as in Figure 10.4.[24]

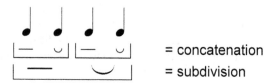

Figure 10.4   Multilevel analysis of accent after Cooper and Meyer

However, using the idea of image schemata and metaphorical mapping, one gets a richer, more multidimensional concept of metre, with the characterization of the relative beats arising from associations with several different areas of bodily experience. This in turn is what permits conductors to exercise their interpretative imagination so flexibly within the standard patterns: the classic distinction between maestro and mere time-beater relies on the distinctiveness and subtlety of the choices a conductor makes in exploiting these qualitative, expressive possibilities built into the formal gestural grammar.

---

[24]   Grosvenor Cooper and Leonard B. Meyer, *The Rhythmic Structure of Music* (Chicago, 1960).

Conclusion

Lakoff and Johnson have aimed to deconstruct the standard Western distinction between body and mind by developing a theory that shows how mental structures arise from bodily experience, which in turn is constituted within shared cultural contexts. In doing so, they have also provided a way to understand conductor gesture that likewise undermines our common distinctions between structure and expression and between nature and nurture.

The analyses in this chapter suggest that distinction between the 'structural' and the 'expressive' elements of conducting technique lies not in the processes by which they construct their meaning, but in the degree to which they are systematically formalized. Dynamic shaping gestures are flexible in the time-frames over which they can be executed, whereas metrical gestures are by their nature more regular. But both map fundamental aspects of bodily experience – size, speed, weight – onto the domain of sound as a means to make sense of it. Not only are the metaphorical processes the same, moreover, but there is a common fund of image schemata that both draw upon to construct their meanings. The emotional turns out to be more cognitive than originally appeared, and the structural turns out to be more expressive.

That even the formal, conventionalized elements of conducting technique are grounded in fundamental physical experience gives weight to those who would claim that conducting is a 'universal language', that it has inherent meanings that are readily and intuitively accessible. On the other hand, musical performers, whether singers, instrumentalists or conductors, undergo the shared bodily experiences that underlie this understanding within particular musical practices. One will have a different relationship with rhythm depending on whether one learns about it by beating time in violin lessons or stepping from side to side while singing in church. Musical culture starts to look not only like a repertoire of ways to imagine music, but like a repertoire of ways to move with music as well.

Moreover, the language we use to talk about musical character and expression draws on the same image schemata by which we communicate about it gesturally. Metaphor theory thus also starts to give an insight into how gestures mediate between language and music, as noted in Chapter 9. The conductor's gestures are not merely 'translations' of a pre-existent musical meaning, but are part of the cultural substrate of Western musical praxis, and thus integral to our musical understanding. Chapter 11 turns to the detail of this process and examines the connection between gesture and thought.

Finally, though, it is worth drawing an artistic conclusion to complement these theoretical points. This is to note how rich the metaphorical mappings are within even the basic gestural vocabulary of conducting technique. Even 'mere time-beating' entails the interaction of two or three image schemata, while dynamic shaping can involve multidimensional mapping across many domains at once. The flexibility and complexity of these interactions gives immense scope for the individual conductor to explore music's imaginative shape, and it is this range of available embodied metaphors that allows their gestural vocabulary to remain expressively inexhaustible.

Chapter 11
Spontaneous Gesture and the Ensemble

Some musicians maintain that a detailed planning of gestures has little value and that if the conductor knows the score thoroughly, gestures will follow automatically. Since the gestures of even experienced conductors are not always adequate at first rehearsals, a novice will profit from such planning. Especially in difficult passages, the student may have to conduct his imaginary orchestra again and again before the sequence of motions is well-balanced and fits the music.[1]

The movement and direction of a melody or voice part can be controlled with a hand gesture. This gives the melodic movement real direction, momentum, and plasticity. … It is of decisive importance that the director thinks of his hands as leading and controlling the melodic flow through every beat of the music. He should never think of his hands as following the music, but always maintain the awareness that there is an indissoluble unity between hand and music and that the director in reality holds every tone 'in his hand'.[2]

Chapter 10's exploration of metaphorical mapping gave an insight into how it is that a conductor can 'look like the music'. Physical motion can resemble sound because each is mapped onto the other via shared, preconceptual image schemata based in lived experience. It also provided some general insight into the way this lived experience shapes the way we think musically: conductor gestures are meaningful because our musical understanding is inherently embodied. What it did not do was explain how this works in the moment-to-moment flow of music-making. When a conductor uses a gesture to express a musical idea, what is the connection between hand and mind? When a singer draws on the musical background they share with the conductor to respond to that gesture, what is the connection between their understanding and their performed sounds? What is going on when a conductor holds the music 'in his hand'?

This chapter turns to the work of gesture theorist David McNeill to help answer these questions.[3] As we saw in Chapter 4, his theories present some difficulties for musicians by their assumption that gesture should be understood in relation to speech. However, his ideas offer a potential to explain fascinating human phenomena that more than compensates for the extra theoretical work musicians have to do when applying them to their own discipline, and the concept of the

---

[1] Max Rudolph, *The Grammar of Conducting: A Comprehensive Guide to Baton Technique and Interpretation*, 3rd edn (New York, 1995), p. 295.
[2] William Ehmann, *Choral Directing*, trans. G. Wiebe, (Minneapolis, 1968), p. 83.
[3] David McNeill, *Gesture and Thought* (Chicago, 2005).

emergent gesture discussed in Chapter 9 will help to bridge this language–music gap. My discussion will focus on two main concepts. The first, the 'growth point', helps us understand how the act of gesturing participates in the act of thinking. The second, 'inhabitance', deals with the way that people share ideas in interpersonal interactions. This will in turn prepare the ground for Part IV's exploration of the conductor–choir bond.

The Growth Point

McNeill is concerned with the emergence of ideas: how we hatch thoughts, and how we express them. He has developed his theories inductively from studying how people use gesture and speech together, and one of their strengths is consequently that it is possible to test the validity of his generalizations by observing people in daily life.

His observational starting-point is to note how people use gesture and speech together: not only are the two routinely and fluently synchronized, but the link between them is strong enough that they are very difficult to separate. For instance, experiments that aim to distract people by playing their own speech back to them with a fractional delay succeed in disrupting their speech patterns, but do not disrupt the way they use gesture and speech in tandem. Likewise, there is a strong positive correlation between the complexity and fluency of gestures and that of speech: as a speaker's words tail off, so do their gestures. Moreover, listeners cannot remember, when asked later, whether they have received any specific item of information from language or from gesture: the two are bound together into a single unit in perception as well as expression.[4]

Gesture and speech are thus co-expressive, but not redundant. That is, they both communicate the same basic idea, but do so in very different modes. So, when we express a thought, we are expanding it in two different dimensions at the same time. The linguistic dimension presents the conventionalized, analytic articulation of the idea, and takes time to unfold – words are placed sequentially through time until the resting point where the thought has finished and the sentence is grammatically complete. The gestural dimension by contrast is imagistic, and encapsulates the complete idea in a single, holistic movement. The two work together such that the main stroke or beat of the gesture either arrives simultaneously with the point in the verbal utterance to which it most directly corresponds or, if it arrives earlier, is held in place until that point is reached.

We can see some good examples of this speech–gesture synchrony towards the end of clip 1.2. When Lucas says, 'it's growing a lot in that', he opens his arms out on the word 'growing'. He goes on: 'It says "*non-crescendo*"', holding thumb and forefinger to suggest a little sound; he forms this gesture with the word 'says', but holds it through the rest of the sentence. He then moves this hand shape back

---

[4] Ibid., pp. 24–7.

and forth horizontally as he says, 'Keep it, keep it there'; the gesture here contains both the idea of the volume to be retained, and also, with the lateral motion, the idea of actively maintaining it. Indeed, the gesture here not only encapsulates the main idea, but presents it more continuously than the spoken version, binding the self-interruption to the original start of the statement.

Key to this model of the expression of thought is the moment at which ideas first arise. McNeill calls this moment the 'growth point', and characterizes it as 'a point of differentiation of newsworthy content from a background'.[5] This background is formed by the current context of speaking, and the more unpredictable the growth point is within this context, the more fully it will be materialized. That is, surprising thoughts produce more elaborate gestures. The growth point is not yet a fully formed thought, however, but a mental package that includes elements from both the static/linguistic and dynamic/imagistic dimensions. As such, it is cognitively unstable, and it is the resolution of this instability that propels speech and thought forwards. The growth point is the initial pulse from which ideas take form. In this sense, McNeill's theory resonates with Merleau-Ponty's idea that expression is not just the presentation of conceptual content, but the process by which thought is brought to fruition; expression is the *completion* of the thought.[6]

Gesture, in this context, is about the way that we think, not about signalling our ideas to others. Indeed, the importance of gesture to the process of thinking has previously been well documented, both experimentally and anecdotally. For instance, Bernard Rimé and Loris Schiaratura discuss the way that, when people's freedom of movement in conversation is restricted, not only do they engage in much more facial movement to compensate, but the verbal content itself becomes less vivid in imagery.[7] And one of the things that the spread of the public use of mobile phones has shown us is just how much people gesture while they talk to people who cannot see them.

This theory, then, appears to deal directly with the question of the relationship of gesture and idea: the physical motion is able to express a thought so clearly because it is an inherent part of the process of thought generation. However, there are three major issues that we need to address in order to apply it to music. The first is its dependence on spoken language as an inherent part of the thinking process; the second is that conductors and choirs are generally presenting precomposed content, rather than making up their material on the spot as conversationalists do; and the third is that conductors work only in the gestural dimension, making no sound.

So, first we need to ask whether musical ideas share the qualities identified by McNeill in linguistic-gestural ideas. Does music have this dual nature of

---

[5] Ibid., p. 19.

[6] Maurice Merleau-Ponty, *Phenomenology of Per*ception, rev. edn (London, 2002).

[7] Bernard Rimé and Loris Schiaratura, 'Gesture and Speech', in Robert S. Feldman and Bernard Rimé (eds), *Fundamentals of Nonverbal Behavior* (Cambridge, 1991), p. 241.

static/analytical and dynamic/holistic dimensions, and do musicians experience growth points?

I think it is quite uncontentious to claim that music does indeed have a sequential, syntactical, analysable structure. All genres have rules of well-formedness that are understood intuitively by their users: any reasonably experienced listener can spot errors and unidiomatic elements when they hear them. Western classical music has undergone an unusual level of theoretical investigation to make these rules explicit, but one does not need to have been trained in these methods to recognize when the rules have been broken.

One of McNeill's criticisms of the discipline of linguistics since Saussure is that, in focusing exclusively on the static dimension of language, most theories have been unable to account for the dialectical tension between static and active that gives the growth point its power to spur thought forward. Musicology's traditional focus on the composer's work as presented in the score, and consequent neglect of music in performance, has undergone a similar critique since the mid-1990s. Carolyn Abbate, for instance, casts orthodox, work-based musicology as the study of musical 'souvenirs' in contrast to the 'real' music that is to be found in live performance.[8] Nicholas Cook, meanwhile, takes a double view of music as both product (work) and process (performance).[9] Lydia Goehr identifies this tension historically in Western musical aesthetics as a dialectic between two ideals: the perfect performance of music and the perfect musical performance.[10] The first is about fidelity to the work, and the performer's job is to let the music through without getting in the way. The second celebrates the particular, real-time skill of the performer, the bringing to life of music in the here-and-now. The first ideal has been dominant in Western classical music of the past two centuries, not least because of a cultural tendency to privilege knowing over doing, but the second has always survived alongside, competing yet connected.

Music's dual nature as both structure and process is thus both well established within music scholarship and widely theorized to exist in a similar state of dialectical tension as McNeill attributes to language. So there is at least the potential for musical ideas to be unfolded across these two dimensions as verbal ideas are. However, this does not tell us whether the growth point, the unstable proto-thought that drives this process, exists musically. Evidence from rehearsal observations, and in particular the category of the emergent gesture, can give us some clues, however.

Emergent gestures are those conducting motions that emerge in the context of issues arising in rehearsal. They usually appear as speech-accompanying or

---

[8] Carolyn Abbate, 'Music – Drastic or Gnostic?', *Critical Enquiry*, 30 (2004): 505–36.

[9] Nicholas Cook, 'Between Process and Product: Music and/as Performance', *Music Theory Online*, 7/2 (2001), available online at: http://societymusictheory.org/mto/issues/mto.01.7.2/mto.01.7.2.cook.html [accessed 25 January 2008].

[10] Lydia Goehr, *The Quest for Voice: On Music, Politics, and the Limits of Philosophy* (Oxford, 2002), p. 140ff.

song-accompanying gestures at the point where the conductor communicates to the ensemble what changes they need to make, and then reappear in the conducting gesture at that point in the music as the choir sings. What is interesting here is the interchangeability of speech and song as the medium in which these gestures emerge. In the examples in Chapter 9, we saw gestures emerge with speech exactly in the way that McNeill describes; these were then used along with vocal demonstration and transferred in turn into conducting gestures. We also saw gestures emerge with vocal demonstrations that then moved back into speech. The song-accompanying gestures, like those accompanying speech, were clearly coordinated with the vocal content, to arrive with the point in the phrase to which the conductor wished to draw attention. This would usually be the focal point of the phrase as it is to be performed, but may involve distorting a phrase's timing and dynamic shape to highlight a feature that, musically, would normally be under-emphasized. A good example of this occurs in clip 4.3, just after the work on the basses' low G, where Halsey traces the first part of the phrase with a pointed finger, slowing down onto the rhythmically weakest note of the phrase to focus on pitch accuracy.

But these are all examples in which the conductor is deciding for him or herself which ideas to express, as we all do in conversational situations. How can McNeill's theory accommodate the fact that the conductor is usually dealing with content that is predetermined by the score?[11] Is this not more akin to reciting a script than improvising a conversation?

The first thing to consider is that the score significantly underdetermines the performance. Notwithstanding the aesthetic tradition of the perfect performance of music, performers need to make significant imaginative investments in the score to bring it to life. Performers who do nothing but follow literally the instructions in the score are accused of 'just singing the notes and words'. Second, conductors need to respond in real time to what performers are producing: the diagnostic work that is unpacked verbally in rehearsal continues gesturally within the flow of the music. The conductor's regulatory function – keeping an ear on and adjusting balance, synchronization, tuning, articulation and dynamic shaping – cannot, by definition, be pre-prepared.

Moreover, we sometimes see emergent gestures that originate within the conducting flow that then move into speech- or song-accompanying gestures, giving direct observational evidence that conductors are hatching ideas within the predetermined content. For example, about a minute and a quarter into clip 4.3, Halsey directs the downbeat in the phrase 'mourn for Adonis' with a gesture akin to the shovel ictus. He then stops the choir, instructs them to sing the phrase with

---

[11] Gospel musicians, of course, do not necessarily work from a score. However, the choral parts are fixed in advance, as are the general harmonic structure and overall form of the song. The lead singers and accompanying instrumentalists may operate improvisationally within this framework, but the material with which director and choral singers work has the score-like quality of being predetermined, even if it is not physically written down.

a *crescendo*, and then demonstrates the effect he wants using a considerably more developed version of the gesture. Indeed, the way that all conductors routinely use different gestures on successive renditions of the same material shows their engagement with musical thought in real time.

So, there are plenty of opportunities for the conductor to experience growth points and bring them to gestural fruition even while working within predefined musical content. However, that these opportunities exist does not necessarily mean that the conductor will take them. I should like to suggest that the difference between time-beating and expressive gesture lies not in the type or function of the gestures, but in the difference between going through the motions versus having fresh musical ideas during the act of conducting. The degree to which a conductor is considered expressive is arguably in direct proportion to the frequency with which they experience growth points within the flow of the music.[12] Indeed, this idea is implicit in the belief that a conductor need only know the music well and the gestures will look after themselves that Rudolph critiques in the passage at the start of this chapter. His advice to student conductors, meanwhile, suggests that engaging with the static dimension of music alone is insufficient preparation for working with a piece in real time because one may have many different ideas about how it will play out in the dynamic dimension.

Incidentally, the distinction between the musician's presentation of the predefined work and the conversationalist's improvisation is probably less clear-cut than it appears, and not only because of the amount of scope that musicians have for creative input into the unfolding musical work (or, to use an old-fashioned phrase, to express themselves). We probably also underestimate how much conversational content is reused. As contemporary critical theory tells us, we do not speak language, language speaks us, and, while we like to think that we are free agents who can make up our own ideas at will, the fact is that much of the time we do not do so.[13] We all have our little catchphrases, and are only too happy to offer advice on the basis of what our grandmothers used to say. The reuse of existing conversational material does not, however, prevent us experiencing our thoughts as meaningful, and so there is little reason to suppose that performing music written by someone else will necessarily divorce us from direct experience of its content either.

---

[12] McNeill suggests en passant that the shape of a gesture changes when it is no longer a 'material carrier', that is, when it is not actively participating in the thought process. He links this with the linguistic idea of 'semantic satiation', although he might also have compared this with the distinction between a 'posed' and 'felt' smile (*Gesture and Thought*, p. 98). Paul Ekman and Maureen O'Sullivan, 'Facial Expressions: Methods, Means and Moues' in Feldman and Rimé (eds), pp. 172–4.

[13] This idea recurs in much of the post-Saussurean structuralist tradition, from Lacan to Helene Cixous; see Lucy Burke, Tony Crowley and Alan Girvin (eds), *The Routledge Language and Cultural Theory Reader* (New York, 2000).

Our third potential obstacle to the application of McNeill's theories to conducting was that conductors unfold their musical ideas in the gestural dimension only. That is, the dual aspect of the growth point is missing in this particular instance, since conductors have that odd and oft-remarked status of being the only musicians who make no sounds. However, we should remember that McNeill is concerned with thought rather than speech. His evidence for the coordination of the linguistic and imagistic content of ideas necessarily comes from spoken utterances, since it would be difficult to record silent thought for experimental purposes. Still, our unspoken thoughts use the same linguistic structures as those we speak out loud. So the absence of audible sound from a conductor is not evidence for the absence of musical thought. Indeed, many novice choral conductors struggle to keep themselves from singing along with their choirs as a matter of course; internalizing musical thought is a skill that needs developing, like learning to read without moving your lips.

The growth point, then, appears to be a concept that works well to explain the connection between conductor gesture and musical thought. The spontaneity and immediacy of a conductor's responses in the flow of the music is possible because their gestures are not translations of musical ideas to be transmitted to performers, but integral to the very process of conceiving those ideas. Gesture is not merely a representation of thought, but participates in the act of thinking itself.

Further, if gesture articulates the imagistic, holistic aspect of a thought, then clearly the gestural types one has to hand affect the types of thoughts one can have. This recapitulates the idea that gestural traditions play a significant role in the maintenance and propagation of performance styles, which arose in the last chapter from the discussion of enculturated bodily experience as the basis for cognitive meanings. But it does so in a more specific way, and with more immediately practical ramifications. It shows why directors coming from one tradition can struggle to get both the rapport and the results they hope for when starting to work with a choir from a different tradition: it is not merely that their gestures look odd to their new choir, but the thoughts that these gestures express also seem alien. It also suggests that Rudolph's concern with technique and well-prepared gestures is not a rejection of spontaneity, but a means to develop the fund of artistic possibilities available for creative use in rehearsal and performance.

Inhabitance

The growth point may give us insight into the conductor's internal imaginative processes, but it does not tell us how this affects the choir. What is going on inside the singers while their director is having these spontaneous ideas? Are they the passive observers of this creative process, or do they also participate in musical thought?

To understand how people can share growth points, McNeill proposes the concept of 'inhabitance'. This draws on the philosophy of Martin Heidegger, and is explained as follows:

> The materialization of one's meaning in a gesture (and speech) is, for the one speaking, not a representation but an updating the of speaker's momentary state of cognitive being. ... The listener, in turn, inhabits the same meaning by updating in parallel his or her own momentary being, communication being a matter not only of signal exchange but of social resonance and inhabitance in the same 'house of being'.[14]

That is, McNeill sees communication less in terms of information transfer than as a process of alignment, with speakers synchronizing their mental processes to develop shared understandings. Again, his examples are all speech-based, but the processes he identifies in conversational situations are also clearly observable in choral rehearsals. The two most readily recognizable instances of this process of inhabitance on the DVD are when Lucas and Brooks each work with a soloist on clips 1.3 and 3.4 respectively. Here, the conductors are in the role of the listener, and we can see them thinking along with the solo singers, and participating in their musical flow both with their gaze and their gestures. The conditions that make this possible on a one-to-one basis can also obtain in a one-to-many relationship, and, as we shall see, this produces an account of the conducting process that resonates strongly with the interaction model proposed by practitioners.

In order to experience this process of inhabitance, people need to establish a shared space in which they can cooperate. McNeill draws on Kendon's idea of the F-formation to describe this space, which Kendon claims to arise 'whenever two or more people sustain a spatial and orientational relationship in which the space between them is one to which they have equal, direct, and exclusive access'.[15] This in turn is built on the idea of the transactional segment, which is the area of space in front of a person into which they look, speak and gesture, and into which they reach to handle objects. The size and shape of this space is framed by posture, orientation of the body and placement of the limbs, and will usually retain its integrity throughout the duration of an activity; the individual will actively maintain it, and others will usually respect it. The F-formation is created when two or more people orient their bodies so as to overlap their transactional segments, thus creating a shared space. Kendon emphasizes that it is the lower body that is primary in defining this formation.

The standard types of choir layout all promote this overlap in transactional space between conductor and choir, although there are some interesting variants on how this is effected. Most choirs are stacked in serried rows, such that each

---

[14] McNeill, *Gesture and Thought*, p. 19.
[15] Adam Kendon, *Conducting Interaction: Patterns of Behavior in Focused Encounters* (Cambridge, 1990), p. 209.

singer's transactional segment can connect with the conductor's, but does not connect very much with singers in front or behind them. The extra intimacy of ensemble that smaller groups can achieve would thus appear to be a result not simply of their number, but also the consequent possibility of singing in a single line, giving all singers the opportunity to participate in the same F-formation. The gentle curvature of choral risers and the layout on three sides of a rectangle, meanwhile, both allow singers more contact with each other than straight rows, and also minimizes the difference in distance from the conductor between singers in the middle and at the ends of rows. The antiphonal layout of the cathedral choir, meanwhile, creates a bond between the two halves of the choir that is potentially stronger than between choir and conductor.

We can see the function of an F-formation's exclusivity of access when a conductor wants to address a subset of the choir, when they will create a new F-formation with those singers, temporarily excluding the others from the interaction. Sometimes this will involve moving closer to the ensemble, as Brooks does when she wants to work with individual singers, and sometimes it will involve changing bodily orientation to change the location of the director's transactional segment. Hence, Lucas's default position faces into space shared between both halves of the choir, but will twist to either right or left to focus on one half or the other, while Halsey inflects his seated position that encompasses the whole chorus by creating a frame with his shoulders to address individual sections. Conversely, the open-armed 'ready' gesture that nearly all directors use in one form or another to presage bringing the whole choir in to sing serves explicitly to re-establish the space shared with the whole group after rehearsing smaller sections.

The one part of Kendon's definition that does not seem to fit choirs at all well is the aspect of equal access to the space in the F-formation. While it is clear that this space is the one in which all participants act – they all look in to it, and the conductor gestures in it while the choir members sing into it – the terms of their access to it are very unequal. As we saw in Part II, a key part of choral discipline is the regulation of access to this space. A disciplined choir is one in which choristers only use this space when invited to by their director: they sing when directed to, and seek permission – occasionally – to speak. However, access to shared space is more unequal even in conversational situations than Kendon's original formulation suggests, as McNeill shows in a study of conversational behaviour among members of the US Air Force.[16] This study identifies a number of ways in which the senior officer maintained dominance, using pointing and gaze as a means to offer the others permission to contribute to the conversation. He was the main source of pointing, but was the least frequent target for others to point at. Conversely, others looked at him more than he looked at them, although when he did look at others, his gaze lasted longer. These observations also describe conductor behaviour very clearly. In choral rehearsals it is rare for anyone but the

---

[16] David McNeill, 'Gesture, Gaze, and Ground', available online at: http://mcneilllab.uchicago.edu/pdfs/McNeill_VACE.pdf [accessed 12 March 2008].

conductor to point at all, and, while it is considered good practice for conductors to retain eye contact with their singers, they may shift their gaze out of the shared space in order to think, or to listen, much more often than singers are allowed to. Indeed, as we saw in Chapter 7, conductors actively insist that that singers look at them continually. That Kendon saw access to the shared space as equal, then, possibly simply reflects the social contexts of the conversations from which he developed the idea of the F-formation, and the other attributes he identified still allow the process to work in less egalitarian situations.

Within this shared space, participants can cooperate to develop ideas together – that is, to share growth points. McNeill uses the term 'hyperphrase' to describe how two or more people may work together, using both verbal and nonverbal elements, to create meaning.[17] This is what happens when one person finishes another's sentence, for instance, or where a speaker adapts what they say or how they say it in response to other people's responses as they speak. Two particular processes are involved in this process of interpersonal synchronization – mimicry and appropriation – and both are germane to musical contexts.[18]

Mimicry is the process whereby one person joins in with another's gestures, and is most likely to happen when those involved are personally close. McNeill interprets this as an act of participation in another person's thought. As the first speaker experiences a growth point that emerges in language and gesture, the second speaker joins in with the idea: the shared gesture is evidence that what they are thinking shares the same imagery as the first speaker. One sees this kind of overtly shared gesture relatively rarely in classical choral contexts, although the sharing of time-keeping between cantoris and decani sides of a church or cathedral choir in the absence of a conductor is a notable exception. It is much more common, however, in musical situations where singers are learning by ear: gospel directors routinely gesture as they teach parts to their singers, and the singers join in with these gestures as a matter of course as part of the learning process. I have documented elsewhere a similar process in the form of social barbershop known as 'tag-singing'.[19]

Appropriation is where one person starts a thought, and another does not merely join in with it, but partly takes it over, actively participating in bringing it to completion. It is a multimodal form of synchrony and splits the linguistic and imagistic parts of a growth point between the participants in a conversation. This may involve a listener gesturing in synchrony with some else's speech, or a speaker verbalizing an idea that another expresses in gesture. In either case, there is a clear sense of people picking up each other's ideas and making them their own. This offers considerable insight into the interaction between conductor and

---

[17] Ibid., pp. 2–3.

[18] McNeill, *Gesture and Thought*, pp. 160–62.

[19] Liz Garnett, *The British Barbershopper: A Study in Socio-Musical Values* (Aldershot, 2005a), Chapter 7. This discussion also includes accounts of the way participants negotiate and maintain an F-formation as members join and leave the group.

choir, not least the nature of the vital connection between them that is celebrated throughout the practitioner literature. The choir participates in the conductor's growth point and completes their gestural image by giving voice to the structural-musical half of the thought. The conductor, meanwhile, responds to the choir; the shape of their gestures emerges in the context of the choir's sound emerging over time. Moreover, while McNeill needed to invent the term 'hyperphrase' to describe cooperatively created meaning shared between participants, this is the standard condition for ensemble musicianship. Conductor and choir are bound together into the same cognitive world by the unfolding musical work.

Inhabitance, then, is the means by which conductor and choir can know 'exactly what each other are thinking'.[20] This is not because of any magical form of telepathy (notwithstanding some of the claims of practitioners), but because the form of the social interaction promotes the sharing of thought processes. When Ehmann writes of the conductor holding the music 'in his hand', he captures the sense of the choirs' voices and the conductor's gesture working together in the shared space created between them.

Two further observations about the idea of inhabitance will help connect it back to the questions of musical identity explored in Part II. The first is the emphasis on being, rather than on representation. Just as McNeill sees expression as integral to the process of thought (rather than a second stage that conveys a thought's content), he sees thought as part of the speaker's state of being at the point of thinking. That is, the thought is not separate from the 'I' who thinks it, but is part of what makes that 'I' cognitively real to itself. Moreover, the 'material carriers' of that thought – words, gestures, and I would add notes and rhythms – are, McNeill claims, 'themselves thinking in one of its forms – not only expressions of thought, *but thought, i.e., cognitive being, itself*'.[21] So, when Neuen claims that 'the really successful conductor *becomes the music itself*', this is not simply a hyperbole to express the degree of metaphorical resemblance between gesture and sound, but a statement about identity and identification.[22] The musical flow forms the 'house of being' that conductor and choir inhabit together, and the process of musical thought inhabits both the psychological present and physical behaviours of all participants.

The second is the importance of social context. Communicative acts always need some kind of common ground, some set of shared expectations and norms, if they are to succeed at all. But McNeill points out that interactions also actually produce their own, local, common grounds through the behaviour of their participants.[23] This builds on Jürgen Streeck's idea of the audience as 'co-author' of a gesture: a speaker adapts their gestures not only to the general expectations and cultural

---

[20] John Bertalot, *How to be a Successful Choir Director* (Stowmarket, 2002), p. 119.

[21] McNeill, *Gesture and Thought*, p. 99, emphasis in the original.

[22] Donald Neuen, *Choral Concepts: A Text for Conductors* (Belmont, 2002), p. 204 (emphasis in the original).

[23] McNeill, 'Gesture, Gaze, and Ground', p. 14.

habits of their listeners, but also to the specific responses they receive in real time.[24] 'Even a seemingly monologic narration is social', suggests McNeill; 'one person does most of the talking but the performance is strongly geared to the listener, and this applies to gestures as well.'[25] The conductor is the archetypal monologic gesturer: they control the agenda of the rehearsal and everyone else's access to the shared communication space. But this does not mean that the ensemble has no role in creating the musical ideas as they unfold. Even if the singers take relatively little part in actively appropriating the conductor's ideas, they form both the general and the local social context in which those ideas are formed.

Conclusion

As Lakoff and Johnson helped show how conducting gestures become meaningful at the level of form, McNeill sheds light on how they work at a level of process. The concept of the growth point helps explain not only our observed category of emergent gesture, but also the time-worn distinction between time-beating and expressive gesture that has remained so intuitively meaningful to practitioners, but difficult nonetheless to describe. Gestures are so intimately evocative of musical shape, it turns out, because they are integral to the way that we think within music. They constitute the holistic, qualitative aspect of musical thought that exists in a permanently productive tension with the notatable, quantitative dimension that emerges in sequences of sounds.

The imagistic content of ideas that emerges in gesture, moreover, is common across the analytical dimensions of both music and language. The director can shift between speech, song and conducting, and the same gesture works in all three contexts. This helps us make the connection between the discursive and the practical dimensions of choral culture discussed in Part II. Not only do musical and extra-musical discourses interpenetrate in the formation of choral cultures, but linguistic and musical meanings interact as directors mould their singers' vocal and musical behaviours into stylistically appropriate forms. As the evolutionary metaphor discussed in Chapter 3 suggests, wider cultural norms set up the general common ground for this endeavour, while the rehearsal process that makes these changes establishes the local common ground through the shared world of inhabitance.

The notion of inhabitance also provides a mechanism for the creation and maintenance of gestural traditions. All conductors will have observed other conductors at work before they pick up the baton for the first time, usually from within a performing ensemble. So, all conductors have had the experience of

---

[24] Jürgen Streeck, 'Gesture as Communication I: Its Coordination with Gaze and Speech', *Communication Monographs*, 60 (1993): 275–99, and 'Gesture as Communication II: The Audience as Co-Author', *Research on Language and Social Interaction* 27/3 (1994): 239–67.

[25] McNeill, *Gesture and Thought*, p. 155.

thinking along with other conductors' musical thoughts, and joining in mentally and vocally or instrumentally with these thoughts as they emerge in gesture. Hence, they have a fund of experience of how to think musically that they draw upon to frame their own musical ideas in gesture: they will conduct as they have been conducted. Besides, inhabitance is not a one-way process; conductors are not the only contributors to the shared state of cognitive being created in the space between them and their performers. Rather, this collective space is a forum in which both the gestural styles of conductors and the performance styles of singers and instrumentalists feed each other, and maintain each other in more or less stable traditions.

All this happens at a level of more or less explicit musical intention. Much of what goes on in rehearsal may be a matter more of practical consciousness than self-conscious control of technique, that is, it occurs at a level whereby participants can operate competently, without necessarily being able to articulate fully what it is they are doing, or how they are doing it.[26] Even so, it takes place within a level that is understood in musical terms: the 'house of being' that the participants build together is constructed using shared stylistic norms and with the clear intention to make music together.

None of the processes discussed so far, however, explain the inadvertent effects a conductor may have on their choir. When a conductor stiffens their neck and the sound hardens, or when they frown and the intonation slips, this is not part of the shared understanding unfolding within the musical flow, and cannot be explained as either a metaphorical process or the product of a structure–imagery dialectic. It is nonetheless a well-documented phenomenon, and provides the focus for Part IV.

---

[26] Lucy Green adopts Anthony Giddens's notion of 'practical consciousness' to music in *Music on Deaf Ears: Musical Meaning, Ideology, Education* (Manchester, 1988).

PART IV
The Conductor–Choir Bond

The origins of this book lie in the early 1990s when I was a postgraduate student. I was already involved as a researcher in the theoretical questions of musical meaning and identity that have continued to inform my work up to and including this project. But it was in one of the choirs that I joined in search of a social life that I found the more directly practical question that has motivated and undergirded this study. Why was it that I ran out of breath singing phrases for our assistant conductor that I had sung with ease for our principal conductor the previous week?

The discussions of culture, identity and the process of semiosis in the previous sections of this book all rest on a more basic question: what is the mechanism by which a singer's voice is directly and unconsciously affected by how a director conducts? Analysing cultural discourses can show us how traditions are maintained and renewed, and theories of gesture and thought can show how musical ideas can be embodied meaningfully. But neither of these approaches can tell us how it is that different conductors from the same musical background directing the same singers can elicit such different results, even when all concerned intend that nothing should change.

Part IV proposes, therefore, to investigate the processes by which 'what they [the singers] see is what you [the conductor] get'.[1] It explores theories from nonverbal communication studies in an attempt not only to provide theoretical insight into this practical experience, but also to explore how the reflective practitioner can use these insights to make the bonds with their own choirs work more effectively. Part IV counterpoises Part II by focusing on the 'nature' end of the nature/nurture spectrum and discussing processes that underlie the shared human heritage of choral performers in any genre.

Chapter 12 starts by examining practitioners' accounts of the process and the few, fragmentary explanations they propose. It then turns to three theories of nonverbal communication that may help to explain this connection between conductor demeanour and choral sound: the 'chameleon effect' and its basis in mirror neurons, 'emotional contagion', and the 'equilibrium model' of interaction. The chapter shows how these theories present strong partial explanations for

---

[1] Rodney Eichenberger and Andre Thomas, *What They See is What You Get: Linking the Visual, the Aural, and the Kinetic to Promote Artistic Singing*, instructional video (Chapel Hill, 1994).

the correlation between gesture and sound, and that where they do not account for every part of an observed process, aspects of the more culturally mediated processes discussed in Chapter 10 can help fill the explanatory gap. While this chapter would appear to represent arrival at the extreme end of the nature/nurture spectrum after the journey through cultural construction in Parts II and III, this is the case only at the level of the processes it outlines. Their operation in practice is still strongly mediated by social norms and expectations within the group. This is significant, because it increases the use that directors can make of these ideas to improve their rehearsals.

Consequently, Chapter 13 considers some of the practical ramifications of these theories for the practitioner. These include the relationship between musical style, vocal production and the musical imagination; the links between morale, mood and vocal craft; and the dynamics of over-conducting. It will explore how aspects of the conductor's craft such as charisma, personality and influence that are often cast as unteachable ('you either have it or you don't') might at least be susceptible to analysis, and possibly also therefore to conscious development.

This explicitly practical final stage to the argument balances the theoretical cast to Part I. The question of what can we and should we do in rehearsal seems in some ways far removed from the questions we started with about how researchers model the conducting process and the implications these models have for research methods. But the links may be closer than they look: the sorts of social interactions discussed in Part IV are at best poorly described by the transmission model of conducting critiqued in Chapter 2. And since that critique was rooted significantly in what practitioners themselves considered important, it makes sense to return to the practitioner's world to test these theoretical constructs on the activities they work with on a day-to-day basis.

Chapter 12
Monkey See, Monkey Do

> If the sound coming back to you is not what you want, you must be willing to accept that the sound is a mirror image of your conducting.[1]

The choral conducting literature is unanimous in its belief that how a choir sounds is affected, if not determined, by the deportment and actions of its director. As Jordan's metaphor of a mirror suggests, the connection is understood as literal and unmediated: the relationship between an object and its reflection is both exact and simultaneous. Indeed, my discussions of individual directors' styles in Chapter 8 relied on this correlation to make sense of their gestures. The barbershop ballad style's perpetual extrusion of the sound from the ictus was understood in terms of the legato vocal delivery, while the punchier articulation of the gospel vocal style was linked with the 'flicking' quality of its directing gestures.

The correlation between conductor demeanour and choral sound goes beyond the meanings discussed in Part III, which circulate and are understood within the terms of the relevant musical style and its choral culture. Rather, it is a more elemental force that can work for good or for ill. At its best it can lead to that sense of creativity and nuance that Bertalot describes as conducting 'so that you hold your singers in the palms of your hands'; at its worst it can result in what Ehmann described as 'beat[ing] the music to pieces'.[2] In either case, it is seen as largely involuntary, and thus impervious to control by the will of either conductor or choir; the singers cannot choose to respond only to their director's artistic gestures, but will reveal both their strengths and their flaws in equal measure. 'What they see is what you get' is thus both a blessing and a curse.

This chapter seeks to understand the nature of this bond. It starts by examining accounts from the practitioner literature, and explores the terms in which they describe the phenomenon. It then presents three models from the nonverbal communication studies literature that can help explain the practitioners' experiences, and tests these against both the written accounts and examples from my rehearsal observations. This will set up Chapter 13's discussion of the practical ramifications of these theories: now that we understand what is happening, what should we, as directors, do about it?

---

[1] James Jordan, *Evoking Sound: Fundamentals of Choral Conducting and Rehearsing* (Chicago, 1996), p. 9.
[2] John Bertalot, *How to be a Successful Choir Director* (Stowmarket, 2002), p. 35; William Ehmann, *Choral Directing*, trans. G. Wiebe (Minneapolis, 1968), p. 110.

Practitioners' Accounts

John Hylton speaks for the choral profession when he states that 'the correct basic posture for a choral conductor is identical to what we seek to develop in singers.'[3] There is a certain intuitive common sense to this: of course a leader should set a good example. But other writers take this idea further, to suggest that, in acting on their own bodies, conductors act on the bodies and voices of their singers. For example, Roe claims that 'the expanded body of the director and his pull and vitality will help the singers keep their ribs expanded and breath under control'.[4] Bostock, meanwhile, advises: 'To facilitate the production of high notes, slightly down-tip the forehead; lifting the head achieves nothing.'[5] Reynolds develops this correlation between conductor action and choral result with the idea that 'his ideal should be to draw out from the choir the sort of sound he would like to make if only he could sing all the parts at once'.[6] The choir is the director's vocal proxy; not only is it his or her musical will that animates their voices, but it is his or her vocal technique that operates them.

A second theme in the literature focuses on the conductor's gestures as the potential source for the artistic or vocal issues they need to deal with. 'If a group is straining to sing loudly', asserts Roe, 'critically analyse the conducting techniques being used; it is likely that too much strength is being used.'[7] Woodgate, meanwhile, contends that 'a rigid beat is inclined to give the performance an inelastic, hard, bitty sound with no flow or curves'.[8] Jordan gives an extended example of this in a 10-page trouble-shooting guide that attributes a myriad of specific performance problems to specific faults in conducting technique.[9] This theme suggests that the sound is affected not only by those bodily actions that the conductor shares directly with the singers, but also by those actions that are unique to their role.

Most practitioners simply assert or assume this connection, with no real attempt to explain it. A few accounts, however, do sketch in some sort of underlying process to rationalize the connection between cause and effect. Decker and Kirk, for instance, imply that the modelling function operates at a conscious cognitive level, by prompting singers to recall elements of technique they have previously been taught:

> Choral sound is affected by a conductor's body language. When the conductor's shoulders are tense, the group may sound tight or pinched. When the conductor's

---

[3] John Hylton, *Comprehensive Choral Music Education* (Englewood Cliffs, 1995), p. 95.
[4] Paul Roe, *Choral Music Education*, 2nd edn (Englewood Cliffs, 1983), p. 231.
[5] Donald Bostock, *Choirmastery: A Practical Handbook* (London, 1966), p. 58.
[6] Gordon Reynolds, *The Choirmaster in Action* (London, 1972), p. 6.
[7] Roe, p. 236.
[8] Leslie Woodgate, *The Choral Conductor* (London, 1949), p. 27
[9] Jordan, pp. 288–97.

posture is not erect, it cannot remind the singers to maintain the posture necessary to support to vocal sound.[10]

Kaplan, meanwhile, sees the effectiveness of singers' control over good vocal habits as dependent on their degree of confidence in the conductor's musical leadership:

> If your arms are tense and strained, the singers will have a hard time following your motions and will eventually become tense themselves. They will therefore not breathe properly and their vocal passages will become constricted.
> If your preparatory beats are not secure, flowing, and relaxed, the chorus cannot breathe properly before starting to sing and is therefore susceptible to vocal trouble.
> If your beat pattern is not clear, some sections of the chorus will be confused by it and will sing hesitantly, another way of losing breath support.[11]

The causal explanations in even these accounts, though, are interspersed with a more basic assumption of a direct, unmediated connection. Decker and Kirk's postural reminder is presented as a subsidiary example to their general point about body language and sound rather than a complete explanation, while Kaplan does not elucidate why an insecure preparatory beat will remove the choir's ability to breathe properly.

Hence, there is considerable agreement among choral practitioners about the nature and experience of the gesture–sound connection. The reasons why it happens, and the means by which it happens, however, are unclear; most writers do not attempt to explain it, and those that do give only brief and partial accounts. Indeed, one could argue that, for practical purposes, an explanation is not necessary: providing one knows *that* the phenomenon occurs, one can use it to make good music. Like dowsing for water, lack of a rational explanation does not make it any less useful. On the other hand, more adequate explanations may prove useful both to practitioners who wish to exploit the phenomenon more effectively, and to instructors faced with sceptical students. One of the hardest things for novice conductors to learn is how many of the musical and vocal issues they want to correct are a direct result of their actions; understanding the mechanisms by which this happens may help them embrace the effect and start to use it to their advantage.

---

[10] Harold A. Decker and Colleen J. Kirk, *Choral Conducting: Focus on Communication* (Englewood Cliffs, 1988), p. 7.

[11] Abraham Kaplan, *Choral Conducting* (New York, 1985) p. 19.

The Chameleon Effect

The 'chameleon effect' is a phenomenon documented by Tanya Chartrand and John Bargh, in which people unconsciously synchronize bodily demeanour with one another in social situations.[12] Chartrand and Bargh report on a series of experiments designed to test the hypothesis that 'the perception of another's behavior (be it facial expression, body posture, mannerism, etc.) increases the tendency for the perceiver to behave in a similar manner, and that this is an entirely passive and nonconscious phenomenon'.[13] They argue that this is a cognitive process, distinct from affective forms of empathy, and contend that the degree to which individuals display the chameleon effect depends on the extent to which they are willing to take on the perspectives of others. Interestingly, they argue that it is the synchronization of behaviour that causes increased liking between interactants rather than vice versa, and they see the purpose of this instinctual behaviour as 'a kind of natural "social glue"'.[14]

The mechanism at the heart of the chameleon effect is the link between perception and behaviour. Chartrand and Bargh base their hypothesis on previous studies that posited shared coding systems for perceiving actions in others and performing those actions oneself. Their findings confirm this link by showing a direct causal effect between seeing an action and copying it: they show how the same person will pick up one mannerism during an interaction with one person, and a different mannerism in conversation with someone else. Further support for this position is also found in a series of neurological studies cited by Arnie Cox.[15] These studies of 'mirror neurons' showed, first, that the same pattern of neurological activity occurs in a monkey's brain when watching the experimenter perform a grasping action as when it performs the action itself, and second, that similar processes appear to occur in human cognition. Cox cites these studies to develop a theory of musical meaning as resulting from a covert imitation of a performer's motor activity in playing or singing; they are also clearly helpful in explaining why the perception of a behaviour makes overt participation in that behaviour more likely.

This theory certainly sheds light on the conductor–choir mirroring documented by practitioners. The mere fact of a singer's perception of the director's demeanour precipitates behaviour to match it. Bertalot's statement that 'if the conductor

---

[12] Tanya L. Chartrand and John A. Bargh, 'The Chameleon Effect: The Perception-Behaviour Link and Social Interaction,' *Journal of Personality and Social Psychology*, 76/6 (1999): 893–910.

[13] Ibid., p. 897.

[14] Ibid., p. 897.

[15] Arnie Cox, 'The Mimetic Hypothesis and Embodied Musical Meaning', *Musicae Scientiae*, 5/2, (2001): 195–212, and 'Hearing, Feeling, Grasping Gestures', in Anthony Gritten and Elaine King (eds), *Music and Gesture* (Aldershot, 2006).

frowns, they [the choristers] frown'[16] can thus be glossed as: 'to perceive the conductor frowning will engage the same neurons in the choristers as frowning themselves, and thus make it likely that they will do so too without even realizing it.' Moreover, the inadequacy of practitioners' explanations makes sense if the chameleon effect is 'automatic, unintended, and passive': involuntary behaviours remain largely opaque to conversant awareness in even the most reflective of individuals.[17]

As Lewis Gordon's diagram of intra-choir relationships cited in Chapter 2 suggests, the chameleon effect can take place between singers as well as between conductor and choir. Choirs often share a common body language, both in stance and movement. For example, in a church choir I visited, one soprano was swaying gently with the music, and dipping her head and torso at major cadence points; by the end of the rehearsal, four or five other singers were echoing these motions. Choir layout also has an impact on this perception–behaviour link: another choir I observed shared posture by row, with the front row sitting up and forward, the middle two leaning back in their chairs, and the back row tending to tilt to one side.

Chartrand and Bargh's discussion of perception is focused on the visual; they document how people join in with behaviours that they see. But there is no reason to suppose that aural perception does not also promote coordinated behaviour. While much choral craft is dedicated to encouraging singers to produce matched vocal qualities and word sounds, there are choirs that achieve this without any particular attention paid to it during rehearsal. I visited one large and well-established choir with a long-serving conductor, where there was no warm-up and the only specifically vocal issue addressed was finessing a high note in the tenors, but which sang with a real sense of unity, both musically and vocally. These singers were clearly accustomed to singing together.

The choral literature's debates over blend also resonate with Chartrand and Bargh's contention that cultural ethos can inflect the extent of behaviour-matching that takes place. Collectivistic societies, they suggest, are more 'likely to be characterized by a relatively intensified attentional and perceptual focus by individuals on the behaviour of others' than individualistic societies, and this ideal of interdependence will lead to more coordinated behaviours, and as a result, smoother social interactions.[18] Hence, one sees and hears more disparate behaviours in a choir with a soloistic ethos that values the individual vocal contributions of singers than in choirs that aim to smooth away what Henry Coward refers to as the 'disagreeable excesses of individuality'.[19] One of the first choir visits in which I became aware of a strongly shared body language was a lesbian/gay/bisexual choir with a strong social and political commitment to solidarity; the director also asked them to sound 'like one voice, like one choir without any individuals

---

[16] Bertalot, p. 35.
[17] Chartrand and Bargh, p. 894.
[18] Chartrand and Bargh, p. 907.
[19] Henry Coward, *Choral Technique and Interpretation* (London, 1914), p. 25.

sticking out'. Conversely, a chamber choir of trained singers showed some of the least matched postures of any of the choirs I visited. Each singer was clearly taking responsibility for his or her own voice, and the director encouraged this sense of artistic responsibility by asking them to 'lead a little more' on entries.

The chameleon effect can thus not only explain that immediate, involuntary connection between conductor and singers and within the choir itself, but it also sheds light on some of the processes discussed in Parts II and III. It strengthens the link between the metaphors embodied in a conductor's gestures and the singers' lived experience: the gestures are meaningful not simply because they recall certain bodily experiences of music, but because they engage the singer in reliving them. This in turn gives more insight into how inhabitance works. The process of alignment, of interpersonal synchrony, relies on a link between perception and behaviour; one can only join in with another's actions and associated thoughts if one has a means by which to participate in their point of view.

The operation of the chameleon effect between singers also provides a mechanism for the storage and propagation of a style's particular body language and vocal production, and thus plays a significant role in the enculturation of new choir members. The appropriate forms of behaviour are defined discursively, but it is through interaction within the group that singers learn to enact them. An interesting example of this process emerged in a large choral society I visited in which there was a strong unity of sound within each section, but quite different sounds between sections. It became apparent during the rehearsal that there were clearly understood stereotypes for both vocal sound and personalities of each section, as well as a degree of good-natured rivalry (particularly between tenors and basses), and these cultural expectations determined both the groupings for behaviour-matching and the resultant approaches to vocal production.

This theory, then, accounts well for both the shared ways of using the body and voice in particular choral traditions and for the direct impact a conductor's demeanour can have on a choir's sound. However, it only provides a full explanation at the level of those elements of conductor behaviour that are directly modelled by singers, such as stance and facial expression. That is, it is clear how conductors' posture, if mirrored by singers, would have a direct impact on their support and resonance; likewise the angle of their head, jaw position and use of facial muscles will all affect the tone quality of their own voice, and, if mirrored, that of their singers. But it less clear how the quality of their downbeat, for example, which will probably not be directly mimicked by the singers, can affect their sound.

One explanation may be that how a conductor uses his or her arms and hands is an integral part of his or her entire demeanour, and thus the qualities of gestures not copied by singers would be consistent with postural qualities that are. For instance, a vigorous beat may cause clavicular breathing in the singers by means of the involvement of the conductor's shoulders in their gesture. Davis proposes this kind of mechanism in his discussion of muscular tension:

> I am convinced that this matter of relaxation is the prime factor in explaining why two different conductors can draw a substantially differing tone quality from the same orchestra or choir employing the same instrumentalists and voices. Tension in a conductor communicates and transfers itself with remarkable rapidity to players and singers, who themselves then become tense, and persons with tense muscles in arms, fingers, lips or throats will produce a less satisfactory sound than those who are relaxed.[20]

Another, less direct, explanation is intimated by Jordan's statement that:

> The gesture of the vocal conductor must at all times reflect the movement of air through the vocal mechanism. Suddenly angular patterns and subdivided rebounds adversely affect the flow of the air and then directly affect the intensity and color of the tone.[21]

This appears to posit a kind of metaphoric mapping across different parts of the body. The hands and arms are mapped onto the phonating larynx, so the musical qualities of gesture emerge as the tonal qualities of the voice. We see this kind of modelling as an explicit part of choral training: the Sistine wrist is used routinely to model both the high soft palate that is a key contributor to the cathedral/collegiate sound, and the long neck with slightly tipped-forward head used to help the placement of high notes. But this kind of mapping also seems to occur outside of explicitly pedagogical contexts, within the general flow of the music. During several rehearsal observations I saw conductors cock their wrists back as they moved into faster tempi, and at the same time lift their chins to create a more acute angle at the back of the neck, suggesting an implicit equivalence between the two joints. Clearly in these cases the resultant change in tone can be attributed to the singers' changing their head positions in tandem with the conductors' rather than to the change in hand position per se. But it does show that directors experience this kind of parallelism across their bodies at an intuitive level, and suggests that choral singers will probably share this understanding as part of their embodied knowledge. Whether this mapping operates within the metaphoric meanings of a musical culture or as part of a more fundamental evolutionary connection between hand and voice is as yet unclear.[22] Nonetheless, Jordan's statement that 'the shape of the hands directly influences the color of the vowel being produced by the choir' certainly resonates with the contrast, on one hand, between the cathedral

---

[20] Leonard Davis, *Practical Guidelines for Orchestral & Choral Conducting: For Those Wishing to Build on their Existing Experience rather than for Complete Beginners* (London, n.d.), p. 6.

[21] Jordan, p. 114.

[22] David McNeill suggests that gestures are so intimately linked with voice because they played a primary role in the development of language; see *Gesture and Thought* (Chicago, 2005), Chapter 8.

tradition's gestural world of the Sistine wrist and the long-fingered, open hands of the Gospel director, and, on the other, the two traditions' very different ideas as to what shape a wide-open mouth should take.[23]

Emotional Contagion

The chameleon effect is a cognitive process, not an emotional one, but it is a prerequisite for a second interpersonal process that can occur in rehearsal, that of emotional contagion. Elaine Hatfield, John Cacioppo and Richard Rapson argue that people's tendency to 'mimic and synchronize [one another's] facial expressions, vocalizations and postures' is the first stage of the process by which they pick up one another's emotions, and, like Chartrand and Bargh, they see this process as largely automatic and uncontrollable.[24]

The second stage of emotional contagion rests on the 'facial feedback hypothesis', which suggests the visible physical manifestations of emotion are not simply the 'results' of internal 'causes', but an integral part of the experience of emotion, and can therefore help induce the internal experience.[25] That is, if one unintentionally assumes the physical disposition of one's interlocutor in conversation, one is liable to experience an emotional state much like that which led them to adopt that posture and expression. Hatfield et al. argue that the experience of felt emotion is a complex of 'conscious awareness; facial, vocal, and postural expression; neurophysiological and autonomic nervous system activity; and instrumental behaviours', and that the causal relationships between these components are context-dependent rather than linear.[26] As a result, it is possible for any one aspect of an emotional experience to trigger the others.

This process has much in common with that of inhabitance. Not only is it a means by which people can align their interior state with one another, but it also relies on the interrelation of expression and experience. That is, it is possible to share another's thought by mimicking their gesture because that gesture is not simply a result of the thought, but part of the act of thinking. In the same way, it is possible to share someone's emotional state by joining in with their facial expression or vocal tone because those perceptible behaviours are part of the emotion itself, not simply the means to signal it to others.

Emotional contagion, then, is a process that is predicated on the synchronization of bodily behaviours; it is possible for the chameleon effect to operate without emotional contagion taking place, whereas the converse is not true. There are

---

[23] Jordan, p. 63.

[24] Elaine Hatfield, John T. Cacioppo and Richard L. Rapson, *Emotional Contagion* (Cambridge, 1994).

[25] See also Paul Ekman, 'Should we call it Expression or Communication?', *Innovations in Social Science Research*, 10/4 (1997): 333–44.

[26] Hatfield, Cacioppo and Rapson, p. 4.

also factors that make it more or less likely to occur. These include individual personality, prevailing affective state and social values and contexts. Hence, extraverts are identified as not only more likely to spread emotional contagion than introverts, but also to be more susceptible to it. Those in positions of relative power are more likely to infect others emotionally, so the conductor is far more likely to 'infect' the choir with their mood than vice versa. The degree to which people like or dislike each other affects how open they are to such infection, as does their general mood: happy people pick up emotions more easily than the angry or depressed, since they will generally be more willing to engage in social interaction.

Practitioner accounts dwell less on emotional contagion than the substrate of unconscious mimicry from which it arises, but there is evidence that it is a common enough experience. Roe refers to an ensemble's 'involuntary emotional responses' to its conductor, for instance, while Woodgate warns that 'the slightest trace of self-consciousness or uncertainty conveys itself like an electric current and your performers will be uncertain as to what you wish them to do'.[27] References to 'rapport' also suggest a form of connection that is at least partly affective.[28] Coward adopts the language of contagion when he states that the conductor's zeal 'must infect his followers'.[29]

One notable factor in the experience of emotions is that they are immediately classified as positive or negative by the person who feels them, who will consequently experience the stimulus that provoked the emotion as inherently attractive or repellent.[30] This kind of polarized response was particularly evident in my choir visits in relation to a choir's level of confidence. More than one director commented about their choir's anxiety when numbers were down due to illness, or simply that a few 'key' voices were missing. 'Amazing how having other people around you bolsters you up', is how one conductor put it. The problem in these cases was not merely the absence of the self-assured behaviours that the conductor wanted the others to match, but the remaining singers' affective response, which was to retreat even more into themselves. Conversely, choirs that displayed a positive emotional state – evidenced particularly through laughter – also seemed to have no problem in singing out confidently. These observations pertain primarily to amateur choirs, of course, since professional ensembles by definition have more confident singers and less time for joking in rehearsal. But similar tendencies can also be seen in expert groups, if in milder forms. Trained singers also recoil when anxious, though they maintain better control over their voices than the untrained, and even the most intensive rehearsal will include a moment or two of laughter if its participants are in good spirits.

---

[27] Roe, p. 273; Woodgate, *The Choral Conductor*, p. 9.
[28] Samuel Adler, *Choral Conducting: An Anthology* (Fort Worth, 1971), p. 8; Robert L. Garretson, *Conducting Choral Music* (Boston, MA, 1970), p. 3.
[29] Coward, p. 251.
[30] Hatfield, Cacioppo and Rapson, p. 3.

The theory of emotional contagion thus suggests a somewhat different mechanism by which a choir may reflect its conductor from that implied by the chameleon effect. The chameleon effect saw the singers' direct matching of the conductor's physical behaviour as providing the framework in which they operated their vocal mechanisms, whereas here the voices' sound is tempered by the emotional states triggered by this coordination. As Roe describes the process, 'Joyous enthusiasm tends to expand the body. Rouse the students to sing vigorously and with freedom.'[31] This is a more mediated process, and has the potential to shape rehearsal experience over longer spans of time than the micromomentary responses of the chameleon effect. While the processes by which emotional contagion occurs are largely unconscious, the experience of an emotional state is accessible to conscious awareness – one can recognize a feeling and give a name to it – and thus may become self-reinforcing. Likewise, the social situation of the choir may allow a mood to be perpetuated and amplified between the members of the group. So, a heavy downbeat might cause a glottal attack, but the director's emotional reaction to that momentary effect can set the tone for the rest of the rehearsal.

The Intimacy Equilibrium Model

These two theories account well for the practitioners' accounts of the isomorphism between conductor motion and choral sound, and for the dynamics of group morale. However, they paint a picture of an ideal world where conductor and singers enjoy a perfect mutual understanding, which does not always match the experience of real musicians in rehearsal. For however frustrating it is to hear the flaws in one's conducting technique shining through in the choir's sound, it is more frustrating still to fail to get any response at all. The final model to be explored in this chapter shows that the connection between conductor and singers is a dynamic form of social contact that needs to be actively maintained if it is to function. We saw some of the spatial and orientational factors involved in Chapter 11's discussion of the F-formation; to understand how other forms of social behaviour interact with this, we turn to the Intimacy Equilibrium Model.

This theory describes how people manage social intimacy, that is, the degree of personal 'closeness' they experience with others in social situations. It was first proposed by Michael Argyle and Janet Dean in 1965, and this paper remains a foundational point of reference for all later studies in the area, not least because subsequent researchers have reliably been able to replicate its results.[32] Their basic finding was that people adjust different aspects of their nonverbal behaviour – in this case, their gaze and physical proximity – so as to maintain a stable level of social intimacy. So, at wider distances people looked at one another more

---

[31] Roe, p. 76.

[32] Michael Argyle and Janet Dean, 'Eye Contact, Distance and Affiliation', *Sociometry*, 28 (1965): 289–304.

frequently and for longer than at closer distances. The two channels of social contact showed a clear inverse relationship; as one increased, the other decreased to keep the overall level of intimacy in equilibrium.

Later studies have inflected these findings with ideas of comfort or appropriateness. When people are generally feeling comfortable with the level of intimacy, they display reciprocal behaviours – that is, the kinds of coordinated actions discussed above.[33] Compensatory behaviour of the types proposed by Argyle and Dean comes into play when people feel either that their personal space has been invaded, or that they are inappropriately socially distant. People experience considerable stress, moreover, should the social imbalance become so great that it can no longer be managed by this dynamic process of mutual adjustment.[34] Later studies have also added to the catalogue of social behaviours that are used in maintaining this equilibrium; as well as proximity and gaze, smiling, topic intimacy (that is, amount of personal information exchanged) and tone and/or volume of voice are also used.[35]

We have already seen how conductors manage the physical distance between themselves and their singers according to what proportion of the choir they are addressing. They will often move in towards the choir when they talk to a single section or small group of individuals, intuitively matching a smaller physical distance to the more intimate temporary social grouping. And when this physical movement is inhibited, such as by the use of a podium, conductors adjust their gaze behaviour to compensate, just as Argyle and Dean's findings would predict. Notice how Halsey makes much more sustained eye contact when he rehearses in sections than when he works with the choir as a whole, such as his work with the altos and basses on the articulation of the phrase 'that isn't known' about two-thirds of the way through clip 4.1.

This model also helps to explain what happens when a choir appears to respond only weakly to a conductor's direction. Given the fixed nature of most choirs' rehearsal layouts, singers have a reduced number of behaviours with which to manage their comfort level in their interactions with the conductor. The primary determinant of social intimacy, that of physical closeness, is not under their control once the rehearsal is under way, although I have seen conductors exhorting their choirs to fill up the seats further forward in their rehearsal halls, suggesting that singers take advantage of such spatial choice as is available to them. Singers do retain control of their gaze behaviour, facial expressions and voices, however. So, if they feel that their conductor's behaviour is intrusive, they may look down at the copies more, or sing with a more neutral facial expression, or simply sing more quietly.

---

[33] Hatfield, Cacioppo and Rapson, p. 201.

[34] John R. Aiello and Donna E. Thompson, 'When Compensation Fails: Mediating Effects of Sex and Locus of Control at Extended Interaction Distances', *Basic and Applied Social Psychology*, 1/1 (1980): 65–82.

[35] Jinni Harrigan, Robert Rosenthal and Klaus R. Scherer, *The New Handbook of Methods in Nonverbal Behavior Research* (Oxford, 2005), p. 175.

My rehearsal observations suggest that this interpersonal dynamic can have a significant effect on a choir's sound. I have watched rehearsals in which an energetic and spirited conductor has worked tirelessly to get more response from singers who continue to sit back in their chairs and hold their copies low; repeated exhortations to sit up and sing out achieve momentary, but never lasting, results. The sound remains somewhat muted for the size of choir. (I should add that I have also conducted rehearsals like this. In describing these rehearsals I intend no criticism, but simply seek to understand an issue that many directors have experienced.) My initial observation was that the choirs' vocal sound in these cases matched their own body language rather than their conductors', and I attributed the relative lack of resonance to the lack of support that comes from a slumped sitting position. However, further observations produced examples where singers who slumped back in their chairs produced sounds that had a real focus and vitality, where one could hear bodily engagement with the music even if one could not see it. While posture is certainly an important factor in voice production, it clearly did not fully account for the difference in resonance between these choirs.

One example was particularly striking for the combination of a full, vigorous sound with bodily behaviours that, seen in isolation, would look rather different from commonly accepted good practice. Both singers and conductor sat with rounded backs; the conductor was sparing with his eye contact, and even more sparing with his smiles. Nonetheless, the chameleon effect was working exceptionally well: his beat was minimal, but every slight change in it was audible in the voices. The emotional tone of the rehearsal, while not jolly, was good-natured and purposeful; the conductor never showed any impatience with the singers, but methodically worked through the issues he wanted to address until he was satisfied with the result.

This, then, was a choir that had found a comfortable equilibrium in which it could engage in closely coordinated reciprocal behaviours. The choirs with over-energetic conductors, by contrast, were using compensatory behaviours, reducing their level of engagement in proportion to the conductor's vigour. These behaviours included the kinds of nonverbal cues that social psychologists have documented – reduction of eye contact, less frequent smiles, physical withdrawal – and these will have had a negative impact on both vocal production and conductor-choir communication. However, I would suggest on the basis of my observations that the reduction in vocal resonance and projection that accompanies these behaviours is not merely the result of the postural changes they entail, but is a distinct compensatory strategy in its own right.

Conclusion

This chapter balances Part II's account of choral practice as a cultural construct by examining the ways it relies on involuntary behaviours that are part of our heritage as a social species. The conductor–choir bond relies on the chameleon effect both at the cognitive level of response to gesture and at the emotional level of empathy and group dynamic. The intimacy equilibrium model, meanwhile, helps us understand what is going on when this bond appears to break down.

These behaviours do not simply underlie the cultural processes, however; they also interact with them. Social norms, power relationships and personality all inflect the degree to which people experience both behavioural and emotional synchrony. Hence, the director has the greatest power to influence the group by virtue of the established balance of power, while the matching of vocal production within an ensemble is mediated by cultural expectations for particular voice parts. Even more intriguingly, the chameleon effect appears to be mediated by a form of metaphoric mapping between different parts of the body: the perception–behaviour link operates between the conductor's hands and various parts of the singer's vocal mechanism.

And it is at this intersection between nature and nurture where the reflective practitioner can intervene to shape the behaviours and beliefs of the singers they work with. With an understanding of how cultural norms frame involuntary responses, and how those responses in turn become the means to propagate the cultural norms, it is possible make conscious choices about which practices one wishes to foster and which to let die out. Accordingly, Chapter 13 works through a number of issues faced by conductors in a range of idioms to show how these theories can inform practical decisions.

Chapter 13
Making Use of the Conductor–Choir Bond

> One of your major tasks as a choral conductor, especially with a non-professional chorus, is to cause that chorus to sing well.[1]

It is all very well to understand the mechanisms that create the conductor–choir connection, but it is also important to explore their practical as well as their theoretical implications. After all, this book's theoretical questions had their origins in practical problems. In this penultimate chapter I am consequently joining the overtly pedagogical ranks of practitioner-writers to work through some of the ways that the theories in Chapter 12 have helped me interpret material from rehearsal observations, and have thereby informed my work as a director and choral educator. It is debatable whether any writing about music is ever entirely theoretical. But critical musicology's commitment to investigating real-world problems and ethnography's obligations to dialogue with its research subjects both suggest that the link back to praxis should be made explicitly. Accordingly, here are some of the ways in which understanding the conductor–choir bond have helped me enable choirs to sing well.

Style and Voice

If we combine our insights into the way that musical meanings draw on socially shared bodily experiences and the way that a choir's vocal production will be affected by their conductor's posture, we can see how the conductor's body language is central to musical style not only at the level of delivery, but also of choral sound. If we want our choirs to sing with a stylistically appropriate vocal production, that is, we need to learn stylistically appropriate ways of using our own bodies.

At one level, this simply restates the practitioner literature's consensus that the conductor should 'look like the music' and that 'what they see is what you get'. However, the context of early-twenty-first-century choral culture makes this both less simple and more important than it first appears. First, there is the general move towards 'authentic' performance; it is no longer considered acceptable to develop a characteristic choral sound and use it for all music. Moreover, the internationalized choral culture discussed in Chapter 5 is increasingly bringing together choirs working in different genres, who are consequently engaging more with each

---

[1] Abraham Kaplan, *Choral Conducting* (New York, 1985), p. 15.

other's repertoires. It is reasonably common at choral festivals, for example, to see the same choir performing in several different classes as different 'types' of choir, especially if they have travelled a significant distance to participate. The winner of the male voice choir class at the 2007 Sligo International Choral Festival, for instance, was also the runner-up in the barbershop and gospel classes.

But, as we saw in Part II, the extension of the idea of stylistically appropriate voice production to styles outside the classical canon has been somewhat problematic, not least because 'correct' choral singing has been defined in part in contradistinction to popular styles. Even within the classical tradition there is a conflict between the recognition of the vocal habits of other styles and one's own local ideas of good practice. Hylton, for instance, states on the subject of the Renaissance style that:

> A perfectly straight, vibrato-less tone is not desirable for any music. Choirs should have the opportunity, however, to listen to performances or recordings by contemporary choirs of men and boys, to hear the tone quality. Then, within the bounds of good vocal production, that sound may be emulated.[2]

This comment suggests that Hylton experiences the imperative to embrace a performance style appropriate to the repertoire as being in direct opposition with his idea of good vocal practice, even when the concept of this historical-stylistic approach is based in the contemporary practices of modern ensembles.

We can understand this reluctance to engage with certain other styles when we consider how our bodily and imaginative experience of music in performance is integrally related with how we experience our sense of self. Chapter 11's exploration of inhabitance showed us that when ensembles share growth points, when they participate in generating musical ideas together, they share not only musical ideas, but also a way of being in the world. To embrace an unfamiliar style with its associated bodily habits may be authentic to the music's origin, but may also feel deeply inauthentic to that performer's sense of musical identity; this is clearly the case in Hylton's problematic relationship with a 'white' tone approach to early music. Furthermore, as we have seen, the boundaries of acceptable vocal and musical behaviours within a style are often constructed in discourse not only with reference to other types of music, but also to social stereotypes drawn from wider culture. It is not surprising, therefore, that many choirs choose – whether consciously or just by default – to perform 'foreign' repertoire in their 'home' style.[3]

---

[2] John Hylton, *Comprehensive Choral Music Education* (Englewood Cliffs, 1995), p. 166.

[3] These decisions, moreover, are not simply about musical correctness, but interact with other areas of cultural politics. Kristina Boerger, for instance, states that 'specific issues of power and privilege are always present whenever White musicians perform Black music in racist America'. ('Whose Music is it Anyway? Black Vocal Ensemble Traditions and

However, my rehearsal observations suggest that our identities in music are not as fixed as this would imply, and that the ideal of stylistic flexibility is not only desirable but, to a considerable degree, attainable. Two case studies will be instructive in showing how directors can help their choirs connect meaningfully to new styles.

The first is of a classical choral society rehearsing a somewhat jazzy arrangement of a Christmas song. The choir was in many ways typical of the amateur choral societies I have visited: around 60 strong, with women significantly outnumbering men, mostly older (50s–70s), with a smattering of 20 to 40-year-olds, and all white. Their first attempt at singing this piece was very staccato – as again is typical of many classical SATB choirs singing 'jazz'. The conductor told them this was not what he wanted, and demonstrated how to sing it; this was still very front-loaded in its attack-decay envelope, but much more connected, and with a sense of collecting the energy slightly before the beat. The demonstration did relatively little to elicit the result he wanted, however, and the choir still responded with a staccato performance. The conductor returned to this piece after a break, and was now much more articulate about the style he sought. He pointed out the performance direction on the score of 'bright swing', linked this to the idea of big band jazz, and told them they needed to feel the syncopations rather than count them. Then when they attempted the piece again, his body language shifted to make similar genre references – he bent one knee slightly to tilt the hips, tilted his head and twisted his body slightly, and clicked his fingers using his thumb and ring finger. This strategy was much more successful in eliciting a style akin to that which he had demonstrated earlier, and also elicited a freer and more supported vocal quality from the singers.

What is interesting about this incident is that the direct demonstration of the musical effect required did not by itself produce the desired result, but a combination of verbal cues that indexed the singers' wider musical imaginations and a style of body language that likewise evoked that stylistic world produced a result much like the earlier demonstration. The choir needed the constellation of associations that made up the cultural category of style in order to be able perceive – and thus imitate – the salient points of the demonstration. Possibly even more interesting is the way that the singers performed more convincingly at a purely vocal level when they were more imaginatively engaged with the musical content. Authenticity to style helped them achieve authenticity to self.

The second case study is of a gospel director working with a group of around 25 young singers that included some who were familiar with the style and others whose only previous experience was in classical choirs. As Brooks does on the DVD, the director required the singers to maintain the sideways step-and-sway as integral to the flow of the music, and then within this used body language appropriate to the individual rhythmic feel of each song to teach the style. A particularly interesting

---

the Feminist Choral Movement: Performance Practice as Politics' (MusAD Dissertation, University of Illinois, 2000), p. 3.)

example was in a reggae-style song. His teaching combined several disparate elements: technical instructions about how to create the rhythmic accents from the diaphragm, verbal metaphors ('it's a bit too ballerina; it needs more of the energy of the street dance') and enrolling the singers into the body language of the piece by modelling the kind of head and shoulder movements he wanted them to use. What was striking here was the way that, as the singers became more fluent in the music's bodily world, they started to pick up aspects of style which he had not explicitly mentioned. For instance, they started to adopt the slightly forward-placed jaw and flat tongue with which he was shaping the words, and with them the characteristically Caribbean vowel sounds that resulted.

These examples suggest that, whether one is inculcating singers into a genre that is entirely new to them or simply varying a choir's stylistic diet, the chameleon effect works at its best when the behaviours a conductor models are part of an overall characterization that engages wider cultural references and does not simply focus on individual stylistic elements. Not only does the richer portrayal of the style help the singers notice – and thus to enact – the pertinent aspects of tone and delivery, but they appear to identify more willingly and wholeheartedly with a style if they can experience it as an integrated, realistic whole. It should be added that this kind of physical and imaginative relationship with style also makes for much more efficient rehearsing. One practitioner I spoke to likened 'technical, left-brain coaching' to 'trying to kill an elephant by clogging up all of his pores', whereas, as our second case study showed, a holistic characterization can inveigle a choir into dealing with multiple technical issues simultaneously and without specific instruction.

Aural Feedback

In a competition in late 2007, I adjudicated a women's choir that had a distinctive and strangely consistent relationship between its sound and its conductor's movements. It was a reasonably competent amateur group: it was not going to win any big prizes, but it sang well enough to allow an audience to feel confident in its performance. However, every time its conductor used one particular gesture, usually deployed at moments of relative emotional intensity, the tuning lost its clarity; the choir still sang the right notes, but they lost the unity within and between sections that gave their prevailing sound its integrity. The gesture itself involved a stroking upwards of the right hand, accompanied by a slight lift in the shoulder and a general shifting of the weight forwards and to the right. The correlation between motion and sound was so dependable that after a while it was possible to predict the quality of tuning by watching the conductor's left heel: as it lifted, the sound lost focus; as it settled back onto the floor, the sound settled too.

This is a clear case where the chameleon effect can work to a choir's disadvantage. The conductor clearly enjoyed a close and responsive rapport with her singers, but this meant that she could undo with a gesture in performance much of the good work on blend she had done in rehearsal. I would hypothesize that it was not the hand movement itself, but the bodily motion behind it that caused the trouble; the change in balance and slight twisting of the body could be enough, even if only covertly mirrored by her singers, to disrupt their otherwise solid vocal support. And the irony is that it was when she most wanted to enrich their sound that she undermined it with this movement.

This kind of problem, however, carries within itself the seeds of its own solution. The sound a choir makes gives a continuous real-time feedback mechanism to report on the effectiveness of a conductor's technique. Indeed, whatever one's stylistic norms in terms of gestural vocabulary or bodily disposition, a technical flaw in one's conducting technique can be defined as anything that induces one's choir to sing less well than they might do otherwise. Effective conductors are those who can use this aural feedback to guide their adjustments to posture and gesture, letting the desired musical outcome shape their actions. Jordan's trouble-shooting guide to conductor gesture and choral sound may be useful as a starting-point, but the real value to conductors lies in developing the skills that make it possible to compile such a list for themselves.

This use of the chameleon effect points back to practitioners' preference for an interactive rather than transmission model of conducting. Careful listening is not merely the means by which to police the vocal and musical behaviours of the singers, but also, ideally, the context in which the conductor's own movements are formed. This in turn helps us understand how some conductors who look as if they have exemplary technique can produce less impressive results than others whom one would not cite as a model of good practice: it is the quality of attention they pay to their singers that makes the biggest difference. This is not to deny the value of conventional gestures per se; as we saw in Chapter 10, standard conducting patterns encode a rich complex of potential musical meanings and thus provide an expressively flexible resource to the conductor as well an accepted lingua franca. But it does suggest that the choral specialist's idiosyncrasies do not necessarily originate in individual egotism or perverseness as the writers who deride them suggest, but evolve in a symbiotic relationship with a choir's developing sound.

Morale

> I don't know how I look to you. Probably as worried as you look to me, but I'm sure if you looked less worried it would do the singing no end of good.

These words were spoken by the director of a small liturgical choir who, like many who serve their communities in this capacity, felt under-confident in the role, and had only undertaken it to save the choir from disbanding. In this moment of anxiety, though, she produced a succinct and insightful account of the relationship between the chameleon effect, emotional contagion, choir morale and choral sound.

It is widely accepted within the practitioner literature that good morale produces better singing, that 'the emotional state of the singer affects the sound of the voice'.[4] And the theory of emotional contagion explains how a mood can spread between singers, and from conductor to choir. There is an easy conclusion to draw here: a conductor who can remain positive even when progress seems slow will solve their rehearsal problems faster than one who shares their frustration with the choir. Berating a choir for singing diffidently is particularly counter-productive.

But we can develop this point further to allow us both greater insight into our choir's emotional state and more capacity to influence it. First, as with the responses to our gestures, we have an ongoing mechanism to monitor our choir's mood in the form of their sound. The knowledge that we can infect our choir with either positive or negative emotions does little good unless we take heed of the effect we are having. Moreover, we have longer to diagnose and act upon our choirs' responses to our emotional state than the fleeting effects of individual gestures, since emotional state involves ongoing visceral reactions as well as behavioural mimicry. If the sound we hear is not what we want, we can ask ourselves not only what effect our posture and gesture is having, but also what the choir needs to make it happy.

This interaction between conductor and choir is not the only feedback loop involved in choral morale, however. Consider the following assertion by Hill, Parfitt and Ash:

> Singing without vibrato can only be achieved by decreasing activity in the muscles involved in the working of the larynx and reducing the energy of the breath. It is clear that such singing also demands a diminished emotional response in the singer, since, willy-nilly, our emotions are expressed through our voices.[5]

I am less interested here in the arguably style-specific beliefs about the expressive meaning of vibrato than in their interestingly recursive view of the relationship between singing voice and emotional expression. The argument is built on the assumption that vibrato is the audible trace that emotional engagement leaves on the voice, that is, that vibrato is a consequence, at least in part, of emotional response. It argues, however, that limiting the degree to which emotion is permitted to be audible will perforce limit the degree to which emotion will be experienced. It promotes, that is, an aural parallel to the 'facial feedback hypothesis', suggesting that the sound of a singer's voice does not merely reflect their emotional state, but can also influence it. Other styles might locate emotional engagement in different elements of vocal sound (barbershop, for instance, would underplay vibrato and

---

[4] David Hill, Hilary Parfitt and Elizabeth Ash, *Giving Voice: A Handbook for Choir Directors and Trainers* (Rattlesden, 1995), p. 26.

[5] Ibid., p. 25.

listen more for 'ring' in the voice), but the principle of this circular relationship between voice and emotion can nonetheless transfer between idioms.

The 'vocal feedback hypothesis', if we may call it that, can strengthen our relationship with our choir's well-being. That is, if the state of singers' vocal production influences as well as reveals their interior state, then a conductor who enables them to sing well is thereby also facilitating the experience of a positive emotional state. We can address the choir's needs through the same medium as we diagnose them, and the use we make of aural feedback to hone our directing skills can also have a positive effect on the choir's morale.

These insights shed light in turn on two issues that repeatedly came up in conversations with both conductors and choir members during my rehearsal visits. The first is the question often raised in amateur groups about the relative importance of musical achievement versus having a good time. People who participate in choirs as a form of leisure can experience an aspiration to musical excellence as a threat to their social life: over-ambitious conductors, they say, take things too seriously and consequently spoil the fun. But an understanding of the interactive connection between voice and emotional state would suggest that the problem here is not so much the musical goal but its pursuit without due regard for the morale of the singers. These conflicts only seem to arise in choirs whose rate of progress is relatively slow compared to the earnestness with which they pursue it. I have yet to visit a genuinely high-achieving choir in which the singers did not feel good about themselves and what they were doing, or in which anyone expressed a wish for more time to chat during the rehearsal.

The second issue is the question of the tyrannical conductor who nonetheless commands a passionate loyalty. Western art music's folklore abounds with anecdotes of conductors whose dictatorial demeanour was tolerated – or even celebrated – because of the musical genius of their performances. Can the sense of achievement afforded by participating in a glorious performance compensate for the damage to the self inflicted by an overbearing manner? Can we assume that aesthetic accomplishment indicates the performers' full-hearted acceptance of the ensemble's moral order? Indeed, less experienced directors may often draw on these examples to justify scolding their singers: if it is good enough for Toscanini, they claim, it is good enough for me. I would suggest, however, that performers respond positively to such expert directors despite a domineering manner rather than because of it, since the vocal and musical results they are able to achieve by their conducting skills outweigh the effects of their social demeanour. Personal rudeness may fade into relative insignificance if singers feel empowered to sing well. If, however, one has yet to learn how to use the chameleon effect to produce a thrilling sound by imaginative gesture alone, one may need to maintain morale using old-fashioned methods such as politeness and good humour.

Over-Conducting

> The conductor of an amateur choral society ... has to coax his performers into giving their best, and that often means bullying, pleading, over-reacting and entreating. ... You will find it necessary as a conductor ... to demonstrate in an exaggerated way exactly what is wanted; most choirs will only respond in a small way to a call for exaggerated effects.[6]

> A former conductor of King's College Choir, Cambridge, Dr Boris Ord ... used to conduct his choir by resting his hands on the music desk alongside his boys, and beating time with one finger of each hand – looking at the senior bass on the other side of the choir, who was looking at him and conducting in the same way. The concentration of those two conductors and all their singers was electric. The choir had to concentrate because the conductors used such small gestures and because the self-discipline of the choir was so strong.[7]

Most conductors at some point in their career have had the experience of working with a group that did not seem to respond, and beating ever more vigorously in an attempt to chivvy them to life. Some go on to spend their lives giving exaggerated pantomimes of their musical wishes, as Ronald Corp presents the lot of the amateur choir's director. Others learn, like Dr Ord, to command attention with the most minimal movements.[8]

The tendency to over-conduct is a particular case of the conductor upsetting the intimacy equilibrium with their choir. It is the gestural equivalent of speaking louder when someone does not understand. Indeed, the gestures themselves tap into several of the bodily metaphors for loudness we saw in Chapter 10: they get larger, they involve the upper arms and shoulders, they entail extra muscular effort, and they may be repeated for emphasis. We identify over-conducting by two factors: first, the gestures are 'louder' than the resultant sound from the choir, and second, they are also 'louder' than the music requires at that moment. That is, they are both ineffective and inappropriate.

It is the initial ineffectiveness that pulls the conductor into the cycle of overstated gesture; failing to get a response, they exaggerate to make the point. But it is the inappropriateness that prompts the choir into compensatory behaviour. Strong gestures make sense in musically robust passages, but vehemence as a means to attract attention tends to prompt social withdrawal. There is a particularly vicious cycle with gaze behaviour. A primary way to compensate for overly intrusive social

---

[6] Ronald Corp, *The Choral Singer's Companion* (London, 1987), pp. 24, 26.

[7] John Bertalot, *How to Be a Successful Choir Director* (Stowmarket, 2002), p. 34.

[8] It might be suggested that this represents the difference in working with amateur and professional singers. I would suggest, however, that the causal chain works in the other direction: one only gets the opportunity to work with the best choirs if one learns not to over-conduct.

behaviour is to reduce eye contact, so a conductor who beats more vigorously at a choir that is not watching enough simply compounds the problem.

Over-conducting is thus a technical, a musical and an interpersonal issue. The disjunction between technique used and musical context disrupts the interpersonal equilibrium, and the singers respond by abandoning their reciprocal behaviours in favour of compensatory tactics to restore it. If we recognize that a choir's relative unresponsiveness is not a product of dullness or lethargy, but a positive strategy to maintain their social comfort level, we can adjust our own behaviours to help re-establish a social environment in which singers will be more at ease and willing to participate in rapport.

Specific actions that a director can do to achieve this include:

- Stand back from the choir, rather than walking in towards them
- Speak more slowly and quietly
- Leave a fraction more silence before speaking, or before bringing the choir in to sing
- Make gestures more contained, and bring them down to sternum or diaphragm level if they have been at shoulder level
- Put less muscular tension into gestures
- Stand tall, rather than leaning in to the conducting space
- Make shorter eye contact with individuals
- Increase the proportion of time the choir sings relative to the conductor speaking.

Some of these actions are standard advice to conductors in all circumstances; conducting manuals are unanimous in their injunctions against talking too much, for instance. Others, such as the reduction of eye contact, seem to go against general advice. However, these are remedial measures: magical as interactive eye contact can be when the conductor–choir bond is working well, the intimacy equilibrium model tells us that staring at a choir will only make them withdraw further when it is broken.

Colin Durrant entitles his chapter on conducting gesture 'Less is More', capturing a truism that every novice conductor is told, and none really believes until they have experienced it for themselves.[9] The intimacy equilibrium model allows us to think of the conductor–choir relationship as an integrated unit in which the total level of energy or effort remains more or less stable, although the relative contributions of conductor and singers may vary considerably. If the director wishes the singers to participate more actively, they will have to reduce their own input commensurately.

---

[9] Colin Durrant, *Choral Conducting: Philosophy and Practice* (London, 2003).

Charisma

> Remember that highly-sensitive brains are a scarce commodity. But though this be so, and the choralists as a body may have, artistically, a low saturation point, they are often quick at following a pattern, and are more enthusiastic with their two talents than others who are blessed with five. This is the conductor's salvation. He can pattern, they will imitate; he can Svengali them into enthusiastic response.[10]

Henry Coward uses the image of the evil hypnotist to articulate the idea of the power the conductor has over a choir. The image is somewhat disturbing from a perspective nearly a century after he was writing, especially when combined with his evident disdain for the artistic capacity of his singers. In one sense, then, this extract represents the epitome of the 'maestro myth', the idea that conductors are a breed apart with special powers that ordinary musicians cannot hope to emulate.[11] At the same time, though, he presents the means by which conductors wield this power in terms of the processes we have been examining in the last two chapters: direct mimicry and emotional contagion.

A conductor's charisma is generally seen to be both indispensable and unteachable. Without the capacity to 'impose his personality' on the ensemble, the conductor is nothing but a 'mere time beater'.[12] Unlike the disciplines of stick technique and musicianship that can be acquired through study and practice, however, this is a quality that is seen to come from within, or, as Jean Bartle puts it, 'from the very essence of the conductor's being'.[13] Instruction manuals may outline the character traits a conductor is expected to possess, but they do little to show how they might develop them if they have not been born with these gifts.

The examples in this chapter suggest, however, that there are specific behaviours conductors can adopt that will increase the effectiveness of the bonds with their choirs, and consequently the extent of their influence over them. That is, the connection a director establishes with their ensemble is determined not simply by the kind of person that conductor is, but can be helped or hindered by what they choose to do. In particular, three key themes have emerged as significant factors in motivating and enabling choral singers:

1. *Holistic imagination.* Engaging with musical style as a complete cultural package elicits greater vocal commitment and a readier understanding from singers than instructions that remain at the level of concrete operations.

---

[10] Henry Coward, *Choral Technique and Interpretation* (London, 1914), p. 252.
[11] Norman Lebrecht, *The Maestro Myth: Great Conductors in Pursuit of Power* (London, 1991).
[12] Leslie Woodgate, *The Choral Conductor* (London, 1949), pp. 4–5.
[13] Jean Ashworth Bartle, *Sound Advice: Becoming a Better Children's Choir Conductor* (Oxford, 2003), p. 45.

This package involves not only diction and delivery, but also the wider use of the self – body language and vocal production – and the wider social beliefs and values associated with the musical practices. When the director 'becomes the music itself', they are entering into the identities and worldviews of the repertoires they embrace, and in doing so they allow their singers to develop a meaningful connection with what they sing.

2. *Responsive attention.* Whether at the level of the conductor's physical effect on the sound, or the choir's current emotional state, paying close attention to the quality of the singers' voices in real time gives continuous and immediate feedback on how well the conductor is directing. When a director lets their actions be guided on a moment-to-moment basis by the current needs of the music and of their singers, they get maximum advantage from the chameleon effect, since it allows them to correct their own postural and gestural flaws and improve their choir's vocal production from within the flow of the music. Since the mirroring effect this is largely unconscious and involuntary, the singers may well experience the resultant improvement in their own performance as deriving from the magical influence of a powerful personality.

3. *Interaction.* The conductor–choir bond is a dynamic, symbiotic relationship that is actively maintained by all participants. If the conductor finds singers opting out of the interaction, this is a sign that they are doing too much themselves. Keeping an awareness of when the choir is matching their behaviour and when they are compensating for it allows the director to regulate their actions so as to keep the choir in the interactive zone. As a side note, this equilibrium is the aspect of the conductor–choir bond that is least well served by a signalling or transmission model of conducting. To disaggregate the equilibrium model into cause and effect is to impose a linear narrative on a synchronized interaction, even if this is conceived recursively. It is just as true to say that a choir's reticence causes a conductor's over-conducting as it is to say that excessively vigorous gestures cause singers to retreat. Indeed, I would hypothesize a correlation between a tendency towards over-conducting and a mental construct of conducting built on the 'conduit' metaphor, since those conductors who worry about 'getting their ideas over' seem to have more trouble with this than those who think in terms of 'eliciting sound' from their singers.

Charisma thus starts to look less like an inborn attribute and more like a technology of the self, that is, a set of operations that conductors can perform on their thoughts and behaviours in order to transform themselves into believable musical leaders. Certainly some will find enacting these processes easier than others. Talents develop or stall in the context of ongoing social identities and relationships, and one's belief structures, previous experiences and the current interpersonal dynamic with one's ensemble will all affect one's capacity to make behavioural changes.[14] But just as we assert our power as choral directors to discipline a miscellaneous collection of individuals into a unified and cohesive choir, so we can assume the power to change our habits of attention and action, and thereby to change ourselves.

---

[14] In particular, the degree to which people persevere in the face of difficulties varies according to whether they attribute their successes and failures to natural talent or their own efforts. See Christopher Peterson, 'Recruiting for Choral Ensemble by Emphasizing Skill and Effort', *Music Educators Journal* 89/2 (2002): 32–5.

Chapter 14
Conclusion

This study has sought to explain two interrelated phenomena:

1. How it is that a conductor's physical demeanour directly affects how a choir sings, and
2. The relationship between a genre's characteristic style of vocal production and delivery, and its distinctive gestural vocabularies/body languages.

The first problem matters to choral practitioners working in any tradition: what they do with their own body may determine the level of musical success their singers can enjoy. The second becomes important when practitioners from different traditions start to work together: to what extent can one practitioner mandate an approach as generic good practice, and to what extent can another refuse it on the grounds that 'we don't do it that way'?

The second problem also matters to scholars investigating music's role in the project of the self. It lies at the seam between scholarly traditions that consider musical substance in 'purely' musical terms and those that consider music in society without necessarily engaging with the detail of sounding substance. It highlights the way that musicology and cultural theory share key vocabulary, but this is sometimes understood in quite different ways: how does performance in a musical style relate to the performance of one's identity? How does authenticity as fidelity to style relate to authenticity as fidelity to self? What does it mean when a director asks his male chorus to 'sing like men'?

As we have seen, these two research problems posit choral singing simultaneously as a single, coherent practice and as a collection of more or less disparate traditions. The tension between these two ways of thinking about choral music opens up what are analogous issues in the practical and theoretical realms. The practitioner wants to know how much the skills and understandings developed in one idiom can transfer across to another, while the theorist wants to know where the social bonds and musical meanings of choral culture sit on the continuum between nature and nurture.

My argument over the preceding chapters has consequently straddled several disciplinary worlds as well as negotiated between these competing interests. This chapter aims, first, to summarize how these disparate elements cooperate to address the book's central theoretical questions. Secondly, it aims to tease out specific findings that have direct implications for praxis. If the balance of the chapter is directed more in the direction of conducting studies than of critical musicology, it is because the subjects represented here are probably less familiar to a practical and pedagogical discipline than to a theoretical one. Musicologists interested in voice, gesture or identity in other forms of music, meanwhile, are unlikely to let the fact that this study deals with a specific set of practices prevent them from adopting or adapting any idea to other musical contexts if they think it potentially useful.

Theoretical Summary

Choral conductors can come to 'look like the music' because their habits of movement, both postural and gestural, are integral to the way that they understand style. Through their inculcation into a choral culture, as first singer then director, they learn a repertoire of bodily ways of being that become part of how they think about musical content. These embodied meanings circulate between directors and singers via the mechanism of the perception–behaviour link, which allows the choir to sound as the conductor looks through three interrelated processes:

1. The mapping of physical gesture onto the domain of sound, via a range of metaphors based in lived experience;
2. The choir's adoption of a bodily demeanour like that of the conductor, which results in a vocal sound akin to that which the conductor would produce; and
3. The sharing of both visual/kinaesthetic and aural cues between singers.

Hence, the automatic 'natural' responses of a choral singer to a conductor's gesture are based in the neurophysiology of humanity as a social species. Our brains have evolved to learn behaviours by imitating others. At the same time, the shape of that gesture and its meaning in a particular musical context are cultural constructs created and maintained within specific social groups; the lived experience that our bodily metaphors draw upon is inevitably experienced within shared cultural settings. Musical gestures are, as Edward Sapir described speech-accompanying gestures, 'the anonymous work of an elaborate social tradition'.[1] We need to understand both of these dimensions if we are to understand both the extent and the limits of what the choral practitioner can control.

Indeed, the cultural environment of the rehearsal may shape how powerfully each of these processes acts at any one moment. Many a new conductor has found it takes time to change both the vocal and musical habits of a well-established choir. The strength of an accustomed bodily relationship with music may be much stronger than the new musical-gestural world the conductor brings to the choir, especially if that embodied understanding is based in physical and imaginative habits that the choir does not share. These mental and embodied modes of understanding

---

[1] Quoted by Adam Kendon, *Conducting Interaction: Patterns of Behavior in Focused Encounters* (Cambridge, 1990), p. 34.

are constructed within discourses that define both what constitutes appropriate choral behaviour and what that behaviour means. These discourses, moreover, draw interchangeably on both musical values and beliefs from wider culture, such that the identity of the choral singer interconnects with and differentiates itself from social categories and musical genres both within and beyond the choral sphere. So the bodily stillness of the classical singer, for instance, is understood in contradistinction to the overt movements of 'lighter' genres in terms of the Western art tradition's values of spirituality and transcending the flesh.

David McNeill's concept of the growth point provides the node at which the gestural, the musical and the discursive meet. This is the moment at which a thought first starts to appear, and it combines both imagistic and analytical components. As the thought comes to fruition, the imagistic elements are materialized in gesture, while the analytical dimension appears sequentially in time either as speech or as music. The gestural component of the thought, meanwhile, remains constant across these two domains, mediating between intra-musical meanings and the verbal discourses we use to discuss them. Gestures may emerge in tandem with speech, with song or in the flow of conducting, and may be transferred seamlessly to accompany the expression of the same idea in a different mode, since the same experiential image-schemata underlie our linguistic, our musical and our gestural ideas. There is a commensurate correlation between the richness and variety of a conductor's gestural vocabulary, their verbal imagery, and the depth and nuance of their choir's performance.

The growth point is also the means by which individuals bring themselves into being as self-aware agents. It is through the conceiving and unfolding of thoughts that people become present to themselves, that they experience their self-identities. At the same time, though, the materials with which the individual creates their thoughts are the learned behaviours and norms of verbal language and musical culture. The act of thought is thus on one hand the place where the subject encounters itself as autonomous, as the author of their own ideas, and on the other is constructed by and within the shared forms of representation that circulate through culture. This is why it is possible for conductors both to present recognizably individual, original artistic profiles and to display clear affiliations to specific musical and gestural traditions.

The circulation of cultural forms is facilitated by the process of inhabitance. Participation in and cooperation with another's growth points involves aligning one's subjective state with both the discursive and imagistic dimensions of the other's thought processes. Sharing this common 'house of being' is also a means by which collective identities are formed: if the generation of a thought brings the 'I' who thinks it into being, then the act of sharing of a thought binds the 'we' who cooperate in its materialization into a communal state of consciousness. Inhabitance is therefore the means by which the subjective becomes inter-subjective. A style's characteristic modes of body language and vocal delivery thus serve three simultaneous functions: as social signals that indicate to co-performers affiliations of musical understanding, as the mechanism by which both the technical and imaginative dimensions of performing traditions are perpetuated, and as an integral part of the way that individuals experience themselves as performing musicians.

Implications for Praxis

Stylistic Mobility

One of my earlier rehearsal observations provides an excellent illustration of how the questions investigated here arise in the week-in, week-out work of conductors and choirs. The group was a well-established male voice choir of over 50 members, with a female director who had been working with them for a few years – long enough to build a stable relationship with the choir, but short enough that both she and the singers talked about her work in terms of what she wanted to change. Her plans had two dimensions: first, a shift in repertoire away from the traditional religious music the choir sang to include more popular and light music as well as some classical pieces such as opera choruses, and second, to change their style of vocal delivery. Much of the rehearsal involved relearning two pieces of established repertoire in order to change old habits, and the detail of this work gave a clear picture of what she was trying to achieve. The main thrust was to move away from what she called a 'shouty' approach to one that involved more 'feeling'. The latter was to be achieved by clearer articulation of the text, a more legato delivery, more dynamic shading and by losing some ingrained rallentandos.

The more subtle, inflected approach she was aiming for certainly offered an addition of artistry in one dimension, but the full-voiced, muscular approach she dismissed as 'shouty' also had its own integrity. There was a real power and ring to the voices as they got into the flow of the music, and there was a clear sense of unanimity between the singers; tuning and section unity were not faultless – some strain in the voices interfered at times – but were true enough to give a convincing sense of ensemble. By contrast, the singers did not appear to connect to the new style of delivery in the same way; there was less support and less focus in the sound, and the result was, as the director put it, 'wishy-washy'. While her interpretative agenda was undoubtedly adding something to the performance, it was also taking something away.

The question this raises is: how can directors make significant artistic changes without undermining the integrity of what is already there? The stylistic leap this director was taking to work with this choir was not even so very great. She was completely at home with the range of compositional styles that the male voice choir tradition draws on, although she clearly did not share any first-hand experience with the tradition's characteristically robust mode of vocal production. If these difficulties emerge in the interaction of relatively close musical worlds, how is the practitioner to cope when making the bigger stylistic leaps necessitated by today's pluralistic choral landscape?

The solution lies, I suggest, in understanding choral singing as an aspect of identity. People experience themselves as performing musicians through the act of musical participation, and the choral practitioner's task is to help singers engage with the music they sing in a way that not only respects the needs of the music, but that can be accepted and embraced by the singer as true to themselves as well. As we saw in Part II, the ways in which people sing, and the terms in which they understand it, not only connect out into their wider social identities but also extend deep into their affective and imaginative states. Indeed, Part IV's discussion of the process of emotional contagion and the associated vocal feedback hypothesis suggests that emotional habits are as much a part of a style as its characteristic vocal and gestural ways of being. Learning new ways to sing thus involves learning new ways to feel; how to sing 'from the heart' has to be discovered afresh in each new stylistic context. The problem that the male voice choir director had, therefore, was in assuming that what she experienced as introducing more 'feeling' into the performance was inherently meaningful to her singers. Their loss of vocal confidence, meanwhile, suggests that what she asked felt quite alien to them.

Once we recognize choral singing as both a common category and a cluster of distinct traditions with varying degrees of overlap, we realize that, while a significant proportion of any one practitioner's expertise and prior experience will transfer usefully to a new idiom, not all of it will, and some will prove positively counter-productive. Moreover, it is not always easy to predict in advance which aspects of craft will fall into each category. Sometimes it is the most basic assumptions that cause problems: practitioners who have only worked with SATB choirs will routinely pitch their warm-up exercises about a fifth too high for women's barbershop groups, for example. Still, there are clues to be found, both in a choir's discourse and in its performance, and staying alert to these clues can help directors mediate between potentially different expectations and values.

Chapter 3's environmental model suggested that a choir has three layers in which behaviours and values are negotiated: the relationship between director and choir (that is, the direct experience of music-making), the choir's social world as an organization, and the choir's musical and institutional allegiances to wider choral traditions. The central layer will work most smoothly if directors pay attention to what people are saying and doing in the outer two. Learning a new style, that is, also involves learning to speak its language. This includes not only the technical vocabulary – counter-subject, tail, swipe – but the vocabularies of value. When directors frame their requests in terms of what a choral culture cares about, whether that be entertainment value, historical authenticity or the glory of God, the singers have the means to connect the new ways of doing things with their established identities as choral singers.

Given the way that musical and extra-musical discourses interact, the ways that directors talk about music with their choirs can also serve wider social agendas. As we saw in Chapter 6, when the metaphors that directors use in rehearsal refer to wider social categories, they can either affirm or exclude individuals, depending on how they relate to those social markers. If recruiting and retaining younger singers is a problem, then it may not be helpful to elicit a tender vocal quality for a Christmas carol by asking one's singers to 'think back to when your first grandchild was born', however much that may affirm one's current membership.

The other set of clues are those that respond to the processes of aural feedback discussed in Chapter 13. While it is clear that different genres have sometimes quite different approaches to using the voice, there are certain indicators that work across choral idioms to tell us how well the singers are aligned with their vocal selves. The first is the size of the sound. As we saw in Chapter 12, a choral sound that is disproportionately small for the size of choir can be a sign of breakdown in the conductor–choir intimacy equilibrium; our male voice choir example, meanwhile, shows that support and resonance suffer when singers are asked sing in a way that feels foreign to them. The second is tuning. This is usually seen as an attribute of skill, but even choirs that are quite artistically unambitious can maintain considerable fidelity of pitch when they are happy and confident. Intonation problems, meanwhile, often result either from loss of support or from other distortions in vocal production, which can be the result of personal discomfort as much as technical inadequacy: people pull themselves out of shape more when they are emotionally unsettled. The third is unity. A common approach to voice production and delivery across a choir shows a stable and shared relationship with both repertoire and style. Problems with ensemble and blend, meanwhile, betray either competing concepts of the desired musical goals or inconsistency across the ensemble in the degree to which singers feel able to commit to them.

These of course are standard areas of choral craft: the practitioner literature is replete with techniques to improve support, resonance, intonation and blend. My point, however, is that if these are not working, this may not simply be a sign of inadequate skill within the ensemble, but may be a symptom of dysfunction in the relationship the singers are experiencing with their vocal identities. The techniques one has always used to deal with these issues may provide an appropriate solution, but it may equally be worth taking a step back to consider what it is causing the singers' vocal alienation, and whether these habitual methods will ameliorate or exacerbate the situation. The problem may be that the singers are resisting identification with a musical and/or vocal mode of being incongruent with their prior sense of self, or simply that they are failing to make the connection between their director's expectations and what they understand through experience as appropriate choral behaviour. If this is the case, more imaginative solutions will be needed. To pursue a standard approach in the face of an only intermittent response is not only inefficient of rehearsal time, it is also to fall back on the brute force of the technologies of power in place of the more effective and thorough-going technologies of the self.

Conceiving Conducting

Part I developed the idea that how we think about conducting will fundamentally shape how we go about studying it. Different mental models of the process lead to different approaches to research design, and different metalanguages allow us to perceive different aspects of it. Our mental representations both highlight and hide elements of the phenomena they describe, and the act of perception is thus always also an act of analysis. What we do is simultaneously constrained and facilitated by the cultural forms we have available to make sense of the world.

This is true not only of research into conducting, of course; it also applies to conducting itself. Directors will behave differently if they think they are signalling to their choirs than they will if they think they are responding to them; gestures will change depending on whether they are conceived them in terms of manipulating metaphorical objects or in terms of the dimensions of space, weight and time. Different modes of thinking about the conductor's craft will make different elements salient, and will thereby give directors the means to observe and control those elements, while other elements remain concealed from the mind's eye. Knowledge is inherently partial – both incomplete, that is, and consequently biased – and it is only through the application of our parochial, culture-bound analytical filters that we can organize the overwhelming onslaught of sense-data that bombards us into meaningful patterns that can give us useable contexts in which to live and act.

Cultivating different mental models and metalanguages thus provides the opportunity to perceive the world through a different lens. Just as conceiving vocal qualities in terms of orchestral sounds makes new aspects of timbre audible and thus permits the development of strategies for choral stacking, thinking about conducting pattern in terms of acceleration and deceleration rather than simply the locations of the beats gives a new insight into the ebb and flow of musical intensity. As we saw in Chapter 13, if one is having trouble getting a response from one's choir, it might help to reframe one's conception of conducting as drawing sound from the singers rather than as an input–output model. Conversely, if one's role is that of chorus master, and a different conductor will be taking over for the performance, it might work better to use a signalling model, so that the singers do not come to rely on their relationship with a specific individual for their musical understanding.

The opportunity for enriched music-making that such reframing permits is, of course, why the increased interaction of different choral idioms in contemporary choral culture has proved not only challenging for those involved, but artistically stimulating as well. Not only do different choral genres have quite different ways of engaging vocally and gesturally with the act of singing, but they bring a similarly varied imaginative vocabulary to bear on what they do. Meeting people who share an activity that is nominally the same, yet which displays a different way of being that is in some ways unimaginable using only one's own frame of reference, can provide the chance to experience both new ways of thinking about singing and new ways of using the self.

Of course, some of these imaginative interchanges are more successful than others: one person's showmanship is another's vulgarity, and one person's purity of sound is another's lifelessness. Still, the dual nature of choral singing as both singular and multiple offers the means to experience both common identity and difference, with the shared definitions providing a clear point of contact from which to make sense of the strange. Commentaries on international events routinely celebrate both of these dimensions, counterpoising the potential for cross-cultural bonding with the richness provided by 'a smorgasbord of choral tastes and styles'.[2] And it seems to be the combination of the two dimensions that leads participants to describe their experiences as 'inspiring': these events both affirm them in their affiliation with a global community of practice and broaden their horizons as to what membership of that community might mean. Hence, Eskil Hemberg, then President of the International Federation for Choral Music, started his invitation to the 2005 World Symposium on Choral Music in Japan by stating that 'the purpose of a world symposium is to promote artistic excellence, cooperation and exchange worldwide by bringing together the finest choirs and choral leaders', and ended it by writing, 'I know from my own experience that now and then I have to re-evaluate art and artistic expressions. I do think that Kyoto … will bring us something new and unexpected that will make my choral world change a bit.'[3]

As we saw in Chapter 13's discussion of style and voice, singers seem to find it easier to grasp the characteristics of a new style when they experience it holistically, as an integrated package of vocal, bodily and discursive traits. Identification with a complete artistic persona appears to come more readily than the adoption of individual elements in isolation. This in turn makes sense of the discursive overdetermination of appropriate choral behaviours discussed in Chapter 6. Forms of action that have a multidimensional definition referencing wider arenas of prior experience can be internalized more effectively than simple physical instructions. Hence it is not surprising that festival participants respond positively to cultural difference when they encounter it directly: there is no more immediate way to gain a rich, fully formed impression of a style's ways of being than to witness it in person.

This reminds us in turn that, when conductors choose the metalanguages and analytical models with which to conceptualize their praxis, they too may respond better to ways of thinking that engage the imagination. Vivid, concrete, nuanced metaphors may be more readily and more productively applied in directing as well as in singing. It may perhaps help to think about conducting in terms more of musical than of didactic gestures.

Technique versus Interpretation

There are two schools of thought about conducting. The first sees the conductor's imaginative engagement with musical content as the source of gesture, while

---

[2] Michael J. Anderson, 'Choir Olympics 2004', *International Choral Bulletin*, 33/4 (2004): 44.

[3] Eskil Hemberg, 'The First Symposium in Asia', 7th World Symposium on Choral Music in Kyoto, Japan, 27 July–3 August 2005, promotional brochure, inside cover.

the other sees the acquisition of technique by physical practice as essential to the conductor's craft. The terms of the dialectic resonate with Lydia Goehr's distinction between the perfect performance of music and the perfect musical performance in Western musical culture discussed in Chapter 11. This dichotomy posed the question: which is more fundamental to the musician's task, technique or interpretation? An emphasis on one risks slick, shallow performances devoid of meaning, while prioritizing the other risks bumbling incompetence in which the musical ideas are obscured by technical clumsiness.

One rarely encounters these positions in their pure forms, of course. The 'music first' camp still acknowledges the importance of a basic grounding in pattern: 'Fundamental conducting patterns, important as they are, are really subservient to the bodily and facial expressions that reflect the mood of the music', states Garretson. 'Nevertheless, they provide a necessary basis from which to start.'[4] Those that advocate technical drill, meanwhile, never lose sight of the musical goal; hence McElheran can state, 'One of the most important principles of this writer's method is to practise conducting as much as one would an instrument', and then a few pages later, 'The beginner must devote much more time to other musical subjects than to conducting itself.'[5]

The maintenance of each of these ethics can be attributed in part to local practices for the training of musicians. A goodly proportion of the British conductors I have observed during the course of my research have commented that they have never had any formal conducting training – and this includes highly proficient and respected professionals. Many British conductors still learn their craft primarily by watching other conductors from within the choirs and orchestras in which they are participant performers, and their capacity and entitlement to direct rests upon their general musicianship and proactiveness in seeking directorships. By contrast, there is a much more developed training infrastructure for conductors in the United States, not least because music teaching in schools there is more about directing ensembles than classroom teaching. And the focus on technical proficiency tends to feature more prominently in the conducting literature published in America. But differences in the ways that people learn their craft do not account fully for these two different emphases. Not only are both views to be found on both sides of the Atlantic, but they also run through both the choral and orchestral literature, and throughout the twentieth century. They are ideologies that persist at least somewhat independently of material circumstance.

The discussion of conductor gesture and musical thought in Part III, however, suggests that the reason why it is impossible to resolve this dialectic is that its two poles – the abstract idea and its material expression – are inseparable. Lakoff and Johnson show how our mental structures are derived from our bodily experiences: our interpretative ideas are inevitably conceived in terms of our technique because

---

[4] Robert L. Garretson, *Conducting Choral Music*, 3rd edn (Boston, MA, 1970), p. 5.

[5] Brock McElheran, *Conducting Techniques for Beginners and Professionals* (Oxford, 1966), pp. viii, 7.

our physical habits are the means by which we understand the world. Chapter 10's analysis of structural/conventional and expressive/interpretive gestures also showed that not only do the same set of metaphorical processes underlie both, but so do many of the same specific metaphors. Technique, it seems, is already interpretative. The concept of the growth point, meanwhile, shows us that, until a thought is unfolded into its material forms, both sounding and gestural, it remains only a potential thought, an inkling rather than an idea. We saw this in action in the form of both the emergent and the musicotopographic gestures: the physical motion surfaced simultaneously with the musical phrase.

What this theoretical awareness offers practising conductors is the opportunity to enhance both gestural control and musical acumen by exploiting the link between the two. Diane Lewis suggests that 'the physical involvement of conducting should begin while the conductor is immersed in score study, with gestural shapes being practised as the aural images are developed', and our insights into the connection between hand and mind show us why and how this is effective.[6] If our usual primary focus in preparing to conduct a piece is on internalizing the music, then a conscious decision to try out different approaches to gesture can help us develop new ways of hearing the piece that we might not otherwise have thought of. Experimenting with the full range of gestural possibilities for dynamic change, for instance, can help one imagine a *crescendo* through a variety of different metaphorical filters, each of which will have different implications for the way that amplitude interacts with other musical parameters such as tone colour and tempo. Conversely, if our preferred method would usually be to work out how to interpret the piece gesturally, then an explicit focus on musical content can act as a means to overcome ingrained gestural habits that might otherwise limit the expressive possibilities of our directing. Analysing a piece's rhythmic structure beyond the level of metre, for instance, can help develop a longer range sense of musical trajectory that organizes and inflects one's treatment of pattern. That is, exploiting the connection between gesture and thought can offer another way to reframe our praxis so as to afford both new perceptions about it and, as a result, greater conscious command over it.

Parenthetically, understanding this connection also sheds light on the practice of conducting along with recordings. This is generally derided as a means to learn how to conduct, since it is entirely derivative and divorces the act of directing from the act of communication. It is presumably a reasonably common activity among aspiring conductors, however, or it would not require such censure. I would suggest that, while it offers no opportunity to develop leadership skills, it probably works quite well as a way to develop a deeper understanding of how another musician has conceived a piece. Conducting along to a recording is an act of cognitive appropriation, participating in the audible traces of another person's growth points while supplying the imagistic component that the recording has erased.

---

[6] Diane M. Lewis, 'Conducting Musical Shape' (DMA dissertation, University of Oklahoma, 1999), p. 112.

Notwithstanding its well-documented shortcomings as a practice method for real-life conducting, then, it remains a potentially useful study tool: it can deepen one's grasp of other conductors' ideas and develop the embodied knowledge base that will inform one's work with live musicians.

The category of emergent gestures showed us how verbal and musical expressions of an idea were based in the same metaphorical content: common gestural shapes show a shared imagistic substrate across words and music. Hence, the possibilities to reimagine one's praxis by oscillating between technique and interpretation as primary focus can integrate well with the possibilities proposed above for reframing one's praxis by changing metalanguage. The vocabulary of verbal metaphors we use to describe our conducting motions and the music we direct can both inform and learn from our gestural imagery and our musical delivery. Gesture becomes the third term that mediates between music and language, while verbal discourse can mediate in turn between music and gesture. Both gestures and music can be *legato*; both gestures and remarks can be pointed. Metaphors flow freely between the three domains, and all can enrich the others, in imagination and in praxis.

William Ehmann claims that 'the search for unity between music and body movements can exist only in theory, or, as the unresolved tension of a dialectical argument'.[7] This dialectical tension, meanwhile, is precisely what generates the thrust of our ideas. And this relationship between hand and mind, between technique and interpretation, can in turn shed light on the tensions between theorist and practitioner explored in Part I: the scholar's disdain for the practitioner's subjective experience, the musician's mistrust of the musicologist, and the consequently conflicting allegiances and obligations of the conductor-scholar. The politics of knowledge that play out in these competing claims to authority are rooted in the same cultural habits of privileging knowing over doing, mind over body, as the debates over the relative priority of technique and interpretation. Western culture has tended to give greater importance to the mental than the physical at the level of personnel as well as of activity.

However, just as Lakoff and Johnson showed us that even abstract concepts are derived from and make sense in the context of our embodied experience, so the capacity for musical scholarship is predicated on a substrate of practical musical participation. At the same time, we need concepts and categories in order to be able to act in the world: even the most intuitive musician is operating within the patterns of representation they have learned through their inculcation into their particular musical sphere. The interests of theorist and practitioner are necessarily going to diverge, since they unfold in different domains of activity, with different goals, success criteria, and, to a significant extent, among different social groups. It may be helpful, however, to see this inherent incompatibility as productive rather than merely discordant. If the act of thinking gains its momentum from the instability of combining two contrasted modes of representation in the same initial

---

[7] William Ehmann, *Choral Directing*, trans. G. Wiebe (Minneapolis, 1968), p. 92.

pulse, perhaps we can experience the tension between action and reflection as the growth point that propels our discipline forwards, opening out into parallel acts of performance and of writing.

Bibliography

Abbate, Carolyn, 'Music – Drastic or Gnostic?', *Critical Enquiry*, 30 (2004): 505–36.

Adler, Samuel, *Choral Conducting: An Anthology* (Fort Worth: Holt, Rinehard and Winston, 1971).

Aiello, John R. and Donna E. Thompson, 'When Compensation Fails: Mediating Effects of Sex and Locus of Control at Extended Interaction Distances', *Basic and Applied Social Psychology*, 1/1 (1980): 65–82.

Anderson, Michael J., 'Choir Olympics 2004', *International Choral Bulletin*, 33/4 (2004): 44.

Archer, Dane, 'Unspoken Diversity: Cultural Differences in Gestures', *Qualitative Sociology*, 20/1 (1997): 79–105.

Argyle, Michael, *Bodily Communication*, 2nd edn (London: Routledge, 1988).

Argyle, Michael and Janet Dean, 'Eye-Contact, Distance and Affiliation', *Sociometry*, 28 (1965): 289–304.

Atherton, Leonard, *Vertical Plane Focal Point Conducting*, Ball State Monograph, no. 32 (Muncie: Ball State University, 1989).

Attinello, Paul, 'Authority and Freedom: Toward a Sociology of the Gay Choruses', in Philip Brett, Elizabeth Wood and Gary C. Thomas (eds), *Queering the Pitch: The New Lesbian and Gay Musicology* (New York: Routledge, 1993).

Bamberger, Jeanne, *The Mind Behind the Musical Ear: How Children Develop Musical Intelligence* (Cambridge, MA: Harvard University Press, 1995).

Bannan, Nicholas, Gillyanne Kayes and Jeremy Fisher, 'Correlations between Tone, Blend and the Experience of Emotion in Group Singing', paper in preparation.

Barthes, Roland, 'The Grain of the Voice', in *Image Music Text*, trans. by Stephen Heath (London: Fontana, 1977).

Bartle, Jean Ashworth, *Sound Advice: Becoming a Better Children's Choir Conductor* (Oxford: Oxford University Press, 2003).

Benge, Timothy, 'Movements Utilized by Conductors in the Stimulation of Expression and Musicianship' (DMA dissertation, Los Angeles: University of Southern California, 1996).

Berlioz, Hector, *Treatise on Instrumentation Including Berlioz's Essay on Conducting*, enlarged and revised by R. Strauss, trans. by Theodore Front (New York: Kalmus, 1948).

Bertalot, John, *How to Be a Successful Choir Director* (Stowmarket: Kevin Mayhew, 2002).

Blacking, John (ed.), *The Anthropology of the Body* (London: Academic Press, 1977).

Blacking, John, *Music Culture and Experience: Selected Papers of John Blacking*, ed by Reginald Byron (Chicago: University of Chicago Press, 1995).

Boerger, Kristina, 'Whose Music is it Anyway? Black Vocal Ensemble Traditions and the Feminist Choral Movement: Performance Practice as Politics' (MusAD dissertation, Urbana-Champaign: University of Illinois, 2000).

Bostock, Donald, *Choirmastery: A Practical Handbook* (London: Epworth Press, 1966).

Boult, Adrian, *A Handbook on the Technique of Conducting*, 7th edn (Oxford: Hall, 1949).

Bowen, José (ed.), *The Cambridge Companion to Conducting* (Cambridge: Cambridge University Press, 2003).

Bräm, Penny Boyes and Thüring Bräm, 'Expressive Gestures used by Classical Orchestra Conductors', in *The Semantics and Pragmatics of Everyday Gestures*, ed. by Cornelia Müller and Roland Posner (Berlin: Weidler Buchverlag, 2004).

Brewer, Mike, *Kick-Start your Choir* (London: Faber, 1997).

Brewer, Mike, *Fine-Tune your Choir: The Indispensible Handbook for Choral Directors and Singers* (London: Faber, 2004).

Burchill, Graham, Colin Gordon and Peter Miller (eds), *The Foucault Effect: Studies in Governmentality* (Chicago: University of Chicago Press, 1991).

Burke, Lucy, Tony Crowley and Alan Girvin (eds), *The Routledge Language and Cultural Theory Reader* (New York: Routledge, 2000).

Burnim, Mellonnee, 'The Performance of Black Gospel Music as Transformation', in David Power, Mary Collins and Mellonnee Burnim (eds), *Music and the Experience of God* (Edinburgh: Concilium, 1989).

Busch, Brian R., *The Complete Choral Conductor: Gesture and Method* (New York: Schirmer Books, 1984).

Butler, Judith, *Gender Trouble: Feminism and the Subversion of Identity* (New York: Routledge, 1990).

Chartrand, Tanya L. and John A. Bargh, 'The Chameleon Effect: The Perception-Behaviour Link and Social Interaction', *Journal of Personality and Social Psychology*, 76/6 (1999): 893–910.

Cleall, Charles, *Voice Production in Choral Technique* (Sevenoaks: Novello, 1970).

Cohen, Harriet, *Music's Handmaid* (London: Faber, 1950).

Cook, Nicholas, *Music Imagination and Culture* (Oxford: Oxford University Press, 1990).

Cook, Nicholas, 'Analysing Performance and Performing Analysis', in Nicholas Cook and Mark Everist (eds), *Rethinking Music* (Oxford: Oxford University Press, 1999).

Cook, Nicholas, 'Between Process and Product: Music and/as Performance', *Music Theory Online*, 7/2 (2001), available online at: http://societymusictheory.org/mto/issues/mto.01.7.2/mto.01.7.2.cook.html [accessed 25 January 2008].

Cooper, Grosvenor and Leonard B. Meyer, *The Rhythmic Structure of Music* (Chicago: University of Chicago Press, 1960).

Corp, Ronald, *The Choral Singer's Companion* (London: Batsford, 1987).

Coward, Henry, *Choral Technique and Interpretation* (London: Novello, 1914).

Cox, Arnie, 'The Mimetic Hypothesis and Embodied Musical Meaning', *Musicae Scientiae*, 5/2 (2001):195–212.

Cox, Arnie, 'Hearing, Feeling, Grasping Gestures', in Anthony Gritten and Elaine King (eds), *Music and Gesture* (Aldershot: Ashgate, 2006).

Cox-Ife, William, *The Elements of Conducting: A Book for the Amateur* (London: John Baker, 1964).

Creswell, John, *Research Design: Qualitative Quantitative and Mixed Methods Approaches*, 2nd edn (London: Sage, 2002).

Cusick, Suzanne, 'On a Lesbian Relationship with Music: A Serious Attempt not to Think Straight', in Philip Brett, Elizabeth Wood and Gary C. Thomas (eds), *Queering the Pitch: The New Lesbian and Gay Musicology* (New York: Routledge, 1993).

Darrow, Gerald F., *Four Decades of Choral Training* (Metuchen: Scarecrow, 1975).

Darwin, Charles, *The Origin of Species*, ed. by J.W. Burrow (London: Penguin, 1968).

Daugherty, James F., 'Choir Spacing and Formation: Choral Sound Preferences in Random, Synergistic, and Gender-Specific Chamber Choir Placements', *International Journal of Research in Choral Singing*, 1/1 (2003): 48–59.

Daugherty, James F., 'On Pursuing Unusually Stubborn and Persisting Efforts to Think by the Intelligent Gathering and Use of Data', *International Journal of Research in Choral Singing*, 2/1 (2004): 1–2.

Davidson, Jane W., 'Communicating with the Body in Performance', in *Musical Performance: A Guide to Understanding*, ed by John Rink (Cambridge: Cambridge University Press, 2002).

Davis, Leonard, *Practical Guidelines for Orchestral and Choral Conducting: For Those Wishing to Build on their Existing Experience rather than for Complete Beginners* (London: Guidelyne Books, n.d.).

Davison, Archibald T., *Choral Conducting* (Cambridge, MA: Harvard University Press, 1954).

Dawkins, Richard, *The Selfish Gene* (Oxford: Oxford University Press, 1976).

Decker, Harold A. and Colleen J. Kirk, *Choral Conducting: Focus on Communication* (Englewood Cliffs: Prentice Hall, 1988).

Decker, Harold A. and Julius Herford, *Choral Conducting: A Symposium* (Englewood Cliffs: Prentice Hall, 1988).

Demorest, Steven, *Building Choral Excellence: Teaching Sight-Singing in the Choral Rehearsal* (Oxford: Oxford University Press, 2001).

Donington, Robert, 'Dynamics' in Stanley Sadie (ed.), *The New Grove Dictionary of Music and Musicians*, Vol. 5 (London: Macmillan, 1980).

Dunn, Dwayne E., 'Effect of Rehearsal Hierarchy and Reinforcement on Attention, Achievement, and Attitude of Selected Choirs', *Journal of Research in Music Education*, 45/4 (1997): 547–67.

Dunn, Lesley and Nancy Jones (eds), *Embodied Voices: Representing Female Vocality in Western Culture* (Cambridge: Cambridge University Press, 1994).

Durrant, Colin, 'Towards a Model of Effective Communication: A Case for Structured Teaching of Conducting', *British Journal of Music Education*, 11/1 (1994): 56–76.

Durrant, Colin, 'Developing a Choral Conducting Curriculum', *British Journal of Music Education*, 15/3 (1998): 303–16.

Durrant, Colin, *Choral Conducting: Philosophy and Practice* (London: Routledge, 2003).

Eco, Umberto, *A Theory of Semiotics* (Indianapolis: Indiana University Press, 1976).

Efron, David, *Gesture Race and Culture* (The Hague: Mouton, 1972).

Ehmann, William, *Choral Directing*, trans. G. Wiebe (Minneapolis: Augsburg, 1968).

Eichenberger, Rodney and Andre Thomas, *What They See is What You Get: Linking the Visual the Aural and the Kinetic to Promote Artistic Singing*, Instructional video (Chapel Hill: Hinshaw Music Inc, 1994).

Ekholm, Elizabeth, 'The Effect of Singing Mode and Seating Arrangement on Choral Blend and Overall Choral Sound', *Journal of Research in Music Education*, 48/2 (2000): 123–35.

Ekman, Paul, 'Should We Call it Expression or Communication?', *Innovations in Social Science Research*, 10/4 (1997): 333–44.

Ekman, Paul and Maureen O'Sullivan, 'Facial Expressions: Methods, Means and Moues', in Robert S. Feldman and Bernard Rimé (eds), *Fundamentals of Nonverbal Behavior* (Cambridge: Cambridge University Press, 1991).

Ekman, Paul and Wallace V. Friesen, *Facial Action Coding System: A Technique for the Measurement of Facial Movement* (Palo Alto: Consulting Psychologists Press, 1978).

Feldman, Robert S. and Bernard Rimé (eds), *Fundamentals of Nonverbal Behaviour* (Cambridge: Cambridge University Press, 1991).

Ford, Kevin, 'Preferences for Strong or Weak Singer's Formant Resonance in Choral Tone Quality', *International Journal of Research in Choral Singing*, 1/1 (2003): 29–47.

Foreman, Lewis (ed.), *British Choral Music: A Millenium Performing Conspectus of Nineteenth and Twentieth Century Music for Choral Societies* (Upminster: British Music Society, 2001).

Foucault, Michel, 'Technologies of the Self', in Luther H. Martin, Huck Gutman and Patrick H. Hutton (eds), *Technologies of the Self: A Seminar with Michael Foucault* (Amherst: University of Massachusetts Press, 1988).

Foucault, Michel, 'Governmentality', in Graham Burchill, Colin Gordon and Peter Miller (eds), *The Foucault Effect: Studies in Governmentality* (Chicago: University of Chicago Press, 1991).

Fricke, Ellen, 'Origo, Pointing, and Speech - The Phenomenon of Two Non-Identical Origos on the Gestural and Verbal Level', paper presented at the First Congress of the International Society for Gesture Studies (University of Texas at Austin, 2002), available online at: http://gossip.ucr.edu/mandana/isgs/papers.php [accessed 27 April 2006].

Fuelberth, Rhonda, 'The Effect of Conducting Gesture on Singers' Perceptions of Inappropriate Vocal Tension: A Pilot Study', *International Journal of Research in Choral Singing*, 1/1 (2003): 13–21.

Fuelberth, Rhonda, 'The Effect of Various Left-Hand Gestures on Perceptions of Anticipated Vocal Tension in Singers', *International Journal of Research in Choral Singing*, 2/1 (2004): 27–38.

Fuller, Gregory, 'Effects of Metric Conducting Patterns, Subdivided Patterns, Managed Preparatory Gestures, and No Conducting on Choral Singers' Precision and Expressiveness at Phrase Punctuation Points less than the Unit Pulse' (Ph.D. dissertation, Columbia: University of Missouri, 2000).

Galkin, Elliott, *A History of Orchestral Conducting in Theory and Practice* (New York: Pendragon Press, 1988).

Garnett, Liz, 'Musical Meaning Revisited: Thoughts on an "Epic" Critical Musicology', *Critical Musicology Journal* (1998), available online at: http://www.leeds.ac.uk/music/Info/CMJ/Index/author.html#garnett_l.html [accessed 12 March 2008].

Garnett, Liz, *The British Barbershopper: A Study in Socio-Musical Values* (Aldershot: Ashgate, 2005a).

Garnett, Liz, 'Choral Singing as Bodily Regime', *International Review of the Aesthetics and Sociology of Music*, 36/2 (2005b): 249–69.

Garnett, Liz, 'Cool Charts or Barbertrash?: Barbershop Harmony's Flexible Concept of the Musical Work', *Twentieth-Century Music*, 2/2 (2005c): 245–63.

Garnett, Liz, 'Research Report: Gesture, Style and Communication', *Mastersinger*, 55 (2005d): 14–15.

Garnett, Liz, 'The Ethics of Choral Blend', paper presented at the *Music and/as Right Action* conference (University of East Anglia, 2007).

Garretson, Robert L., *Conducting Choral Music*, 3rd edn (Boston, MA: Allyn & Bacon, 1970).

Geertz, Clifford, 'Thick Description: Towards an Interpretative Theory of Culture', in *The Interpretation of Cultures: Selected Essays* (New York: Basic Books, 1973).

George, Vance, 'Choral Conducting', in José Bowen (ed.), *The Cambridge Companion to Conducting* (Cambridge: Cambridge University Press, 2003).

Gibbons, Stella, *Cold Comfort Farm* (London: Penguin, 1932).

Giddens, Anthony, *Modernity and Self-Identity: Self and Society in the Late Modern Age* (Cambridge: Polity, 1991).

Goehr, Lydia, *The Quest for Voice: On Music Politics and the Limits of Philosophy* (Oxford: Oxford University Press, 2002).
Goldbeck, Frederick, *The Perfect Conductor: An Introduction to his Skill and Art for Musicians and Music Lovers* (London: Dennis Dobson, 1960).
Gordon, Lewis, *Choral Director's Rehearsal and Performance Guide* (West Nyack: Parker Publishing, 1989).
Green, Elizabeth, *The Modern Conductor: A College Text on Conducting based on the Technical Principles of Conductor Nicolai Malko as set forth in his 'The Conductor and his Baton'*, 6th edn (Englewood Cliffs: Prentice Hall, 1997).
Green, Lucy, *Music on Deaf Ears: Musical Meaning, Ideology, Education* (Manchester: Manchester University Press, 1988).
Gritten, Anthony and Elaine King (eds), *Music and Gesture* (Aldershot: Ashgate, 2006).
Harrigan, Jinni, Robert Rosenthal and Klaus R. Scherer, *The New Handbook of Methods in Nonverbal Behavior Research* (Oxford: Oxford University Press, 2005).
Hart, Steven Robert, 'Evolution of Thought and Recurrent Ideas in Choral Conducting Books and Secondary Music Education Texts Published from 1939 to 1995' (Ph.D. dissertation, Boulder: University of Colorado, 1996).
Hatfield, Elaine, John T. Cacioppo, and Richard L. Rapson, *Emotional Contagion* (Cambridge: Cambridge University Press, 1994).
Hatten, Robert S., *Musical Meaning in Beethoven: Markedness, Correlation, and Interpretation* (Bloomington: University of Indiana Press, 1994).
Heinlein, Robert, *Stranger in a Strange Land* (London: New English Library, 1961).
Hemberg, Eskil, 'The First Symposium in Asia', 7th World Symposium on Choral Music in Kyoto, Japan, 27 July–3 August 2005, promotional brochure, inside cover.
Hibbard, Therees Tkach, 'The Use of Movement as an Instructional Technique in Choral Rehearsals' (DMA dissertation, Eugene: University of Oregon, 1994).
Hill, David, Hilary Parfitt and Elizabeth Ash, *Giving Voice: A Handbook for Choir Directors and Trainers* (Rattlesden: Kevin Mayhew, 1995).
Hindemith, Paul, *A Composer's World: Horizons and Limitations* (New York: Anchor Books, 1952).
Hoffmann, E.T.A., 'Beethoven's Instrumental Music', in David Charlton (ed.), *E.T.A. Hoffmann's Musical Writings: Kreisleriana The Poet and the Composer Music Criticism*, trans. by Martyn Clarke (Cambridge: Cambridge University Press, 1989).
Holst, Imogen, *Conducting a Choir: A Guide for Amateurs* (Oxford: Oxford University Press, 1973).
Holt, Michele Menard, 'The Application to Conducting and Choral Rehearsal Pedagogy of Laban Effort/Shape and its Comparative Effect upon Style in Choral Performance' (DMA dissertation, Eugene: University of Hartford, 1992).

Houle, George, *Meter in Music 1600–1800* (Bloomington: Indiana University Press, 1987).
House, Richard Earl, 'Effects of Expressive and Nonexpressive Conducting on the Performance and Attitudes of Advanced Instrumentalists' (DMA dissertation, Arizona State University, 1998).
Huxley, Aldous, *Brave New World* (London: Vintage, 1932).
Hylton, John, *Comprehensive Choral Music Education* (Englewood Cliffs: Prentice Hall, 1995).
Jacobs, Arthur, 'Spohr and the Baton', *Music and Letters*, 31/4 (1950): 307–17.
Jacobson, John, *Riser Choreography: A Director's Guide for Enhancing Choral Performances* (Milwaukee: Hal Leonard, 1993).
Johnson, Mark, *The Body in the Mind: The Bodily Basis of Meaning Imagination and Reason* (Chicago: University of Chicago Press, 1987).
Johnson, Peter, '"Expressive Intonation" in String Performance: Problems of Analysis and Interpretation', in Jane W. Davidson (ed.), *The Music Practitioner: Research for the Music Performer Teacher and Listener* (Aldershot: Ashgate, 2004).
Johnson, Peter, Review of Richard Parncutt and Gary E. McPherson (eds), *The Science and Psychology of Music Performance: Creative Strategies for Teaching and Learning* (Oxford University Press, 2002), *Musicae Scientiae*, 9/1 (2005): 196–202.
Jordan, James, *Evoking Sound: Fundamentals of Choral Conducting and Rehearsing* (Chicago: GIA Publications, 1996).
Kahn, Emil, *Elements of Conducting*, 2nd edn (New York: Schirmer, 1975).
Kaplan, Abraham, *Choral Conducting* (New York: Norton, 1985).
Kappas, Arvid, Ursula Hess and Klaus R. Scherer, 'Voice and Emotion', in Robert S. Feldman and Bernard Rimé (eds), *Fundamentals of Nonverbal Behavior* (Cambridge: Cambridge University Press, 1991).
Kearney, Richard, *Poetics of Imagining* (London: Routledge, 1991).
Kendon, Adam, *Conducting Interaction: Patterns of Behavior in Focused Encounters* (Cambridge: Cambridge University Press, 1990).
Kendon, Adam, 'An Agenda for Gesture Studies', *Semiotic Review of Books*, 7/3 (1997): 8–12, available online at: http://www.univie.ac.at/wissenschaftstheorie/srb/srb/gesture.html [accessed 12 March 2008].
Knapp, Mark L. and Judith Hall, *Nonverbal Communication in Human Interaction*, 5th edn (London: Wadsworth/Thomas Learning, 2002).
Knight, Victor, *Directing Amateur Singers* (West Kirby: JUBAL Music Publications, 2000).
Kopelson, Kevin, *Beethoven's Kiss: Pianism Perversion and the Mastery of Desire* (Stanford: Stanford University Press, 1996).
Lakoff, George and Mark Johnson, *Metaphors We Live By* (Chicago: University of Chicago Press, 1980).
Lakoff, George and Mark Johnson, *Philosophy in the Flesh: The Embodied Mind and its Challenge to Western Thought* (New York: Basic Books, 1999).

Lebrecht, Norman, *The Maestro Myth: Great Conductors in Pursuit of Power* (London: Simon & Schuster, 1991).

Lee, Eric, Marius Wolf and Jan Borchers, 'Improving Orchestral Conducting Systems in Public Spaces: Examining the Temporal Characteristics and Conceptual Models of Conducting Gestures' (2005), available online at: http://media.informatik.rwth-aachen.de/materials/publications/lee2005a.pdf [accessed 7 December 2007].

Lemke, Thomas, 'Foucault, Governmentality, and Critique' (2004), available online at: http://www.thomaslemkeweb.de/publikationen/Foucault%20Gover nmentality%20and%20Critique%20IV-2.pdf [accessed 11 February 2008].

Lewis, Diane Margaret, 'Conducting Musical Shape' (DMA dissertation, Norman: University of Oklahoma, 1999).

Lewis, Joseph, *Conducting without Fears: A Helpful Handbook for the Beginner, Part I: Conducting - a General Survey* (London: Ascherberg, Hopwood and Crew, 1942).

Lewis, Joseph, *Conducting without Fears: A Helpful Handbook for the Beginner, Part II: Choral and Orchestral Conducting* (London: Ascherberg, Hopwood and Crew, 1945).

Lindlof, Thomas R., *Qualitative Communication Research Methods* (London: Sage, 1995).

Litman, Peter, 'The Relationship Between Gesture and Sound: A Pilot Study of Choral Conducting Behaviour in Two Related Settings', *Visions of Research in Music Education*, 8 (2006), available online at: http://www-usr.rider.edu/~vrme/v8n1/vision/Litman_Article.pdf [accessed 13 March 2008].

Lodge, David, *Changing Places* (London: Martin Secker & Warburg, 1975).

Lodge, David, *Small World* (London: Martin Secker & Warburg, 1984).

Luck, Geoff, 'An Investigation of Conductors' Temporal Gestures', paper presented at the *Music and Gesture* Conference (University of East Anglia, 2003).

Luck, Geoff and Sol Nte, 'An Investigation of Conductors' Temporal Gestures and Conductor-Musician Synchronization, and a First Experiment', *Psychology of Music*, 36/1 (2008): 81–99.

Lyotard, Jean-François, *The Postmodern Condition: A Report on Knowledge* (Manchester: Manchester University Press, 1984).

MacDonald, Raymond, David J. Hargreaves and Dorothy Miell, *Musical Identities* (Oxford: Oxford University Press, 2002).

MacKinnon, Catharine, *Toward a Feminist Theory of the State* (Cambridge, MA: Harvard University Press, 1989).

McElheran, Brock, *Conducting Techniques for Beginners and Professionals* (Oxford: Oxford University Press, 1966).

McNeill, David, *Hand and Mind: What Gestures Reveal about Thought* (Chicago: University of Chicago Press, 1992).

McNeill, David (ed.), *Language and Gesture* (Cambridge: Cambridge University Press, 2000).

McNeill, David, *Gesture and Thought* (Chicago: University of Chicago Press, 2005).
McNeill, David 'Gesture, Gaze, and Ground' (n.d.), available online at: http://mcneilllab.uchicago.edu/pdfs/McNeill_VACE.pdf [accessed 12 March 2008].
Mellor, David H. (ed.), *Ways of Communicating* (Cambridge: Cambridge University Press, 1990).
Merleau-Ponty, Maurice, *Phenomenology of Perception*, revised edn (London: Routledge, 2002).
Meyer, Leonard B., *Music, the Arts and Ideas: Patterns and Predictions in Twentieth-Century Culture* (Chicago: University of Chicago Press, 1967).
Mockus, Martha, 'Queer Thoughts on Country Music and k.d. lang', in Philip Brett, Elizabeth Wood and Gary C. Thomas (eds), *Queering the Pitch: The New Lesbian and Gay Musicology* (New York: Routledge, 1994).
Molnar, John W., 'The Selection and Placement of Choir Voices', *Music Educators Journal*, 36/6 (1950): 48–9.
Monks, Susan, 'Adolecent Singers and Perceptions of Vocal Identity', *British Journal of Music Education*, 20/3 (2003): 243–56.
Moore, Carol-Lynne and Kaoru Yamamoto, *Beyond Words: Movement Observation and Analysis* (New York: Gordon and Breach, 1988).
Mulder, Axel, 'Hand Gestures for HCI', Hand Centred Studies of Human Movement Project, Technical Report 96-1 (1996), available online at: http://xspasm.com/x/sfu/vmi/HCI-gestures.htm [accessed 22 January 2008].
Nakra, Teresa Marrin, 'Inside the Conductor's Jacket: Analysis, Interpretation and Musical Synthesis of Musical Gesture' (Ph.D. dissertation, Massachusetts Institute of Technology, 2000).
Nattiez, Jean-Jacques, *Fondements d'une Sémiologie de la Musique* (Paris: Union Générale d'Editions, 1975).
Nattiez, Jean-Jacques, *Music and Discourse*, trans. by Carolyn Abbate (Princeton: Princeton University Press, 1990).
Nettl, Bruno, 'Mozart and the Ethnomusicological Study of Western Culture: An Essay in Four Movements', in Philip Bohlman and Katherine Bergeron (eds), *Disciplining Music: Musicology and Its Canons* (Chicago: University of Chicago Press, 1996).
Nettl, Bruno, *The Study of Ethnomusicology: Thirty-One Issues and Concepts* (Urbana: University of Illinois Press, 2006).
Neuen, Donald, *Choral Concepts: A Text for Conductors* (Belmont: Schirmer/Thomson Learning, 2002).
Nicholson, Sydney Hugo, *Practical Methods in Choir Training*, RSCM Handbook No. 2 (London: Royal School of Church Music, n.d).
Palmer, Anthony, 'Ethnic Musics in Choral Performance: A Perspective on Problems', *The Choral Journal*, 40/5 (1999): 9–18.
Peraino, Judith, *Listening to the Sirens: Musical Technologies of Queer Identity from Homer to Hedwig* (Berkeley: University of California Press, 2005).

Peterson, Christopher, 'Moving Musical Experiences in Chorus', *Music Educators Journal*, 86/6 (2000): 28–30.

Peterson, Christopher, 'Recruiting for Choral Ensemble by Emphasizing Skill and Effort', *Music Educators Journal*, 89/2 (2002): 32–5.

Pfautsch, Lloyd, 'The Choral Conductor and the Rehearsal', in Harold A. Decker and Julius Herford (eds), *Choral Conducting: A Symposium* (Englewood Cliffs: Prentice Hall, 1988).

Philip, Robert, *Early Recordings and Musical Style: Changing Tastes in Instrumental Performance 1900–1950* (Cambridge: Cambridge University Press, 1992).

Phillips, Kenneth H., *Directing the Choral Music Program* (New York: Oxford University Press, 2004).

Plank, Steven Eric, *Choral Performance: A Guide to Historical Practice* (Oxford: Scarecrow, 2004).

Poch, Gail B., 'Conducting: Movement Analogues through Effort Shape', *The Choral Journal*, 23/3 (1982): 21–2.

Poizat, Michel, *The Angel's Cry: Beyond the Pleasure Principle in Opera*, trans. by Arthur Denner (Ithaca: Cornell University Press, 1992).

Potter, John, *Vocal Authority: Singing Style and Ideology* (Cambridge: Cambridge University Press, 1998).

Potter, John (ed.), *The Cambridge Companion to Singing* (Cambridge: Cambridge University Press, 2000).

Price, Harry E., Editorial introduction to Julie A. Skadsem, 'Effect of Conductor Verbalization, Dynamic Markings, Conductor Gesture, and Choir Dynamic Level on Singers' Dynamic Responses', *Journal of Research in Music Education*, 45/4 (1997): 508.

Putnam, Robert, *Bowling Alone: The Collapse and Revival of American Community* (New York: Simon & Schuster, 2001).

Rabinow, Paul (ed.), *The Foucault Reader: An Introduction to Foucault's Thought* (London: Penguin, 1991).

Randel, Don Michael, *The New Harvard Dictionary of Music* (Cambridge, MA: Harvard University Press, 1986).

Reynolds, Gordon, *The Choirmaster in Action* (London: Novello, 1972).

Rimé, Bernard and Loris Schiaratura, 'Gesture and Speech', in Robert S. Feldman and Bernard Rimé (eds), *Fundamentals of Nonverbal Behavior* (Cambridge: Cambridge University Press, 1991).

Rink, John (ed.), *The Practice of Performance: Studies in Musical Interpretation* (Cambridge: Cambridge University Press, 1995).

Robinson, Kim Stanley, *Blue Mars* (London: HarperCollins, 1996).

Roe, Paul, *Choral Music Education*, 2nd edn (Englewood Cliffs: Prentice Hall, 1983).

Rosen, Charles, 'Music à la Mode', *New York Review of Books*, 41/12 (23 June 1994): 55–62.

Rudolph, Max, *The Grammar of Conducting: A Comprehensive Guide to Baton Technique and Interpretation*, 3rd edn (New York: Schirmer Books, 1995).

Sakata, Jon, 'The First Recitative-Chorus from Haydn's *The Creation*: Rendering Forces of Darkness and Light Audible', *SAPAAN* 1 (2003), available online at: http://www.sapaan.com/vol1/sakata.htm [accessed 9 January 2008].

Saslaw, Janna, 'Forces, Containers, and Paths: The Role of Body-Derived Image Schemas in the Conceptualization of Music', *Journal of Music Theory*, 40/2 (1996): 217–43.

Scholes, Percy A., *The Oxford Companion to Music*, 10th edn (Oxford: Oxford University Press, 1970).

Schuller, Gunther, *The Compleat Conductor* (Oxford: Oxford University Press, 1997).

Schumann, Robert, 'Berlioz' *Symphonie Fantastique*', in Henry Pleasants (ed.), *The Musical World of Robert Schumann: A Selection from Schumann's Own Writings* (New York: St Martins Press, 1965).

Scott, Alan P., 'Talking about Music is like Dancing about Architecture' (2006), available online at http://www.pacifier.com/~ascott/they/tamildaa.htm [accessed 9 January 2008].

Skadsem, Julie A., 'Effect of Conductor Verbalization, Dynamic Markings, Conductor Gesture, and Choir Dynamic Level on Singers' Dynamic Responses', *Journal of Research in Music Education*, 45/4 (1997): 509–20.

Smart, Mary-Ann (ed.), *Siren Songs: Representations of Gender and Sexuality in Opera* (Princeton: Princeton University Press, 2001).

Smeyers, Paul, 'Qualitative versus Quantitative Research Design: A Plea for Paradigmatic Tolerance in Educational Research', in Mike J. MacNamee and David Bridges (eds), *The Ethics of Educational Research* (Oxford: Blackwell, 2002).

SPEBSQSA, *Directing a Barbershop Chorus: Method Techniques and Philosophies* (Kenosha: SPEBSQSA, 1999).

Spitzer, Michael, *Metaphor and Musical Thought* (Chicago: University of Chicago Press, 2004).

Spohr, Louis, *Grand Violin School*, trans. by C. Rudolphus (London: Edwin Ashdown, n.d.).

Spohr, Louis, *Louis Spohr's Autobiography* (London: Longman, Green, Longman, Roberts and Green, 1865).

Stravinsky, Igor, *Poetics of Music in the Form of Six Lessons*, trans. by Arthur Knodel and Ingolf Dahl (Cambridge MA: Harvard University Press, 1947).

Streeck, Jürgen, 'Gesture as Communication I: Its Coordination with Gaze and Speech', *Communication Monographs*, 60 (1993): 275–99.

Streeck Jürgen, 'Gesture as Communication II: The Audience as Co-Author', *Research on Language and Social Interaction*, 27/3 (1994): 239–67.

Strimple, Nick, *Choral Music in the Twentieth Century* (Portland: Amadeus Press, 2002).

Swan, Howard, *Conscience of a Profession* (Chapel Hill: Hinshaw Music Inc, 1987).

Swan, Howard, 'The Development of a Choral Instrument', in Harold A. Decker and Julius Herford (eds), *Choral Conducting: A Symposium* (Englewood Cliffs: Prentice Hall, 1988).

Ternstrom, Sten, 'Choir Acoustics: An Overview of Research Published to Date', *International Journal of Research in Choral Singing*, 1/1 (2003): 3–12.

Thiemal, Matthias, 'Dynamics', *Grove Music Online*, ed by L. Macy, available online at www.grovemusic.com [accessed 22 January 2008].

Thurman, Leon and Graham Welch (eds), *Bodymind and Voice*, revised edn (Minneapolis: The Voice Care Network, 2000).

Turk, Edward Baron, 'Deriding the Voice of Jeanette MacDonald: Notes on Psychoanalysis and the American Film Musical', in Leslie Dunn and Nancy Jones (eds), *Embodied Voices: Representing Female Vocality in Western Culture* (Cambridge: Cambridge University Press, 1994).

Valent, Joseph A., 'An Examination of the Conducting Method of Hideo Saito' (DMA dissertation, Muncie: Ball State University, 2000).

VanWeelden, Kimberly, 'Relationships between Perceptions of Conducting Effectiveness and Ensemble Performance', *Journal of Research in Music Education*, 50/2 (2002): 165–176.

Venn, Edward, 'Towards a Semiotics of Conducting', paper presented at the *Music and Gesture* Conference (University of East Anglia, 2003).

Wagner, Richard, *On Conducting: A Treatise on Style in the Execution of Classical Music*, trans. by Edward Dannreuther (London: William Reeves, 1897).

Weingartner, Felix, *Weingartner on Music and Conducting: Three Essays by Felix Weingartner*, trans. by Ernest Newman, Jessie Crosland and H.M. Schott (New York: Dover, 1969).

Welch, Graham F., 'Developing Young Professional Female Singers in UK Cathedrals', paper presented at the 2nd International Conference on the Acoustics and Physiology of Singing (Denver, 2004), available online at: http://www.ncvs.org/pas/2004/pres/welch/WelchPres_files/frame.htm [accessed 5 August 2005].

Welch, Graham F. and David M. Howard, 'Gendered Voice in the Cathedral Choir', *Psychology of Music*, 30/1 (2002):102–20.

Willetts, Sandra, *Beyond the Downbeat: Choral Rehearsal Skills and Techniques* (Nashville: Abingdon Press, 2000).

Williams, Simon, *Emotion and Social Theory: Corporeal Reflections on the (Ir)rational* (London: Sage, 2001).

Wis, Ramona, 'Gesture and Body Movement as Physical Metaphor to Facilitate Learning and to Enhance Musical Experience in the Choral Rehearsal' (Ph.D. dissertation, Evanston: Northwestern University, 1993).

Woodgate, Leslie, *The Chorus Master* (London: Ascherberg, Hopwood and Crew, 1944).

Woodgate, Leslie, *The Choral Conductor* (London: Ascherberg, Hopwood and Crew, 1949).

Yarbrough, Cornelia and Paul Henley, 'The Effect of Observation Focus on Evaluations of Choral Rehearsal Excerpts', *Journal of Research in Music Education*, 47/4 (1999): 308–18.

Zbikowski, Laurence, 'Metaphor and Music Theory: Reflections from Cognitive Science', *Music Theory Online*, 4/1 (1998), available online at: http://mto.societymusictheory.org/issues/mto.98.4.1/mto.98.4.1.zbikowski.html#FN23 [accessed 12 May 2006].

Zbikowski, Laurence, 'Conceptual Models and Cross-Domain Mapping: New Perspectives on Theories of Music and Hierarchy', *Journal of Music Theory*, 41/2 (1997): 193–225.

Index

Abbate, Carolyn 156
Adler, Samuel 23, 28, 48, 83, 101, 123, 177
American Choral Directors Association 3, 66, 67, 68
appropriation
    cognitive 162–3, 204
    cultural 84
Archer, Dane 54
Argyle, Michael 21, 178–9
Ash, Elizabeth 22, 23, 64–5, 78, 188
Association of British Choral Directors 65, 75
Atherton, Leonard 45
Attinello, Paul 96
auditions 82, 91–3
aural feedback 28, 186–7, 189, 200
authenticity
    of expression 45, 64,
    in performance 83, 84, 183–5, 195
    to self 78–80, 96, 184–5, 195
authority 7, 81, 83, 205
    of conductor 13, 40, 75, 96, 101–2
    of scholar 18, 19, 38, 41, 74, 104

Bannan, Nicholas 56
barbershop 1, 12, 14, 32, 38–9, 68, 111–15, 162, 184, 199
    ballad style 70–71, 72, 112–4, 169
    quartet 111, 115
    vocal production 65–6, 138, 188
Bargh, John 172–3, 176
Barthes, Roland 5–6
Bartle, Jean 192
baton 26, 105, 127, 129, 141, 145, 149
Berlioz, Hector 103, 131, 147
Bertalot, John 23, 32, 91, 95, 96, 97, 163, 170, 172–3, 190
Birmingham Community Gospel Choir 115–18
Black musics 14, 72, 83–4, 184
Blacking, John 1
blend 69, 70, 78, 94, 100, 200

and chameleon effect 173–4
vs. soloistic ethos 79, 85, 92
body
    control 77–80, 87, 96, 98–9
    demeanour 1, 130, 172, 177, 187
    language, 1, 2, 10, 11, 35–6, 37, 57, 112, 114–15, 140, 148, 170–71, 173–4, 180, 183, 185–6, 193, 195, 197–8; *see also* posture
    movement 50, 71, 84, 98, 114, 116, 124, 173, 186, 205
    relationship with music 1, 6, 26, 96, 114–15, 121, 127, 128–30, 139, 150, 151, 174, 180, 184, 185–6, 196–7, 202, 203
Bostock, Donald 22, 170
Boult, Adrian 129, 142, 145, 149–50
Bräm, Penny Boyes 48–9, 139–41, 148
Bräm, Thüring, *see* Bräm, Penny Boyes
Brewer, Mike 22, 78, 101
Brooks, Maxine 115–18, 125, 130, 132, 138, 140, 148, 160, 161, 187
Busch, Brian 55, 125, 143, 145

Cacioppo, John T. 176–8, 179
cathedral tradition 1, 12, 38, 57, 65, 81, 96, 99, 104, 107–11, 118, 121, 126, 161, 162, 175–6
    and the music profession 15, 67, 107–8
chameleon effect 167, 172–6, 178, 180, 181, 186, 187, 189, 193
charisma 75, 168, 192–4
Chartrand, Tanya, *see* Bargh, John
Chilcott, Bob 65
choir layout 37, 108, 111, 119, 126, 160–61, 173, 179; *see also* stacking
choir type 64, 66–9, 73, 123, 184
choral society 66, 67, 84, 85, 91, 97, 99, 174, 185, 190
ChoralNet 68, 105
choreography 71–2
chorus master 118, 201

City of Birmingham Symphony Chorus 118–21
classical music 3, 6, 32, 39, 44, 66, 68, 73, 82, 83–4, 88, 89, 118, 156, 162, 184, 185, 197, 198; *see also* Western art music
Cleall, Charles 69, 80, 81, 85, 86, 98
Clements, Jim 109, 143
communication 1, 16, 18, 28, 43, 64, 81, 102, 134, 180, 204
    as inhabitance 160–64
    models of 20–25, 26, 29, 140
    nonverbal 4, 10, 27, 127
community choir 12, 92
conducting gesture 18, 23, 46, 51, 103–4, 129, 133, 137, 138, 140, 157, 164, 190–91
    beat location 113, 114, 120, 124, 147; *see also* conducting gesture, pattern
    down-beat 36, 57, 109–10, 112, 115, 117, 120, 121, 147, 157, 175, 178
        as in-beat 125, 148
    dynamics 96, 109, 142–146
    expressive gesture 45, 48, 53, 69, 72, 105, 121, 125, 131, 139, 140, 147, 150, 151, 158, 164, 204
    grammar 45, 53, 105, 150
    hand function 25, 26, 45, 47, 48, 104, 113, 116, 125, 125–8, 133, 139–41, 142, 143, 146, 148
    ictus 27, 36, 44, 45, 50, 57, 109, 110, 113, 114, 120, 129, 143, 145, 169
        'shovel' ictus 109, 110, 121, 125, 138, 148, 157
    left-hand gestures, *see* conducting gesture, hand function
    'mere' time-beating 53, 131, 141, 151, 158, 164
    pattern 22, 25, 27, 44, 47, 53, 69, 70, 71, 104, 105, 109, 112, 114, 120, 121, 123–5, 126, 127, 130, 133, 137, 139–41, 142, 145, 147–50, 171, 175, 187, 201, 203, 204
    pitch-patterning 117, 124, 130, 138–9
    technique 1, 16, 26, 32, 44, 45, 47, 53, 70, 95, 101, 104, 109, 113, 120, 123, 125, 138, 141, 142–50, 160, 170, 178, 187, 191, 203–5

conductor–choir bond 48, 154, 172, 180, 183–194, 200; *see also* chameleon effect; emotional contagion; inhabitance; intimacy equilibrium model
Cook, Nicholas 7, 58, 156
Cooper, Grosvenor 128, 150
Corp, Ronald 190
Coward, Henry 13, 23, 55, 70, 80, 85, 86, 92, 173, 177, 192
Cox, Arnie 172
critical musicology 2–4, 7, 184, 195
cultural politics 3, 6, 66, 82, 87, 114, 184

Darwin, Charles 32
Davison, Archibald 23, 36, 41, 48, 70, 78, 79, 101, 125
Dawkins, Richard 33
Dean, Janet, *see* Argyle, Michael
Decker, Harold 22, 105, 125, 132, 142, 144, 170, 171
Demorest, Steven 82
diction 69, 70, 85, 120
    and social identity 80–82, 93, 193
discipline
    choral 91, 96, 100, 101, 108, 161, 194
    self-discipline 61, 91, 101, 190
discourse 5, 9, 13, 77, 89
    analysis 10, 59–61, 63
    musical 11, 164, 199
    of the natural 79–80
    rehearsal 35, 82
    of scholarship 10, 38, 39, 41, 45
    of the universal 63–6, 72
Dunn, Dwayne 30
Durrant, Colin 23, 74, 75, 97, 191

Eco, Umberto 21
effort shapes, *see* Laban, Rudolf
Efron, David 51, 53
Ehmann, William 23, 86, 105, 124, 125, 128, 132, 153, 163, 169, 205
Ekman, Paul 49–50, 158, 176
emic/etic 38
emotion 10, 45, 50, 54, 79, 92, 97, 99, 126, 142–3, 146, 151, 177, 188, 189, 193, 199, 200; *see also* emotional contagion

emotional contagion 57, 167, 176–8, 180–81, 192, 199
　and morale 177, 187–9, 193, 200
empirical studies
　of conducting 8, 9–10, 17–18, 19–30, 38, 50–51, 75
　of performance 8, 56
enculturation 10, 59–62, 174
enforcement 15, 77, 85, 91, 94–7, 100, 101, 116
epistemology 17, 31; *see also* knowledge
ethnography, *see* research methods
ethnotheory 34, 44–6, 51, 55, 56
evolution 31–2, 61, 164, 175
extra-musical 89, 95, 164, 199
eye contact 96, 109, 132, 162, 179, 180, 191; *see also* gaze behaviour

facial expression 10, 11, 21, 26, 49–50, 98, 143, 155, 172, 174, 176, 179, 203
facial feedback hypothesis 176, 188; *see also* emotional contagion
faith choirs 14, 67, 92, 102
F-formation 160–62, 178
Fisher, Jeremy, *see* Bannan, Nicholas
Ford, Kevin 19, 27
Foucault, Michel 5, 59, 75, 94, 97
Friesen, Wallace, *see* Ekman, Paul
Fuelberth, Rhonda 25, 47
Fuller, Gregory 25

Galkin, Elliott 140
Garretson, Robert 9, 22, 80, 85, 95, 99, 103, 105, 142, 144, 177, 203
gay/lesbian/bisexual choir 173
gaze behaviour 21, 26, 124, 132, 160, 161, 162, 178–9, 190; *see also* eye contact
Geertz, Clifford 34
genre
　classification by 68–9, 72, 74, 77, 82–4
　differences between 15, 88, 107, 126, 186
　legitimacy of 65, 73, 74, 87
George, Vance 88, 102
gesture; *see also* conducting gesture; gesture types; hand shapes
　classification systems 46–7, 51–4

and speech 11, 53, 54, 131–2, 133, 134, 154–5, 157, 162, 163–4
and thought 11, 52, 103–4, 123, 131–2, 134, 151, 153–65, 176, 197, 201, 202–5
vocabularies 1, 2, 15, 36, 45, 58, 70, 104, 105–6, 107–21, 123, 134, 145, 151, 176, 195, 196–7
gesture studies 11–12, 18, 51–4, 133–4
gesture types
　deictic 53, 131, 134–5
　depictive 131–2
　emergent 133–4, 135, 139, 145, 154, 156, 157, 164, 204, 205
　ergotic 54, 110, 125, 126, 148
　figural 124, 137
　iconic 53, 118, 137, 141
　metaphoric 49, 53, 118, 134, 148, 137–52
　musical/didactic 95, 130–31, 133, 134, 202
　musicotopographic 131–2, 133, 204
　spontaneous 45, 53, 57, 104, 131, 133, 134, 153–9
　symmetrical 111, 117, 125–8, 148
Giddens, Anthony 2, 60, 165
Goehr, Lydia 156, 203
Gordon, Lewis 24, 33, 105, 173
Gospel 1, 12, 14, 32, 45, 68, 83, 115–18, 137, 157, 169, 176
　devotional practices 70, 72
　rehearsal process 81, 94, 96, 115, 162, 185–6
　step-and-sway 116, 124, 128
governmentality 74–6, 100
Green, Elizabeth 26, 105, 143, 145–6, 149
Green, Lucy 165
Gritten, Anthony 139
growth point 11, 154–9, 160, 162–3, 164, 184, 197, 204, 206

Halsey, Simon 118–21, 127, 129, 133, 135, 139, 148, 157, 161, 179
hand shapes 48, 127, 130, 143, 154, 175–6
　'bullhorn' hand 110, 121, 127
　pointed finger 95, 100, 110, 127, 131, 134–5, 137, 157, 205
　'Sistine' wrist 57, 110–11, 121, 175, 176

Hargreaves, David 5
Hart, Steven 36, 69, 72
Hatfield, Elaine, *see* Cacioppo, John T.
hegemonic power 97, 102
Heidegger, Martin 160
Hemberg, Eskil 202
Hill, David, *see* Ash, Elizabeth
Hindemith, Paul 22
Holst, Imogen 28, 78, 86, 87, 101, 142, 144
Houle, George 140
Hylton, John 22, 65–6, 70, 71, 73, 74, 80, 82, 170, 184
hyperphrase 162–3

identity 60, 96, 167, 195, 202
  choral 12, 13, 14, 15, 71, 76, 87, 89, 197, 199
  corporate 2, 91, 93, 197
  musical 2, 4–6, 163, 184–5, 193
  social 5, 13, 14, 67, 77, 80–82, 87, 93, 193, 197, 199
  vocal 5–6, 96, 200
image schema 138, 144–6, 148–51, 153, 197; *see also* metaphor
imagination 45, 77, 99, 103, 104, 120, 128, 130, 131, 132, 138, 150, 157, 168, 184–6, 192–3, 196, 198, 199, 201–2, 205
inhabitance 154, 159–65, 174, 176, 184, 197
International Federation for Choral Music 75, 202
intimacy equilibrium model 178–80, 181, 200
  and over-conducting 190–91
involuntary behaviours 1, 61, 169, 173, 174, 177, 180, 181, 193

Johnson, Mark 20–21, 48, 58, 104, 138–41, 146, 151, 164, 203, 205
Johnson, Peter 8, 27
Jordan, James 9, 23, 28, 64, 74, 105, 126, 130, 169, 170, 175–6, 187

Kahn, Emil 45, 142, 143, 144, 145, 148
Kaplan, Abraham 1, 94, 101, 124, 171, 183
Kayes, Gillyanne, *see* Bannan, Nicholas
Kendon, Adam 11, 52–3, 160–62

King, Elaine, *see* Gritten, Anthony
Kirk, Colleen, *see* Decker, Harold
Knight, Victor 79, 80–81, 87
knowledge 17–18, 44, 51, 56, 58, 61, 100, 201, 205
  bodies of 4–12, 18, 20, 27, 30, 31, 74
  embodied 40, 175, 205
  experiential 31, 33, 39–40
  systematic 9–10, 13, 17, 63, 69, 73, 74–6

Laban, Rudolf 47, 49, 110, 117
Lakoff, George, *see* Johnson, Mark
Lewis, Diane 204
Lewis, Joseph 77, 79, 85, 98–9, 102, 130
Lindlof, Thomas 18, 40
Litman, Peter 47
Lucas, Adrian 107–11, 129, 131, 132, 135, 143, 146, 154–5, 160, 161
Luck, Geoff 27

MacDonald, Raymond, *see* Hargreaves, David
McElheran, Brock 22–3, 203
McLean, Sally 111–15, 125, 129, 131, 133, 135, 139, 140, 145
McNeill, David 11, 52–4, 104, 153–65, 175, 197
male voice choirs 12, 15, 32, 38, 76, 84, 89, 184, 198–200
marked terms 68
Merleau-Ponty, Maurice 155
metalanguage 17, 18, 43–58, 201, 202, 205
  analytical 46–7, 51–4, 55
  ethnotheory 34, 44–6, 51, 55, 56
  metaphorical 47–9, 205
  objective 49–51, 55–6
  relationship with knowledge 43–4, 51, 56, 58, 201
metaphor 47–8, 54, 201, 202
  conduit 20–22, 24, 29, 193
  gestural 53, 58, 113–14, 118, 125, 134–5, 137–49, 153, 163, 174, 175, 181, 190, 196, 204, 205
  musical 139, 175, 205
  as social marker 81–2, 199
  theory 48–9, 58, 104, 138–41, 151
  verbal 35, 58, 98, 186, 205

metre 109, 112–13, 114, 116, 117, 120, 124–5, 128–30, 140–41, 147–50; *see also* rhythm
Meyer, Leonard B. 21; *see also* Cooper, Grosvenor
Miell, Dorothy, *see* Hargreaves, David
mimicry 162, 176, 177, 188, 192
mirror neurons 167, 172–3
Mockus, Martha 6
model (of conducting) 17–18, 19–30, 34, 44, 58, 168, 187, 193, 201, 202
　interactive 18, 23–5, 31, 33–4, 41, 96, 160
　transmission 20–22, 25–6, 140
Molino, Jean 35
morality 77, 84–6, 87, 91, 92, 95, 102, 189
morale 168, 178, 187–9
Mulder, Axel 54, 127, 142–3
musical literacy
　as genre marker 82–3, 87, 93, 119
　relationship with conductor gesture 141
musical meaning 3, 7, 21, 36, 53, 64, 88, 103, 138, 144, 150, 164, 167, 172, 195, 197; *see also* metaphor
　circulation of 8, 33, 140, 159, 169, 174, 196
　embodied 104, 140, 151, 153, 159, 167, 174, 175, 196
　generation of 8, 16, 33, 37, 146

Nakra, Teresa Marin 50–51, 127, 129
Nattiez, Jean-Jacques 20, 21, 43
nature/nurture 2, 4, 15, 61, 78, 151, 167–8, 181, 195
Nettl, Bruno 33, 61
Neuen, Donald 9, 65, 79, 88, 93, 95, 103, 163
Nicholson, Sydney 69, 123
nonverbal communication studies 10–12, 21, 44, 51, 167

orchestral conducting 9, 34, 48, 53, 101–2, 103, 104, 105–6, 120, 125, 129, 141, 143, 203
Ord, Boris 190
over-conducting 168, 190–91, 193

Parfitt, Hilary, *see* Ash, Elizabeth

peer research, *see* research methods
perception–behaviour link, *see* chameleon effect
performance studies 7–8, 10, 18, 34, 123
performativity 2, 60
personality (of conductor) 75, 100, 168, 181, 192, 193
Pfautsch, Lloyd 98
Philip, Robert 7–8
Phillips, Kenneth 85–6
Plank, Steve 140
pointing
　in conducting gestures 95, 100, 110, 127, 131, 133, 134–5, 137, 157, 205
　and social dominance 161–2
Poizat, Michel 6
popular music 198
　studies 4, 5
　and voice production 6, 65, 82, 87, 184
posture 21, 36, 69, 104, 115, 160, 170, 171, 172, 173–4, 176, 180, 183, 187, 188; *see also* body, language
Potter, John 6, 65, 85, 97, 99
practitioner literature 8–10, 12–14, 17, 19, 25, 28, 44, 105, 123, 125, 126, 163, 183, 200
　discourse analysis of 10, 59, 63, 66–76, 77, 93
　as ethnotheory 34, 55–6, 167, 170–71, 177, 178, 188
Prausnitz, Frederick 46–7
Price, Harry 19
project of the self 2, 195
punishment, *see* discipline

rapport 29, 159, 177, 186, 191; *see also* conductor–choir bond; inhabitance
Rapson, Richard, *see* Cacioppo, John T.
rehearsal 45, 49, 59, 130–35, 159, 165, 178
　diagnostic processes 23, 94–7, 133
　discourses 81, 82, 86, 99–100, 199
　as environment 31–5, 37, 161–2, 164, 174, 177, 179, 196
　filmed 36–8, 104, 107–21, 123, 131, 160
　observations 12, 14, 18, 31, 34–6, 38–9, 47, 50, 56, 77, 95, 99, 123, 130–35, 156, 169, 173, 175, 180, 185, 189, 198

techniques 25, 28, 66, 69, 70, 94, 98, 100, 144, 168, 188, 200
research ethics 8, 18, 20, 33, 34, 40–41, 43
research methods 4, 9, 11–12, 15, 17–18, 44, 50, 56, 168
  empirical 4, 8, 9–10, 17–18, 19–30, 32, 38, 44, 49, 56, 75, 103
  ethnographic 31–40, 183
  peer research 8, 18, 31, 39, 40–41
Reynolds, Gordon 87–8, 93, 101, 142, 144, 170
rhythm 114, 116, 120, 121, 140, 163; *see also* metre
  accuracy 27, 135, 147
  analysis 128, 139, 150, 204
  and the body 109, 114, 124, 128–30, 139, 151
  melodic rhythm 109, 113, 114, 117, 124
  qualities 71, 83, 86, 114, 148, 185–6
Rimé, Bernard 11, 51, 155
Roe, Paul 23, 28, 73, 86, 87, 98, 102, 130, 142, 142, 144, 145, 170, 177, 178
Rose, Bernard 43
Rosen, Charles 43, 58
Rudolph, Max 22, 45, 103, 105, 126, 142, 143, 144, 145, 153, 158, 159

Saito, Hideo 45
Sakata, Jon 56
Sapir, Edward 196
Saslaw, Janna 49, 138
Schiaratura, Loris, *see* Rimé, Bernard
Schuller, Gunther 101, 102, 126
Schumann, Robert 43, 103
semiotics 10, 18, 20, 21, 68, 143, 167
singing by ear 35, 115
  as genre marker 93
  relationship with conductor gesture 124, 162
Skadsem, Julie 28
social psychology, *see* nonverbal communication studies
Spitzer, Michael 49, 139
Spohr, Louis 140–41
stacking 55, 160, 201; *see also* choir layout
stance 1, 10, 69, 77, 78, 98, 113, 173, 174; *see also* posture
Stravinksy, Igor 22, 118

Streeck, Jurgen 54, 163–4
Strimple, Nick 63, 64
structure vs. expression 45, 53, 126–7, 131, 137–52, 204; *see also* conducting gesture, hand function
style 1–2, 36, 46, 66, 69, 72–4, 159, 168, 169, 188, 195, 196, 197–8
  boundaries of 6, 15, 65, 82, 83
  gestural 15, 45, 53, 70–71, 104, 105, 107–21, 134, 147, 165
  and identity 3, 32, 84, 87, 93, 140, 174, 183–6, 193, 202
  pluralism 2, 70, 198–200, 201–2
surveillance 61, 91, 94–6, 98, 100, 102
Swan, Howard 23, 76, 96
symphony chorus 45, 104, 105, 118, 120

technologies of power 93, 94–7, 99, 100, 131, 200
technologies of the self 93, 97–100, 102, 131, 193, 200
thick descriptions 34–5
Turk, Edward Baron 6

Venn, Edward 21, 47
videography 26, 28, 36–8, 54, 58
vocal feedback hypothesis 189, 199
vocal production 69, 70, 77, 80, 168, 174, 180, 181, 189, 200; *see also* voice
  breathing 55, 69, 77, 78, 86, 87, 99, 110, 111, 112, 125, 126, 148, 170, 171, 174, 188
  mouth shape 96, 176
  and style 1–2, 6, 65–6, 82, 84, 87, 93, 104, 169, 183–6, 193, 195, 198
  range 6, 67–8, 88–9
  resonance 77, 79, 114, 174, 180, 200
  support 55, 95, 100, 113, 133, 171, 174, 180, 185, 187, 198, 200
  vibrato 55, 70, 79, 84, 86, 184, 188
voice 82, 84, 85, 99, 163, 167, 170, 174, 175, 178, 179 183–6, 188–9, 193, 196, 198, 200; *see also* vocal production; voice types
  and identity 2–3, 4–6, 96, 202
  natural 6, 77–80
  trained/untrained 55, 78–9, 84, 177
voice types 6, 55, 57

alto 67, 78, 87, 88, 107, 117, 121, 130, 139, 179
bass 78, 88, 107, 120, 121, 133, 157, 174, 179, 190
baritone 88
countertenor 68
tenor 67, 78, 88, 89, 94, 107, 132, 146, 148, 173, 174
soprano 6, 14, 68, 78, 87, 88, 99, 121, 173
stereotypes 87–8, 174

warm-ups 35, 70, 84, 98, 99, 119, 173, 199
Western art music 4, 6, 32, 39, 40, 68, 72 84, 120, 156, 189, 197, 203
as Grand Narrative 66, 73–4

White Rosettes 111–15, 131, 143
Willetts, Sandra 81, 82, 88, 98
Wis, Ramona 30, 48
Wood, Elizabeth 6
Woodgate, Leslie 22, 85, 125, 142, 143, 144, 145, 170, 177, 192
Worcester Catherdral Choir 107–11

Zbikowski, Laurence 49, 138

CPSIA information can be obtained
at www.ICGtesting.com
Printed in the USA
LVHW020912011119
636049LV00009B/178/P